T0397035

# CORSAIRS
## AND
# CAPTIVES

# CORSAIRS
## AND
# CAPTIVES

## NARRATIVES FROM THE AGE OF THE BARBARY PIRATES

## ADAM NICHOLS

PEN & SWORD

**HISTORY**

AN IMPRINT OF PEN & SWORD BOOKS LTD.
YORKSHIRE – PHILADELPHIA

First published in Great Britain in 2024 by
**PEN AND SWORD HISTORY**
An imprint of
Pen & Sword Books Ltd
Yorkshire – Philadelphia

Copyright © Adam Nichols, 2024

ISBN 978 1 03610 607 2

The right of Adam Nichols to be identified as Author of
this work has been asserted by him in accordance with the Copyright,
Designs and Patents Act 1988.

A CIP catalogue record for this book is available from the British Library.

All rights reserved. No part of this book may be reproduced or transmitted in
any form or by any means, electronic or mechanical including photocopying,
recording or by any information storage and retrieval system, without permission
from the Publisher in writing.

Typeset in Times New Roman 10.5/13 by
SJmagic DESIGN SERVICES, India.
Printed and bound in the UK by CPI Group (UK) Ltd.

Pen & Sword Books Limited incorporates the imprints of Atlas, Archaeology,
Aviation, Discovery, Family History, Fiction, History, Maritime, Military,
Military Classics, Politics, Select, Transport, True Crime, Air World, Frontline
Publishing, Leo Cooper, Remember When, Seaforth Publishing, The Praetorian
Press, Wharncliffe Local History, Wharncliffe Transport, Wharncliffe True Crime
and White Owl.

*For a complete list of Pen & Sword titles please contact*
**PEN & SWORD BOOKS LIMITED**
George House, Units 12 & 13, Beevor Street, Off Pontefract Road,
Barnsley, South Yorkshire, S71 1HN, England
E-mail: enquiries@pen-and-sword.co.uk
Website: www.pen-and-sword.co.uk

or

PEN AND SWORD BOOKS
1950 Lawrence Rd, Havertown, PA 19083, USA
E-mail: uspen-and-sword@casematepublishers.com
Website: www.penandswordbooks.com

# Contents

## NARRATIVE TEXTS

# Introduction

Barbary pirates! White slavery! The centuries-long conflict—the clash of civilizations—between Islam and Christian Europe! Most everybody has heard the stories. For nearly three hundred years (from the early-mid sixteenth century to the early nineteenth), Barbary pirates from North Africa swarmed first the Mediterranean and then the Atlantic, seizing enormous amounts of booty and tens of thousands of captives. Those they did not kill outright they brought back to the slave markets in their home ports and auctioned off to the highest bidders—men, women, even small children.

Ruthless pirates—slavers—armed with scimitar and musket and boarding pike, bellowing 'Allahu Akbar!' as they terrorized European shipping and coastal areas.

Well... yes—and no.

Technically speaking, Barbary pirates were not pirates. They were privateers.

Privateers were employed by governments of the time—both European and North African—as a sort of auxiliary navy. The government issued an official letter of authorization (in Europe it was typically referred to as a letter of marque) that gave privateers the legal right to attack and loot enemy shipping. The booty they brought back was then sold at auction. Privateering expeditions were financed by wealthy investors, by consortiums of the less wealthy, or by the privateers themselves. The profits were shared between the investors, the privateers, and the government, and the whole operation was considered a perfectly legal commercial enterprise—and, of course, a boon to cash-strapped governments.

This was exactly how Barbary pirates operated. There was indeed an element of *jihad* in what they did—sometimes referred to as *al-jihad fil-bahr* (the holy war at sea)—and attacking Christian infidels was deemed a righteous religious act. Imams encouraged young men to participate in the *jihad* instead of making the *hajj* to Mecca, for completing the *hajj* only benefited the individual, while participating in the *jihad* benefited the entire Muslim community. But Barbary pirates were not religious fanatics (or at least not *only* religious fanatics). Neither were they lawless pirates out for purely personal gain. Instead, they participated in a large-scale business enterprise, legally sanctioned and regulated by North African city states like Algiers, Tunis, Tripoli, and Salé. Barbary corsairs were, above all else, ruthless businessmen looking to take as much booty and as many captives as possible to sell at a profit back in their home ports—a cruel and inhumane business, but a business all the same.

So Barbary corsairs were legally sanctioned privateers rather than outlaw pirates. Practically speaking, though, Barbary corsairs—like privateers everywhere—*behaved* like pirates: they violently attacked ships and coastal settlements and stole whatever they could—including people. As a result, they have been incorporated into the literature of pirate yarns. Most of the stories told about pirates are exaggerations at best; at worst, they are romantic fabrications. This holds for Barbary corsairs as much as for any other kind of pirate. As a result, Barbary corsairs, and the world in which they operated, are often depicted in an oversimplified, distorted way.

In the summer of 1639, an Englishman name William Okeley had the misfortune to be captured by Barbary corsairs from Algiers. After spending five years as a slave in that city, he managed to escape with four other captives in a hand-made, canvas-covered boat the men had laboriously constructed in secret. In 1675, thirty years after his return to England, Okeley published an account of his experiences. In the Preface, he makes the following comment about narratives such as his:

It is very true that every narrator is under strong temptation to season his discourse to the gusto of the time, not imposing any very severe law upon himself to report what is true, but accommodating his story to the liquorish appetite of others. I have observed that some men are ashamed to recount mean and humble matters if they bring us anything below prodigy and miracle...

There is also a sort of story, which, by way of courtesy, we miscall histories, that scorns to give us an account of anything but dreadful and terrible battles, and how one great man above all the rest chopped off heads and arms, and cut off some sheer by the waist, and with his trenchant blade mowed down whole files of armed enemies, the field all this while running with streams of blood and purple gore, and all this with total confidence and exactness in every minute circumstance.

To secure the reader against the fear of such entertainment in this narrative, let him know that he shall meet with nothing in fact but what is precisely true. [1]

---

1. William Okeley, *Eben-Ezer, or, A small monument of great mercy appearing in the miraculous deliverance of William Okeley, William Adams, John Anthony, John Jephs, and John ____ carpenter, from the miserable slavery of Algiers*, pp. i-ii.

# Introduction

Like Okeley, I can reassure the reader that the purpose of this book is not to recount wild tales of dreadful battles, trenchant blades, and fields running with streams of blood and purple gore. Rather, the narratives gathered together in this book are 'precisely true'. That is, they are all first-hand accounts.

Barbary corsairs may indeed seem like cruel villains, but the era in which they lived was not a simple one. At times, half the corsair captains hunting the Mediterranean and the Atlantic were European renegades (men who had converted to Islam and taken up new lives as corsairs). The best way to get an accurate sense of the Barbary corsairs, their captives, the period in which they all lived, and the larger conflict between North Africa and Europe is to go to the original sources. This book does just that. It presents a collection of narratives, most dating from the seventeenth century—the century of the Barbary corsairs' ascendency—that come from a variety of documents: accounts written by escaped or ransomed captives, a track penned by an ex-pirate about how to combat piracy, the account of a French Trinitarian friar who voyaged to Algiers to ransom captives there, even a transcript from a trial held by the Canary Islands chapter of the (in)famous Spanish Inquisition. Few of these sources are familiar to casual readers. Quite a few of them have never before been translated into English. They are, in other words, a collection of previously untold stories.

There is a problem with four-hundred-year-old sources, however: they are often difficult to make sense of. More importantly, perhaps, they are, generally speaking, not very good reads. Instead of being *stories*, they often consist of mere chronologies of events, often recorded in stultifying detail—extremely useful for scholars, of course, but not very entertaining for casually interested readers. This book tries to address that problem. Buried in the dry chronologies are human stories filled with pathos and danger, fear and bravery, betrayal and friendship—and love. The original sources just need a bit of editing to bring out the story element in them.

The notion of editing original sources is anathema to serious scholars. But this book is not intended for serious scholars. It is for readers interested in true stories—stories told by those who experienced the events themselves—of the world of North African piracy. They are not stories of swashbuckling pirates. Neither are they stories of a clash of civilizations between Muslim North Africa and Christian Europe. The problem with the 'clash of civilization' approach is that it assumes an 'us' and a 'them' facing off against each other across an impermeable barrier. Things were more complicated than that. The struggle between North Africa and Europe was a military conflict, but not *just* that; it was a religious conflict, but not *just* that; it was a social and economic conflict, but not *just* that.

Above all, it was a *human* conflict, with all the confusion, blurred lines, and inherent messiness of such things, and the stories it generated were complicated.

People found themselves stuck on one side or the other, or caught in between, or driven to painful extremes. Not all the stories have happy endings. Not everybody survives. But they are all *interesting*.

It was the gleam of these stories—these interesting human stories—buried under the bland chronologies that drew me to write this book.

The narratives presented here are of two types. The first consists of relatively short narratives of individual people, on both sides of the Mediterranean, taken from a variety of original sources. These I have rendered in my own words to make them more accessible. These narratives, particularly the early ones, contain an element of historical background to help set up the context in which the events took place, for the world of four hundred years ago was not the world of today, and some aspects of it need explaining. The second type of narrative consists of translations of seventeenth-century French texts (all translations are my own), or of lightly edited and abridged versions of mostly seventeenth- (but also eighteenth- and nineteenth-) century English texts. These first-person narratives recount the direct experiences of the authors in their own words, mostly as slaves in North Africa. They provide vivid accounts of what it was like to *be there*. Taken together, the two sorts of narratives provide a series of glimpses into a world long gone from us now, a world very much tougher to live in than our own, and one in which ordinary people faced risks and dangers we no longer have to consider.

It is not the world most people imagine when they think of Barbary pirates.

It is more interesting than that.

# NARRATIVES

# *CORSAIRS*

# The Barbary Corsair Enterprise

Barbary corsairs, remember, were not pirates, at least not the sort of wild buccaneering freebooters—like Captain Kidd or Blackbeard—that the word 'pirate' typically brings to mind. Barbary corsairs certainly behaved like pirates, in that they boarded ships and took by force everything they could (often including the ships themselves), but they were not lone wolves out purely for illicit personal gain. Neither were they simple religious fanatics. The *corso* (as the act of corsairing was sometimes known; the word derives from various romance language versions of the Latin root word 'cursus,' to run and, by extension, to chase) may have begun as part of *al-jihad fil-bahr*—the holy war at sea—but the North African city states quickly became economically dependent on it. And as with most business enterprises, prosperity required growth.

Hordes of corsair vessels swarmed the Mediterranean and, later, the Atlantic, taking everything and anything they could, both at sea and on land. The pilfered merchandise and captured people these corsairs brought back were auctioned off in the *souks* (markets). The city authorities took a cut at every stage. The financial backers of the expeditions also took a cut. The corsairs themselves divided up what remained. All of these parties spent their profits in the local economies, invigorating them. A kind of financial feeding frenzy ensued: the more merchandise and captives that came in, the more the profits soared... and the more the demand increased. Men became rich, some very, very rich—especially on the buying and selling of human beings. All this meant that the larger corsair enterprise could not be allowed to stop, or even to slow down. For if the pirated booty ceased to flow, the North African city states faced financial ruin.

As a result of all this, the *corso* became a massive enterprise, far larger than most people imagine. It included not only the taking of European ships, goods, and captives at sea, but also extensive raiding of coastal settlements all along the Mediterranean littoral, the Atlantic coasts of Europe, and even Iceland on one occasion. It has been estimated that from the early-middle of the sixteenth to the early part of the nineteenth centuries—a period of just about 300 years—corsairs operating out of North African ports captured and enslaved upwards of a million Europeans. It is difficult to accurately calculate the cost of the goods they stole and/or destroyed, but it was enormous.

Here is a description of the situation, written in the late sixteenth century, that shows just how powerful the Barbary corsairs were at that time and how vulnerable Europeans felt themselves to be:

The corsairs traverse the eastern and western seas [of the Mediterranean] without the least fear or apprehension, as free and absolute sovereigns thereof. Nay, they roam up and down as if chasing hares for their diversion. Here they snap up a ship laden with gold and silver from India, and there another richly fraught from Flanders; now they make prize of a vessel from England, then of another from Portugal. Here they board and lead away one from Venice, then one from Sicily, and a little further on they swoop down upon others from Naples, Livorno, or Genoa, all of them abundantly crammed with great and wonderful riches.

At other times, carrying *renegados* [Christian renegades who 'turned Turk' and converted to Islam] with them as guides, of which there are in Algiers vast numbers of all Christian nations—nay, the generality of the corsairs are no other than *renegados*, and all of them exceedingly well acquainted with the coasts of Christendom, and even the country inland—they very deliberately, even at noon-day, or indeed just when they please, leap ashore, and advance without the least dread and march into the country ten, twelve, or fifteen leagues or more. Poor Christians, thinking themselves secure, are surprised unawares. Many towns, villages, and farms are sacked, and infinite numbers of souls— men, women, children, and even infants at the breast—are dragged away into a wretched captivity. With these miserable, ruined people, and loaded down with other valuables, the corsairs retreat leisurely to their vessels, with eyes full of laughter and content.

In this manner, as is too well known, these corsairs have utterly ruined and destroyed Sardinia, Corsica, Sicily, Calabria, the neighbourhoods of Naples, Rome, and Genoa, all the Balearic Islands, and the whole coast of Spain, in which last most particularly they feast as they think fit, on account of the Moriscos [Spanish Muslims who had been forced to convert to Christianity] who inhabit there. Being more zealous Mohammedans than are the very Moors born in Barbary, these Moriscos receive and caress the corsairs and provide them with whatever information they desire.

As a result of all this, before these corsairs have been absent from their abodes much longer than perhaps twenty or thirty days, they return home rich, with their vessels crowded with captives, and ready to sink with wealth. With scarce any trouble, they reap the fruits of all that the Mexicans and Peruvians have dug from the bowels of the earth with such toil and sweat, as well as that which merchants, facing manifest perils, have been scraping together for so long, and that they have travelled so many thousand leagues to fetch away, either from the east or west, with inexpressible danger and fatigue. Thus the corsairs have crammed most of the houses, the magazines, and all the shops of this Den of Thieves [Algiers] with gold, silver, pearls, amber, spices, drugs, silks, cloths, velvets, etc., whereby they have rendered this city the most opulent in the world, so that the Turks call it, not without reason, their India, their Mexico, their Peru.[1]

Things were not quite as bad as they are depicted in the quote above—it is unlikely that corsairs returned to their ships carefree and at their leisure 'with eyes full of laughter' during a shore raid—but they were bad enough. European merchant ships faced the constant danger of attack, so constant that those involved sometimes felt that European merchant shipping would soon collapse entirely. Here is one view on the matter by an English pamphleteer in the early seventeenth century:

If it does not please God to move the heart of His Majesty and other Christian Princes and states to join together for their [the Barbary corsairs'] speedy suppression and the disjointing of their lately strengthened forces, which are continually increased by ships of England and Holland that they daily surprise, it will be discommodious to the state, and so dangerous to the common wealth, in succeeding times, that Christendom must expect no traffic at sea.[2]

Merchant traffic did continue at sea, of course, but losses were high. So if you were on a European ship anywhere in the Mediterranean or along the

---

1. Joseph Morgan, *A Complete History of Algiers, from the Earliest to the Present Times*, Volume 2, pp. 593-594. The extract from Morgan presented here is his translation of a passage from an early seventeenth century Spanish work titled *Topographia e Historia General de Argel* (*Topography and General History of Algiers*), written by Antonio de Sosa—a work we will come back to later in this book.

2. Anthony Nixon, *News from Sea of two notorious Pyrates, Ward the Englishman, and Danseker the Dutchman, with a True Relation of all or the Most Piracies by them Committed unto the sixth of April, 1609*, from the dedication to 'his worshipful, worthy and singular good friend Master T. I.' (this is a pamphlet with no page numbers). I have lightly edited the original text to make it more accessible.

Atlantic coast of Europe during this period, you scanned the ocean constantly for potential trouble. The corsairs were aware of this, of course. If they were travelling in a fleet and had overwhelming superiority of numbers, they would attack European ships outright without hesitation. If they did not have a clear advantage, though, they often resorted to subterfuge rather than outright assault.

In the next chapter, we will look at some of the tricks Barbary corsairs employed when attacking European shipping.

# Corsair Methods of Attack

Throughout the sixteenth and well into the seventeenth centuries, Barbary corsairs sailed in oared galleys—long, sleek ships, usually with a single lateen (triangular) sail, a covered pavilion at the stern (where the captain and officers stayed), rows of manacled oarsmen chained to the rowing benches, and a narrow projecting beak on the prow, often ironclad. One or more cannons were mounted on the prow, at the base of the beak. Like other ship's guns of the period, these forward-pointing guns could not be swivelled. To aim the guns, the captain had to aim the ship.

Galleys could move with the wind, but the thing that made them deadly was that, essentially, they were a form of motorboat—powered by human muscle. This meant they could operate independently of the wind when needed, which gave them a significant tactical advantage in the age of sail that enabled them to take on much larger vessels.

Galleys had their limitations, though. The enslaved oarsmen—a large corsair galley could have upwards of 120 or more—required serious quantities of food and water, so they had to make frequent stops for reprovisioning. Also, their long, low design made galleys unsuitable for the turbulent waters of the open Atlantic, restricting them in the relatively placid waters of the Mediterranean.

Starting at the beginning of the seventeenth century, European renegades from the Netherlands and England taught Barbary corsairs how to build, sail, and navigate European-style, square-rigged sailing ships, and galleys began to be phased out. Sailing ships were larger and more stable in rough water than oared galleys; they could make long voyages without having to stop for provisions (since they did not need huge numbers of slaves to manage them); and, perhaps most importantly, were far better armed. Since a galley's sides were lined with oars and oarsmen, the only place to mount cannon was in the bow or stern. Square-rigged ships, however, could line the entire side of the ship with cannons. Depending on the size and armament of the vessel, a square-rigged ship in the seventeenth century could employ anything from half a dozen to thirty or more cannons (of various calibres) per side. Firing such a bank of cannons in a broadside could have a devastating effect.

Because of the movies, we tend to imagine corsair attacks as violent and brutal affairs: a series of overwhelming broadsides followed by a horde of men swarming aboard, knives clutched between their teeth, brandishing cutlasses and blunderbusses, hacking people to pieces and blowing holes through them.

A dramatic image, but not always a very accurate one.

Such violence did indeed occur. From the point of view of the corsairs, however, the very last thing they wanted was ferocious combat. The *corso* was a business enterprise, remember. If your aim is to gain booty and captives which you can sell at a profit, there is little point in destroying that booty when you encounter it—whether it be merchandise or human beings.

Plus... corsairs—like pirates in general—were essentially predators. Like predators everywhere, they sought vulnerable victims. Whether you are a pirate, a cheetah, a weasel, or a trap-door spider, if you injure yourself attacking your prey, you are in trouble; if you injure yourself badly enough, your chances of survival become slim. So being a predator means playing a constant game of risk and reward. Successful corsair captains would have developed a very fine-tuned sense of what risks were worth taking and what were not.

So Barbary corsairs made careful and limited use of the firepower available to them. Their aim was to intimidate their intended prey—to thoroughly cow the crew and passengers aboard any ship they intended to capture—rather than to engage in open battle and destroy things. Every one of their own men killed or injured, every part of their own ship damaged, reduced their chances of continued success.

A corsair galley would usually employ its forward-pointing cannon to fire warning shots across the bows of a vessel it planned to capture rather than to directly target the vessel itself, or the corsairs might load a couple of bow cannons with grapeshot and fire them to clear the decks of a ship they were about to board. A square-rigged corsair ship might indeed fire off a broadside, but it was often more for intimidation than destructive effect. Brutal clashes certainly did occur—we will look at one in the *A Game of Risk and Reward* chapter below, and one of the accounts in the *Narrative Texts* section describes in detail a violent corsair attack—but it was not unusual for confrontations to result in the prey ship surrendering without a shot being fired.

Aside from this sort of outright intimidation, Barbary corsairs also employed subterfuge.

Ships of this period flew flags to declare their nationality. Barbary corsair ships regularly flew false flags, posing as countrymen or allies of those aboard a ship they intended to capture. If the corsairs were in a European-style square-rigged ship, from a distance there was no sure way to know their identity. And since corsair crews often included renegades from a variety of European countries, there was likely to be one or more men aboard who spoke the language of their intended prey and could engage in conversation shouted from ship to ship... as the corsair ship all the while edged nearer and nearer.

Since the whole point in shipping goods across the sea was to make a profit, the crews aboard European merchant ships were kept as small as possible to help bring down shipping costs. Corsair vessels, on the other hand, had crews as large as possible—for their intimidation value. So if a corsair ship (with most of its crew hidden below decks) could use the ruse of a false flag to draw close enough to a prey ship... it was all over. To the horror of those aboard the prey ship, the decks of the supposedly friendly vessel were suddenly swarming with heavily armed corsairs, and it was too late to mount any sort of effective resistance—even if they wanted to.

There was yet another stratagem that Barbary corsairs employed, more devious than the others.

The various European powers were continuously embroiled in a bewildering round of wars, truces, peace treaties, alliances, betrayals, renewed conflicts, renewed truces. During all this, they were also negotiating with the individual Barbary States.

The Barbary States could more accurately perhaps be referred to as the Barbary City States. They consisted essentially of Tripoli, Tunis, Algiers, and Salé. The first three were nominally under Ottoman control, but in reality, they were largely independent. So it was not enough for European powers to enter into treaty relations with the Ottoman Sultan in Istanbul; they had to negotiate with each Barbary city state individually. Morocco was never absorbed into the Ottoman Empire, and so Salé was always an independent entity that European powers had to deal with separately.

Treaties with Barbary city states were designed to guarantee the safety of the European signatory's shipping. The standard arrangement required ships of the European nation to carry special passes. Corsairs were permitted to stop and board the European ships to inspect the passes. If the European ship could present the right pass, the corsairs were obliged to release the ship.

There were complications to these arrangements, though.

If, for example, England concluded a treaty with Algiers, this meant that English ships, English nationals, and English goods were inviolable. It did not, however, guarantee the safety of non-English nationals or merchandise aboard English ships. If an English ship was carrying, say, Spanish wine, or had Spanish crewmembers or passengers aboard, Algerine corsairs could board the ship, abduct the Spaniards, confiscate the Spanish merchandise, and depart—all while abiding by the dictates of the treaty.

Some corsairs took this legal nicety a step further and forced the captains of captured vessels to state that they were transporting goods not covered by the treaty. In 1624, the States-General of the Republic of the Netherlands—which had entered into a treaty with Moulay Zaydan, the Sultan of Morocco—sent a formal letter of protest to the Sultan complaining of this very thing:

On the 14th of October last, near Cape Finisterre, fifteen leagues from the shore, Captain Eeuwout Henricxz. was attacked by a pirate from Salé, al-Hadj Ali, who seized his ship. And though the said Captain Henricxz. declared and proved, by his bills of lading and other documents, that he had on board only Dutch goods destined for Amsterdam, the aforementioned al-Hadj Ali ignored these documents and, wishing to obtain from the Captain a statement contrary to truth, by which he could justify his conduct, he had the said Captain and a sailor named Jan Pietersz. brought on deck and tied together. He instructed them to declare that their cargo consisted of French goods. When they refused, he had them whipped most painfully. Eventually, the torments, the pain, and the threat of being thrown into the sea, still bound together, led the said Captain to declare, in order to avoid further suffering and death, that the goods onboard belonged to the French. Thereupon al-Hadj Ali took possession of the said ship and cargo and brought them to Salé.[1]

One of the clearest and most vivid descriptions of Barbary corsair trickery can be found in the autobiography of Thomas Phelps, who captained the ship *Success*, out of London, when he was captured by Salé corsairs off the coast of Portugal in the autumn of 1684. After being taken to Salé, he wound up in Meknes, the capital of the Alaouite Sultan Moulay Ismail Ibn Sharif. Moulay Ismail had grandiose plans to construct an immense royal palace, dwarfing Versailles, using hordes of slaves to do so. Conditions for these slave workers were atrocious. Phelps and several companions escaped and fled overland to Salé, where they made it onto an English warship fortuitously anchored outside the harbour. Back in England, Phelps became an acquaintance of Samuel Pepys, the great (though at the time secret) diarist.

Perhaps it was Pepys' influence. Perhaps not. In any case, Phelps published a detailed account of his experiences as a captive and a slave. His autobiography begins with a description of how his ship was captured.

In order for the excerpt below to make sense, you need to know the following: England and Algiers had a recognized treaty in effect when Phelps' ship was approached by a Barbary corsair vessel, a treaty that officially guaranteed

---

1. Henry de Castries, éd., *Les sources inédites de l'histoire de Maroc, première séries, dynastie saadienne : archives et bibliothèques des Pays-Bas*, tome IV (*The Unpublished Sources of the History of Morocco, First Series, Saadian Dynasty: Archives and Libraries of the Netherlands*, Volume 4), p. 74.

Algerine corsairs would not molest English ships. However, the treaty did give the Algerines the right to board English ships and to inspect English ship captains' passes to make sure they were genuine.

Here is Phelps' account of his capture.

❁

Upon the 5th of October (being then a hundred leagues west of Lisbon) we saw a sail to windward of us, which immediately gave us chase. We made what sail we could to get away from him, and, night coming on, we had, for about two hours, lost him. But at the rising of the moon, he got sight of us and quickly came up with us, hailing us to enquire whence we were from. We answered from London, demanding the like of him. He made answer: from Algiers, and withal commanded us to hoist out our ship's boat, which we refused to do, but we lowered our headsails for him. Immediately, he sent his own ship's boat towards us. When it was got almost by our side, we gave them three shouts, which so surprised them that they thought it convenient to retire aboard their own ship. We were not a little cheered at their departure and made away from them with all the sail we could make, for we had not one great gun, and as for powder, I believe one single pound was the utmost of our store.

We had got above two miles from him, which made me think we were clear of him—and that the ship must indeed be an Algerine. She appeared so great that, according to the stories in England, I thought no such ship could belong to Salé. But I found myself within a little while mightily mistaken, for as soon as his ship's boat was hoisted in, he presently fetched us up again: We had tried sailing all ways but found we could not get free of him. So seeing him astern, and a thing impossible to lose sight of, I put out a light for him, notwithstanding I was possessed at that time (God knows) with fear enough, but I thought, in the dark, my seeming confidence and resolution might impose upon him, so as to fancy I was of some force. And truly, afterwards he confessed to me that he thought I had six guns aboard and that I did intend to fight him.

He kept astern of me all night. In the morning he put out Turkish colours, which I answered with our English. Then he came up and saw I had no ship's boat in sight, for my boat was stowed down betwixt decks. He commanded me therefore to brace my headsails, and he then sent his ship's boat to demand my Pass. Aboard her was an ancient Moor who formerly had been a slave in England and spoke good English, and who was set at liberty by our late Gracious King Charles the second. He, seeing us in readiness with what arms we had, asked me if I had a mind to break the peace. He told me I needed not trouble myself to keep them out of our vessel, for none of them could be persuaded to come aboard me.

I brought him my customhouse documents, but I had no official Pass: The Moor aforesaid carried them to his Captain, but soon after returned and told me that such documents would not satisfy the Captain unless the Master himself would come. I made answer that I would not come, and that I had done what I was obliged to by the Articles between England and Algiers. The boat a second time put away for their ship, and while they were hoisting it aboard, I made what sail I could and was got a mile or more from them again, entertaining better hopes than I was in the night before. But as soon as the boat was in and stowed, the Moors made sail and came up with me again. Their Captain then commanded me that if I refused to come aboard his ship, he would come aboard me with his ship.

I answered that I doubted he was from Algiers. He swore in English to me that he was, else before this he would have shown himself, and he told me that if I did not come aboard, he would straightway sink me. And so he hoisted out his ship's boat, which then came aboard. I asked the Moor who spoke English what ship of Algiers this was. He very readily, without stammering, told me she was called the *Tagerene*. I then went into his ship's boat. So soon as I came aboard his ship, the Captain asked me why I was so hard of belief. My distrust was such that I asked the Captain, now that he had me aboard in his power, to tell me whether he was a Salé-man or not. He swore to me again that he was of Algiers, and that I should not be wronged. He made me sit down and caused them to set dates and figs before me.

A little after, the Captain told me that he was informed by his men that they saw two Portuguese aboard my ship, and that he would have them out, and then I should be gone about my business. I told him I had none such aboard. But he insisted on seeing the two men. So two men were sent for. After that he told me there were three more, and them he must have also. Well, to be short, at last he was suspicious that I was a Portuguese also, and to convince me that I was one, I found my entertainment presently withdrawn. Thus did this faithless barbarian serve me, until he had wheedled all my men aboard him except two. And then the valiant Moors entered my vessel with abundance of courage, heaving the two remaining Englishmen over the head of the vessel into the boat.

Thus were we all stripped, the vessel plundered in a moment, which they did resolve to have sunk, because they were too far at sea distant from their own coast. But immediately we saw five ships bearing down upon us, which startled the Moors, putting them into a great fright, obliging them to quit my vessel with abundance of beef and three boxes of dry goods left aboard, which their fear would not give them leisure to rummage for. In some small time the five vessels discovered us when they came within two leagues of us. Had they bore down afterwards with that resolution that they threatened before, the pirate would never have stood to look them in the face. But alas, like distracted fearful game, every one of the five ships took a different course, and, it being now night, they all escaped.

I am pretty well satisfied for that small time that I was amongst them, (although it was too long for my profit) that no Salé-man will fight a ship of ten guns, which I found true by observation of a ship from Bristol, while I was aboard. We came up with this ship and hailed him, and would have had him put out his boat, but he refused, and withal showed himself ready in his own defence, upon which the Salé-men were glad to leave him.[2]

Capturing a ship, cargo, crew, and any passengers onboard by subterfuge like this was the goal many corsairs strove for. The most famous and successful corsair captains—and the ones everybody wanted to go out on a *corso* cruise with— were the ones who had perfected this approach, for it meant there was little danger to the corsairs themselves. Next to plain old good luck, the most desirable characteristic in a corsair captain was the ability to be a successful trickster.

If the trickery failed, though, he had to also be a capable commander in a fight. Look at the following brief description, for example:

Off Cape Finisterre, we were very unhappily surprised by two Sallee Rovers [corsairs from Salé], and, after such small resistance as we could both make, we were taken and carried as prisoners on board the infidels' ship, as was also the next day Captain Ferris of London, in a ship of much greater strength than ours, having twenty men, eight swivel guns, and eight carriage guns. Though they behaved in the bravest manner, fighting ten hours, and with a noble resolution, putting the Moors off from boarding them three times and killing many, they were eventually overpowered by the superior forces of the Moors and were obliged to submit, and to become our comrades in captivity.[3]

This kind of desperate encounter was exactly the sort of thing corsairs wished to avoid whenever possible. The whole point, remember, of cruising around looking for prey was to be able to bring back booty and captives to sell at a profit. To be successful in such an enterprise, craftiness was a more useful asset than either brawn or guns.

---

2. Thomas Phelps, *A True Account of the Captivity of Thomas Phelps, at Machaness in Barbary*, pp. 1-5. I have slightly abridged the original, modernized the spelling and punctuation, and replaced some archaic words and expressions to make the text more readable.

3. Thomas Pellow, *The History of the Long Captivity and Adventures of Thomas Pellow, in South-Barbary*, p. 7. I have simplified the original text to make it more readable.

# The Economics of Booty, Captives, and Ransoms

In a city like Algiers in the seventeenth century, the *corso* was big business.

Algerine corsairs brought back enormous amounts of booty and hundreds—sometimes thousands—of captives every year. Captives and booty were both sold in a *souk* (an outdoor market) known as the Badestan.

The Badestan was a large place, something like 25-30 metres (80-100 feet) long and half that wide, lined with shops, bustling and crowded. Booty—merchandise such as sugar, salt, oil, fish, timber, leather goods, woollen cloth, silk, wine, spirits, tobacco, and much, much more—was offered at cut-rate prices (it was stolen goods, after all). Specialized brokers paraded new captives through the Badestan, loudly proclaiming their sale, and then put them up for auction to the highest bidder. In order to show their physical condition, captives were ordered to jump up and down, run on the spot, bend and twist. Buyers examined their teeth and their hands. Potentially beddable female captives were taken to a private examination area to determine whether or not they were virgins.

Three main considerations determined captives' sale prices:

- Their skill set. Those with useful skills—carpenters, shipwrights, surgeons, bookkeepers, etc.—fetched higher prices because of their utility to their new owners
- Their sexual attractiveness. Young, attractive women (and boys) fetched high prices
- Their background. Captives from wealthy backgrounds fetched high prices because they had the financial wherewithal to pay ransoms.

This last consideration is why inspecting captives' hands was so important. Calloused hands meant the person did manual work. A man with calloused hands might be anything from a farm labourer to a fisherman to a master carpenter, so calloused hands did not necessarily mean a low sale price. But it was a pretty good indicator that the captive was not wealthy. Non-calloused hands, however, likely indicated just one thing: that the person was rich, or at least rich enough to be able to avoid the drudgery of daily menial tasks. And that meant that such people likely had the financial resources to pay ransoms.

And ransoms were where the really serious profits lay.

Every prospective slave owner in North Africa was on the lookout for a rich captive whom he (or she) could buy. Such captives were encouraged—sometimes quite ruthlessly—to write letters back home requesting the ransom funds needed to free them. If a captive was wealthy enough, his or her owner could easily turn a profit of 500 per cent or more.

That profit did not just go to the captive's owner, though.

The proceeds from the *corso*—booty and captives—were the driver of the Algiers economy (as they were for the other Barbary corsair capitals as well). *Everybody* took a cut of the profits. So when a ransom payment was successfully negotiated, the actual cost was significantly higher than the 'asking price'. The Pasha of Algiers (the Ottoman Governor of the city) took his percentage. There was a port tax. The official in charge of collecting the port tax (the Emmini) took his cut. Each ransomed captive needed to purchase an official document (a Hücett) certifying that s/he was now freed. The interpreter who facilitated the ransom negotiations, the Turgeman (also sometimes referred to as the Dragoman), took his share. The janissary soldiers who guarded and transported the newly freed captives took their cut (janissaries were Ottoman troops stationed in Algiers; there were thousands of them). The money changers who acted as bankers—ransoms were paid either in merchandise or in cash transported in large sacks or chests filled with coins that needed to be valued and exchanged from one currency to another—took their percentage, too.

We know all this from several sources. One of the most interesting and revealing is a letter, dated October 15, 1622, written by Wynant de Keyser van Bollandt, the Dutch consul in Algiers at the time. In this letter, de Keyser complains about all the extra costs that were added to a ransom payment. He includes an itemized list of the expenses of a generic ransom to back up his complaints. That list is included below. It was originally written in Dutch. Instead of trying to present a literal translation, I have simplified the text and reorganized the list a little where I thought it would be helpful. All prices in the list are in *doubles*, a silver coin which was the standard unit of currency used in Algiers at the time:

Here is the list:

| Captive's ransom price in doubles | 1,000 |
|---|---|
| To the Pasha, 10% | 100 |
| For the port tax, 1% | 10 |
| To the Emmini [the port tax collector], 2% | 20 |
| For the Hücett [the certificate of liberty] | 46 |
| To the Yasakçi [the janissary guards] | 46 |
| To the Yasakçi guarding the Dutch nationals | 9 |
| To the Turgeman [Dragoman, interpreter] | 18 |
| To the Dutch Consul | nil |
| For the exchange of the above amount of money, 30% at least, if the money is in large denominations of coin, otherwise more, counted in doubles | 377 |
| Total amount in doubles | 1,636[1] |

As you can see, according to this list, the extra charges increased the original ransom price by more than 60 per cent. Little wonder that de Keyser complained about these added expenses.

It was the way things worked, though. The details differed from ransom to ransom, and from decade to decade, but the principle remained the same. The most important revenue stream Algiers had was from the proceeds of the *corso*, and ransoms were a large part of that. Those paying the ransoms—whether they were individual wealthy families, governments, monarchs, or redemptionist religious orders like the Mercedarians or the Trinitarians—had little choice but to cough up the money demanded and pay the added costs. It was either that or let their family members/citizens/subjects/co-religionists languish in slavery.

It was a ruthless, exploitive business model that worked for the better part of three hundred years.

A sobering thought.

There is an underlying aspect to all this, however, that it is important to remember.

---

1. K. Heeringa. ed., *Bronnen tot de geschiedenis van den levantschen handel* (*Sources of the History of the Levant Trade*), Book 1, Part 2, p. 903.

Corsair capitals like Algiers, that depended economically on profits from piracy, prospered in large part because of the exorbitant ransoms demanded for people the corsairs captured. However, such cities also prospered because they could sell the masses of stolen merchandise that flowed into the city. The buyers of this booty were often European merchants who were complicit with the Barbary corsair enterprise because it was so extremely profitable for them. Such merchants purchased the stolen European goods cheaply and then shipped them back to ports like Livorno, in Italy, to be sold for a hefty profit— sometimes to the fury of the original owners, who recognized their stolen property being sold off for other people's profit but could do nothing about it (proving legally and indisputably that it was their property was extremely difficult).

Profit trumped all other considerations.

Sound familiar?

# A Game of Risk and Reward

As we saw in the *Corsair Methods of Attack* chapter, since Barbary corsairs' overall aim was to gain booty and captives to sell at a profit, they preferred intimidation and trickery to violent confrontation.

Much of the time, intimidation and trickery worked. Sometimes, however, it did not.

We are going to look at one of those times.

In September of 1614, a galley arrived unexpectedly in the harbour at Algiers. It was an impressive vessel sporting flags and embroidered silk banners streaming in the wind. As it eased into port, trumpeters onboard announced its arrival with brassy fanfares.

The commander was the *Caja* (the Lieutenant) of the Pasha (the Ottoman Governor) of Tripoli. The *Caja* had come to Algiers on a particular mission: to purchase two hundred and fifty slaves on behalf of his Pasha. The Pasha, in turn, planned to send these slaves as a special gift to the Sultan in Istanbul.

It took time to buy slaves, though, and the *Caja*'s galley sat moored at the quay in the Algiers harbour day after day as negotiations to buy slaves in the town slowly proceeded.

Meanwhile, Alli Pegelin, the head of the Taifa (from *taifat al-ru'asa*, meaning the 'community of the captains') was preparing to launch one last *corso* cruise to end the season—with the onset of winter, ships generally (though not always) stopped going out; the weather was too cold and rainy and conditions at sea too rough. The Taifa, a sort of combination union, ruling council, and political party, represented the interests of the corsair captains of Algiers and was a powerful force in the city. Its head was an important man. When Alli Pegelin went out on the *corso*, others wanted to go with him, for he had a reputation for not only being a tough, competent, aggressive captain, but also lucky.

By the time everything was prepared, the expedition consisted of four oared galleys, manned by corsairs and janissaries, rowed by slaves chained to the oar benches.

The *Caja* from Tripoli, stuck aboard his splendid galley twiddling his thumbs while negotiations dragged on in the city, decided he could better occupy his time by accompanying Alli Pegelin on his *corso* expedition. So he joined forces with Alli Pegelin, and five galleys eased out of the Algiers harbour and went hunting.

After several days at sea, they encountered a large English merchant ship. Such vessels typically carried valuable cargo—and a lot of it. There was a problem with this particular ship, though. It was armed with something like forty cannons.

Alli Pegelin urged the other galley captains to attack immediately, arguing that a sudden, overwhelming show of force would intimidate the English captain into surrendering. And if not, if they attacked quickly enough, the English captain would not have time to organize any sort of coherent defence. The other captains held back. The idea of a direct assault on such a well-armed ship seemed too risky—even if the assault was merely intended for show and intimidation. The discussion turned into a heated argument that went on until nightfall with no clear resolution.

At which point, the English ship slipped quietly away to safety in the darkness.

Alli Pegelin was furious, but there was nothing he could do except berate the galley captains for their timidity.

The next morning, the disgruntled corsairs sailed on in search of new prey.

Alli Pegelin's vaunted luck did not hold. The five galleys quartered the Mediterranean as far as the waters around Majorca without seeing so much as a single sail on the horizon. When they finally did sight a ship, it proved to be a small coastal boat with only a handful of people aboard. Such a minnow was not worth their time.

More argument ensued. Alli Pegelin accused the other captains of outright cowardice and blamed them for the expedition's ill luck. The captains scowled and muttered sullenly among themselves. Finally, under Alli Pegelin's irate goading, they all committed to directly attacking the next ship they spotted—no matter what sort of ship it might be.

Alli Pegelin smiled at this and said that now, finally, their luck would return.

It took a couple of days before they spotted another ship, but when they did, all the signs were good. It was a Dutch merchant vessel. Such ships were famous for being crammed with valuable cargo. It was manned by about forty men, a fairly large crew, but armed with no more than twenty cannons. Best of all, there was little to no wind, so the Dutch ship could not use its sails to escape, nor even to manoeuvre.

The Dutch ship was, as the old cliché goes, a sitting duck.

There was no argument among the captains this time.

The five galleys set about preparing themselves, readying everything so that they could swoop down upon the hapless Dutch ship in a pack and strip it of everything of value—merchandise and men.

The five Algerine corsair galleys drew up in formation just out of cannon range from the Dutch merchant ship, which, because of the lack of wind, was unable to manoeuvre.

Alli Pegelin sent out an emissary—a Dutch renegade—with a white flag. Easing up to within hailing distance of the Dutch ship, this emissary called out: 'The great Captain General, Alli Pegelin, has sent me to tell you that if you will yield now, without a fight, he vows he will set you and all your men free on Christian ground. This he has sworn by the Grand Seignior's head.'

The Dutch captain said nothing.

'If you are wise,' the emissary went on, 'you will accept the offer I make to you from the great Captain General while there is still time.' He paused. 'Otherwise... I fear you will repent your error.'

The Dutch captain remained silent for a long few seconds. Then he said, 'This ship belongs to its owners, and the cargo it carries belongs to the merchants who paid to have it shipped. I cannot surrender that which is not mine to give. Moreover, I know Alli Pegelin's reputation far too well to place any trust in him, for I was a slave in Algiers once. Tell him I will not yield. But if he wishes to have this ship, let him, instead, come aboard, and he shall see whether we can satisfy him or not.'

The renegade returned with this answer.

Alli Pegelin was infuriated by what he considered the Dutch captain's insolence, and he ordered the galleys to immediately draw up into a half-moon formation and row towards the stern of the Dutch ship, for the Dutch captain could not defend himself from that direction since there were no cannon mounted on that part of the ship.

At that moment, however, there was a small breath of wind, just enough to allow the Dutch captain, who was a seaman of extraordinary skill, to swing his ship about. This caused immediate confusion among the corsairs in the galleys, who suddenly found themselves looking into the mouths of ten cannons arrayed along the side of the Dutch ship's hull.

In a frantic effort to regroup so that they were once again in position facing the stern of the Dutch ship, several of the galleys fouled each other.

Only Alli Pegelin's galley churned ahead. Bellowing encouragements, Alli Pegelin ordered a contingent of his men to board the Dutch ship. As the prow of his galley crashed into the Dutch ship's hull, close to seventy corsairs scrambled aboard, brandishing scimitars and guns, tossing home-made grenades ahead of them first to clear the decks.

The Dutch captain, however, anticipated this manoeuvre and had withdrawn his men into the protection of the cabins in the ship's bow and stern. As the corsairs hauled themselves onto the midship deck, the Dutchmen opened fire on them with muskets, catching the corsairs in the crossfire.

Alli Pegelin's galley, meanwhile, pulled away, for he had realized that the Dutch ship was so heavily laden and rode so low in the water that the belowdecks cannons were on a level with the corsair galleys, and he did not at all wish to be caught by a broadside at point blank range.

The galley's sudden withdrawal caught the corsairs who had boarded the Dutch ship by surprise. Those who could swim leaped hastily overboard and tried to rejoin the retreating galley. The wounded, and those who could not swim, were forced to remain. In a desperate attempt to take the ship, they rushed the forecastle cabin but were driven back.

At this point, the Dutch captain commanded his belowdecks gunners to fire a broadside. The gunners had loaded their cannons with musket balls, nails, and pieces of iron. When they fired off the broadside, dozens of corsairs were cut to pieces and killed. The Dutch captain ordered another broadside, and another. Before the corsair galleys could all get completely out of range, nearly two hundred of the men aboard them had been slain or gravely wounded.

Meanwhile, the corsairs who had boarded the Dutch ship were still desperately assaulting the stern and bow cabins. They could not dislodge the Dutch crew from their positions, and, left with little in the way of options, those who could began climbing the rigging to try to get the advantage of height. The Dutch crew immediately poured out onto the deck and shot the corsairs down from where they hung from the shrouds and about the masts, picking them off one by one.

And so ended Alli Pegelin's final *corso* expedition of the season.

Close to half the galley crews were killed or mutilated, including many of the slaves on the rowing benches who were needed to get the galleys back to port. Two of the galley captains were killed, and the *Caja* of Tripoli lost an arm and was wounded in the belly.

The galleys limped back to Algiers as best they could.

When they were first spotted approaching the harbour, the people of Algiers were puzzled. They could make out five galleys, but two of them had no flags flying. At first, it was thought that these were Spanish galleys that had been captured. Soon enough, though, it became clear that this was Alli Pegelin's *corso* expedition returning, and that the lack of flags meant the captains of those vessels had been killed.

When an Algerine *corso* expedition had been successful, the ships fired off a celebratory cannonade as they entered the harbour. Alli Pegelin's galleys came in slowly, from the lack of rowers, and fired off no cannons. Those on shore had been poised to rejoice in yet another victorious *corso* cruise by the celebrated head of the Taifa. But their hopes turned to dismay as the details of what had happened became known.

The wounded were brought ashore, including the *Caja* of Tripoli. The *Caja* called immediately for his personal surgeon, a European slave who was renowned for his skill. 'Cure me,' he said, 'and I will grant you your freedom and give you as well a hundred patacoons.' But the *Caja*'s belly wound was too severe. Try as he might, there was nothing the surgeon could do.

The *Caja* resigned himself to death then and made out his will. In it, he granted freedom to his slaves, including the surgeon.

His body, draped in a silk covering, was carried through the narrow Algiers streets in a solemn procession. His freed slaves marched before it. The surgeon came behind. In his hand he carried a cleft staff, with a letter in the cleft containing the official document attesting to his freedom. He wept openly, as was expected of him at the passing of his master.

Some people, though, said he wept for joy.

Alli Pegelin, wily commander that he was, had survived the disastrous confrontation with the Dutch ship without any hurt. He wasted little time on regrets. Since he was hugely wealthy —he personally owned something like 500 slaves and, among other things, had financed the construction of a great mosque that bears his name and still stands in Algiers today—he could absorb the loss. During that winter, he focused his energy on restocking his supply of galley slaves and refitting his galleys for the coming *corso* season.

The next spring he went out again. That season, though, he chose a different set of galley captains to hunt with and had far better luck.

The Dutch captain delivered his cargo safely and continued to ply his trade.

Rough times.

Rough men.[1]

---

1. The story of the Dutch sea captain, Alli Pegelin, and the Tripolitan *Caja* is based on 'Relation II, De la valeur d'un Capitaine Hollandois qui se deffendit seul contre cinq Galeres Turques, & les mit en déroute' ('Of the valour of a Dutch Captain who defended himself against five Turkish Galleys and routed them') in Emmanuel d'Aranda, *Relation de la captivité et liberté du sieur Emanuel d'Aranda, mené esclave à Alger en l'an 1640 & mis en liberté l'an 1642* (*Relation of the captivity and freedom of Sieur Emanuel d'Aranda, Enslaved in Algiers in 1640 & released in 1642*), pp. 43–51.

# Of Piracy, Profit, and Prudence

Legally speaking, remember, Barbary corsairs were privateers rather than outlaw pirates. They were officially authorized by their governments to attack 'enemy' shipping and coastal areas, and any captives or booty they returned with was shared out in a carefully prescribed manner with the various city authorities, the financial backers of the expedition, and themselves. The *corso* was an extremely profitable business that everybody wanted in on. There was a time in the history of America when, if a young man wanted to go out into the world and 'seek his fortune', he was told 'Go west, young man. Go west.' If a young man in a place like Algiers wanted to seek his fortune, he went to sea in a corsair ship.

This is the story of one such young man.

His name was Mustaffa, and he was a Turkish soldier in Algiers—a janissary. There were thousands of janissaries stationed in Algiers. They served as a combined police/military force, keeping the peace within the city and protecting it from attack. Each summer, a contingent of them marched out into the wild hinterland surrounding Algiers to collect taxes. They also served as marines aboard Algerine corsair ships. As we saw in previous chapters, corsair captains preferred subterfuge to direct frontal assault, but when subterfuge failed, they sent in the janissaries to swarm the ships they attacked and overwhelm the crews. It was, of course, dangerous work.

Mustaffa served as one of these marines, risking his life at sea in the hopes of earning enough money from his share of the spoils to enable him to finance a better, more secure future for himself. Janissaries received regular monthly salaries but got no additional pay for serving aboard corsair ships. Instead, they signed on for a small percentage of the profits. In order for his share of the take to ever be large enough to enable him to change his life, any ship Mustaffa served on would have had to capture a monstrously profitable prize—a Spanish galleon filled with silver and gold returning from the New World, for instance.

For Mustaffa, nothing of the sort had happened. The *corso* was a game of chance as much as anything. In the vast expanse of the Mediterranean (vast if you were in a modest sized wooden sailing ship or an oared galley) you had to run into just the right ships at just the right time in order to be able to capture them. Corsair captains who did so were considered lucky. Crews flocked to them. Investors lined up to bankroll their excursions.

Mustaffa had never had the good fortune to sail with such a captain.

Over time, however, he had managed to amass 200 pieces of eight—the famous Spanish silver coins, which were in common use in Algiers at the time. That might not sound like very much by today's standards, and it was nowhere near enough to enable him to embark on a new life, but it was still a respectable amount of money.

Enough to buy a small ship.

With a ship of his own, he would be a captain, and a captain earned a significant percentage of the take from any successful corsair expedition.

So Mustaffa decided to take the risk. In the spring of 1639, he bought a small ship, so small that it did not even have decks. It was a solid, seaworthy little craft all the same, though. His 200 pieces of eight were enough to both buy the ship outright and outfit it for a *corso* cruise, including not only rigging and tackle and victuals for the voyage, but also muskets—the boat was too small to mount cannon, but his crew needed to be armed.

Mooring his new ship in the harbour near the Mole (as the long breakwater that enclosed the Algiers harbour was called), Mustaffa raised a flag indicating that he was looking for crew. Soon enough, he had attracted a collection of sixteen men, both Muslims and renegades, who were willing to sail with him for a share of any booty they took.

They left Algiers at the beginning of the summer—the *corso* season—and sailed westwards across the Mediterranean and through the Strait of Gibraltar. These were dangerous waters, patrolled by Spanish warships, but they managed to slip through. Then they began to cruise along the Spanish coast near Cadiz, looking for prey.

At first, they found nothing. The sea seemed empty. But then they got lucky—very lucky.

By sheer chance, there happened to be a group of merchants in Cadiz at that very moment who were trying to smuggle a considerable quantity of silver out of the country. During this period in Spain, it was a capital offense to export silver without a royal warrant. So the merchants had made secret arrangements with an English ship to clandestinely smuggle sixty bars of silver onto it.

The plan was that a hired band of eighteen men, armed with swords and muskets, would convey the load of silver ingots quietly through the streets in the dead of night, load it aboard a boat waiting in the harbour, and transfer it to the English ship.

These men collected the silver, hauled it across town without incident—successfully avoiding the king's Officers of Justice—and loaded it into the waiting boat. Then, in dim pre-dawn light, they set off across the harbour and out into the choppy waters beyond, in search of the English ship.

Mustaffa and his crew spotted them as they emerged from the calmer waters of the harbour. Mustaffa brought his ship close and ordered his men to fire a volley. The Spaniards immediately returned fire. Mustaffa realized, however, that they had far fewer muskets than his own crew. So he kept firing, making multiple passes just within musket range, raking the Spanish boat with volley after volley.

After an hour of this, they had killed four of the Spaniards and wounded quite a number of others, and the rest surrendered.

Mustaffa and his crew had been on the edge of despair. Despite all their cruising of the Spanish coast, they had so far been unable to take a single prize. They had sustained their attack on the small Spanish boat partly because its size made it vulnerable, but also because they desperately needed to take some sort of prize—*any* sort of prize—even if it did not amount to much.

So they boarded the Spanish boat without much in the way of expectations. Weary and still with the jitters from the fighting, they quickly took the surviving occupants of the boat prisoner, binding them so they could not cause any trouble, and began transferring them to their own small ship.

And then they found the silver.

Sixty bars of silver was a *lot* of silver. Mustaffa and his crew must have stood there on the rocking boat staring at the stacked, dully gleaming ingots in utter astonishment. After which, no doubt, they all sent heartfelt prayers of thanks to Allah.

With a prize like this, they did not need to stay out any longer. They abandoned the Spanish boat and let it drift, with the dead sprawled stiffly in it. Then they raised sail and headed out, threading their way safely through the Strait of Gibraltar and onwards until they reached the harbour at Algiers.

Dividing up booty was a formal process. The Pasha (the Ottoman Governor of the City) was entitled to one eighth of all captives and merchandise, and any captive ships brought into the city were his and his alone. There were also the usual port taxes and fees to be paid—all part of the process by which the city profited from *corso* activity.

Mustaffa would have paraded his captives through the streets to the Pasha's residence, for, by long custom, the Pasha got first pick of any captives. It would not have made much of a parade, though, compared with what larger expeditions could produce: Mustaffa and his small crew and perhaps a dozen or so limping captives, some of whom were suffering from musket-shot wounds. It is likely that they did not generate much of a crowd. It is likely, too, that the Pasha himself did not pay much attention or have much in the way of expectations. After all, Mustaffa was returning from his first *corso* expedition, in a small boat, leading a paltry number of captives. The most the Pasha could have expected for his one-eight share would have been a captive or two, in bad shape, possibly wounded.

And then he—and everybody else—learned about the silver.

Mustaffa became an overnight sensation.

As captain of his own ship, Mustaffa was entitled to half of all the profits remaining after the Pasha received his share. The other half was divided among the crew. On larger ships, where the crew was composed of men with varying tasks—soldiers, gunners, seamen, carpenters, etc.—there were elaborate formulas that determined what share each sort of crewmember was eligible for. On a small ship like Mustaffa's, the sixteen-man crew received equal shares. A larger ship would also have required the backing of a number of investors in order to finance the expedition, and they would have demanded their share in the profits. Mustaffa had no such investors to deal with.

Everything was carefully assessed and calculated. The Pasha took his one-eighth portion of everything—both captives and silver—and the city authorities received their various taxes and fees. When it was all over, Mustaffa's share amounted to a value of thirty thousand pieces of eight. Again, that may not sound like a huge amount by modern standards, but it was the equivalent of close to £1,000,000 today.

Captain Mustaffa had suddenly become a seriously wealthy man.

He was now referred to as Mustaffa Reis—Captain Mustaffa; 'Reis' being Turkish/Arabic for 'Captain'—and he was everybody's darling. The city's important merchants all wanted to marry their eligible daughters to him. Freelance crew all wanted to serve on board his next expedition. The wealthy backers who financed *corso* expeditions entertained him with sumptuous dinners, offering him ships and crew and seed money for his next excursion.

For Mustaffa had shown he possessed the one crucial quality that all great and successful corsair captains needed: luck.

Having demonstrated that, he could now launch an entirely different sort of life than he had first intended. He could become a corsair captain. If his luck held, he could become a *famous* corsair captain, celebrated by one and all, a man of wealth and importance.

*If* his luck held.

It was one of those watershed moments in a man's life. Two roads… One led to a life of excitement, danger, and, if he succeeded, incredible riches and lasting fame. The other led to a quiet life in a villa somewhere with a wife and children and, perhaps, a garden.

The wealthy backers were pressing him for a decision.

'Mustaffa,' they said, one evening over dinner. 'Allah has smiled upon you. Take our ship, pillage the infidels. Make us all rich.'

Mustaffa leaned back, looking at them. They were well dressed men all, sleek and comfortable. Most had never set foot aboard the ships they financed. 'As a soldier,' he said to them, 'I endangered my life many times. Now you are suggesting I do so again?'

'You are a lucky man,' one of the wealthy backers said. 'A brave man. The danger will be as nothing to you.'

'Think of the fame!' one of the others said.

'You could become head of the Taifa,' suggested a third. 'An influential and important man!'

Mustaffa nodded. 'All you say is true. A new life beckons me, a life of riches and importance.'

'Yes!' the wealthy backers all agreed.

Mustaffa paused. 'But… I have sufficient money now to maintain myself for as long as I live. Why should I go to sea again? I have endangered my life enough… I think I shall spend the rest of my days ashore and laugh at the dangers of the sea.'

Which is exactly what Mustaffa did.

He married the pretty daughter of a wealthy Morisco merchant and bought a small but elegant villa in the countryside outside the city. There he lived a quiet life with his wife and children, watching the sun rise and set and the seasons pass, with seldom a thought for the sea. As he aged, his beard whitened. Occasionally one of his old crew might visit. He served the man tea, and they would reminisce about their famous exploit. Afterwards, Mustaffa strolled through the green aisles of his garden, listening to the songbirds, until dinner was ready.

Mustaffa's story is a reminder of something important: people are people.

Barbary corsairs—like their European counterparts—practised a violent profession that included armed robbery, abduction, and human trafficking. But they did not practise this profession because they were inherently wicked people. They did it for… many reasons, some good, some bad. Such men were products of the time and place in which they lived.

This is not to say that armed robbery and human trafficking is excusable. But history, if it is to rise above the level of dry dates and lists of events—or blatant propaganda—is about people, individual people and the lives they led. Those individual lives offer a means to understand the past in a direct way. More importantly, perhaps, they can act as a counterweight to overly simplistic broad generalizations about the past.

Barbary corsairs were ruthless, violent men, but they were still human beings for all that. It is useful, sometimes, to remind ourselves that everybody is indeed human, and that most everybody is searching for essentially the same thing in life: a home, somewhere to belong, somewhere to live in peace with oneself and others.

Sometimes, people do ugly things to accomplish that goal.[1]

---

1. Mustaffa's story comes from Relation XXIV, 'De la prudente retraite d'un corsair' ('Of the Prudent Retirement of a Corsair'), in Emanuel d'Aranda, *Relation de la captivité et liberté du sieur Emanuel d'Aranda, mené esclave à Alger en l'an 1640 & mis en liberté l'an 1642* (*Relation of the captivity and freedom of Sieur Emanuel d'Aranda, Enslaved in Algiers in 1640 & released in 1642*), pp. 131–134.

# *CAPTIVES*

# The Tale of the Good Ship *Jacob*

In the autumn of 1621, a merchant ship named the *Jacob*, out of Bristol, set sail for the Mediterranean. She was a modest-sized vessel, with a carrying capacity of 120 tons, about 26 metres (85 feet) long, lightly armed with a few cannons, and with a crew of about a dozen or so.

She made good time through the English Channel and down past the Atlantic coasts of Portugal and Spain. But at the mouth of the Strait of Gibraltar, the *Jacob* had the bad luck to run into a fleet of corsair ships from Algiers. The crew refused to be intimidated and put up a fight, firing off their cannons, but it was no use. The corsairs overwhelmed them, and all the men aboard the *Jacob* were taken captive. The corsairs combed through the ship, stripping away anything of value they found, no matter how small. The crew was transferred to one of the corsair ships and manacled in the dank recesses of the hold.

The *Jacob* was a stout ship, though, and, after some discussion, the corsairs decided that instead of scuppering it, they would put a skeleton crew aboard and have them sail the *Jacob* back to Algiers, where they could re-outfit it as a corsair vessel. The corsair captain appointed thirteen men from among the contingent of janissary soldiers aboard his ship to man the *Jacob*. These men were soldiers rather than sailors, though, and the *Jacob* was a new and unfamiliar ship to them. So the corsair captain chose four of the *Jacob*'s crew—the youngest and therefore least likely to pose a threat—to manage the sails on the voyage back to Algiers.

While the corsair fleet sailed on in search of new prey, the *Jacob* began the voyage back to Algiers.

The four young sailors—John Cooke, William Ling, David Jones, and Robert Tuckey—were in despair. The janissaries aboard the *Jacob* were all armed with muskets, scimitars, and long knives. Their *Çavuş* (sergeant) was a squat bull of a man, implacably stern, unyielding as an iron post. If the young sailors did not do as they were ordered quickly enough—and none of the janissaries spoke proper English, so the orders were always unclear—they were slapped and punched, thrashed with ropes, or pricked with the wickedly sharp point of the *Çavuş*'s knife.

And they had only worse to look forward to. They had all heard stories of what it was like to be a slave in Algiers, to be chained and beaten, to labour continuously from sunup till dusk, fed only on coarse bread and water, to have nothing but damp, hard boards or bare stone for a bed. Or... cruellest fate of all, to be assigned to one of the corsair raiding galleys as a slave at the oars, to row for hour after hour, day after day, endlessly—until they collapsed and died of exhaustion or sickness and were slung overboard like so much unwanted refuse.

If the young men had come from well-to-do families, they might have been able to count on being ransomed. But they were all poor. There was no chance of ransom for any of them.

When they were not up in the shrouds managing the sails, the four young sailors sat about listlessly, staring mutely at each other, overwhelmed by the horror of what awaited them.

For five days things went on like this, with the young sailors growing more and more despairing.

And then, in the black middle of the fifth night, a storm struck.

When a storm hit like this, the ship's sails had to be shortened quickly, or they risked being ripped to shreds by the violent winds. Worse, with all her canvas up, the *Jacob* would be blown charging blindly before the wind... to be smashed to bits on any unseen rocks that might lie ahead in the dark. So the four young sailors scampered quickly up into the shrouds to haul in the topsails. This was no easy task. It was black dark, lit only by the occasional flash of lightning. They had to work by feel, straddling the yardarms nearly fifteen metres (fifty feet) up in the air, the ship rocking and heaving like a live thing under them. But they had done this task before. And they knew their ship. They soon had both the main- and the foretopsail furled.

It was not enough.

The *Jacob* still had too much canvas up, and she was hurtling forward blindly into the darkness, driven by the howling storm wind. The mainsail had to be taken in. But that was the largest sail on the ship, and its rain-sodden bulk was too much for the four young sailors to handle by themselves.

So they called on the janissaries to help.

Janissaries were soldiers rather than sailors, and they were of little use up in the shrouds of a storm-driven ship. But they could haul rope. The young sailors scrambled down to the deck to organize the janissaries. They managed to explain by shouts and signs what was needed and set two men to haul on the starboard mainsail halyards. Moving to the port halyards, John Cooke and David Jones found only one man there: the *Çavuş*. They looked about for others, but there was nobody in sight anywhere on the pitching deck.

The *Çavuş* stood braced awkwardly against the gunwale, trying to keep his balance. He pointed aloft, stabbing his finger upwards angrily, and shouted something that the howl of the storm wind drowned out.

John Cooke and David Jones looked at each other. The deck in this part of the ship was still empty—just the two of them and the *Çavuş*.

The man who for five long days had bullied them and tormented them with the knife he still carried.

Without a word, they rushed him, grabbed him up by the belt, and heaved him overboard.

The *Çavuş* was a strong man, though, and agile for all his bullishness. He managed to grab hold of a trailing rope as he fell and started to haul himself back on board. John Cooke sprinted to a nearby bilge pump, tore the handle off it, and flung it to David Jones. As the *Çavuş* pulled himself over the gunwale, shrieking in fury, Jones smashed him across the head with the bilge pump handle with all the force he could manage, cracking the man's skull open and sending him toppling backwards into the sea.

John Cooke and David Jones stood as they were, frozen, gasping for breath. A bolt of lightning lit the ship. They could see the dark, tossing sea, the white faces of William Ling and Robert Tuckey across from them on the deck.

'Stay here!' John Cooke shouted to his companions, his voice barely audible over the storm wind. He turned and sprinted for the *Jacob*'s stern, where the captain's cabin was. Six or seven janissaries stood clustered before the cabin, grasping at stanchions, or railings, or each other to stay on their feet, staring wide-eyed at the heaving sea—soldiers, not sailors.

They all shouted at John as he came rushing up the deck stairs. He skidded to a stop uncertainly... but then pressed ahead. Ignoring their calls and the grasping hands they reached to him, he elbowed a way through and into the captain's cabin.

High on a shelf in the back wall of the cabin, John knew, the English captain (now in chains in the hold of the Algiers corsair ship that had captured the *Jacob*) kept a pair of cutlasses. John had raced to the cabin in the hope that the corsairs had not found them.

They had not.

With the cutlasses in his arms, still in their scabbards, John burst out of the cabin, through the startled janissaries, and down onto the main deck.

The other young sailors were clustered there uncertainly. John held up the cutlasses with a triumphant flourish. For a long few moments, nobody moved. Then William Ling grabbed one of the cutlasses and yanked it from the scabbard. John did the same.

Together, the two of them rushed the janissaries still waiting on the *Jacob*'s port side for the signal to haul away on the mainsail halyards.

Neither of the young sailors had any training in how to use a sword. But a cutlass is a straightforward hacking weapon, and this was not swordplay. It was more like butchery. They swung the curved blades as they would have swung an axe at a tree bole, feeling the steel cut into flesh and grate jarringly against bone. The janissaries shrieked and tried to draw their own blades, but it all happened much too fast. And they lacked the shipboard agility the young sailors had.

The janissaries bled out their lives sprawled on the heaving deck, their eyes wide in disbelief at what had happened to them.

The other two young seamen grabbed up the butchered janissaries' scimitars, and the four of them rushed the stern deck.

This proved to be a harder fight. The element of surprise was gone, for one of the janissaries in front of the captain's cabin saw them coming up the stairs and warned his fellows. When the young Englishmen reached the stern deck, the janissaries were already drawing their scimitars.

John Cooke leaped forwards. The others hesitated a heartbeat, and then followed.

The janissaries were all seasoned soldiers. In anything like a normal fight, they would have cut down the young sailors in short order. But this was not a normal fight. They were on the deck of a heaving and pitching ship, in the dark, rain hammering down on them, able to see clearly only in brief spasms when lightning sizzled and boomed across the sea. And they had nobody to get them properly organized, for their *Çavuş* was gone.

The young sailors might not have known how to properly use the swords they held, but they knew their ship and instinctively anticipated each upwards or sideways heave of the deck. They swarmed the janissaries with desperate energy, agile as monkeys, trying to do as much damage as they could before their charge lost momentum.

In hardly more than an eyeblink, they cut down two of the janissaries and wounded several others.

The janissaries broke and fled.

The young sailors chased them across the deck, whirling their swords over their heads, howling like wolves, terrified and exultant and half mad.

The janissaries took shelter belowdecks, crowding down through one of the hatches.

The young sailors fastened that hatch, then raced about the ship and fastened all the other hatches until they had the janissaries safely trapped belowdecks.

Then they collapsed to the deck, gasping, too drained even to feel the cold rain on their faces.

'What do we do now?' one of them said when they had enough breath back to speak.

The storm was easing off, and the horizon showed the first pale light of dawn.

'The whipstaff,' John Cooke gasped.

The four of them rushed to the *Jacob*'s stern. (This was in the days before ships' wheels, and the helmsman steered the ship by using a long pole, called the whipstaff, attached to the rudder.) When they got there, they discovered that the janissaries, from their position belowdecks, had disengaged the whipstaff from the rudder, and the *Jacob* was beginning to tumble and role unguided in the still boisterous sea.

The four young men looked at each other.

'The muskets,' John Cooke said.

They scrounged up some of the janissaries' muskets, packed away in various parts of the ship. It took them some time to get the guns' barrels and priming pans cleaned and dried, and to find powder that had not been soaked by the storm. But eventually they had several of the muskets successfully primed and loaded.

John Cooke and William Ling walked to the nearest hatch, stuck the muzzles of their muskets through the grating, and fired.

A volley of surprised shouts came from below.

They loaded and fired into a different hatch, and then another, over and over, racing from one hatch to the next, until their arms ached and their ears rang.

Eventually, one of the janissaries called out in broken English that they were willing to reconnect the whipstaff and surrender.

By this time, the morning was well advanced. The storm had broken up, and swaths of blue sky showed overhead. The rain-soaked deck steamed in the morning sun. The four young sailors looked at each other wearily.

'What now?' William Ling asked.

'We head for the closest Christian port we can find,' John Cooke said.

That port proved to be Saint Lucas, Spain. As Englishmen, they were treated at first with the deepest suspicion. But after they had told their story, and brought the captive janissaries up on deck, they became far more popular. The local Spanish authorities offered to buy the janissaries and put them to work as slaves on the oarbenches of one of the galleys of the Spanish navy.

The four young Englishmen took the money, bought supplies, and headed home, triumphant.[1]

It is hard to know how accurate the details of this story about the *Jacob* and the plucky young English crewmen might be. It was likely based on true events. But it was also likely modified to make the young Englishmen look especially courageous and staunch. In the ongoing struggle between the European states and the Barbary corsairs, stories such as this, with its triumphal, happy ending, were no doubt needed to keep people's spirits up.

---

1. The story of the four intrepid young English sailors can be found in Samuel Purchas, *Hakluytus Posthumus or Purchas His Pilgrimes: Contayning a History of the World in Sea Voyages and Lande Travells by Englishmen and Others*, Volume VI, originally published in 1625, pp. 146-151.

# Nicolaus the Unlucky

In the early 1600s, a young French sailor named Nicolaus, from Havre-de-Grâce (modern-day Le Havre, on the northern coast of France, where the Sein empties into the English Channel) went to sea to seek his fortune. Instead of finding riches, however, he encountered disaster. His ship was attacked by corsairs from Algiers, and he, along with everybody else aboard, was captured.

Nicolaus was taken to Algiers and sold there in the Badestan—the slave market. For years, he endured the misery of his enslavement, forced to do hard labour without hope of liberation. Eventually, out of desperation, he 'turned Turk' (as the expression was then) and converted to Islam, becoming a renegade.

When a Christian slave converted, he was circumcised, given a new Muslim name, and paraded through the streets of Algiers triumphantly. He also acquired a new status.

In marked contrast to the rigidly stratified European societies of the time, Algiers was a meritocratic culture. Neither race nor ethnic background nor class origins mattered—as long as you were a Muslim. When Nicolaus converted, he became a member of a privileged group, a group in which he was treated as an equal (or at least a potential equal). A new future opened up for him. Conversion did not automatically mean that Nicolaus became a free man—things were not that simple—but it opened up opportunities for him that otherwise would have been impossible.

For some European Christians, conversion to Islam was a genuine matter of adopting a new faith. For others, it was merely a way of formally aligning themselves with the ruling group in order to further their careers (this was the tactic of a number of European pirates who chose to operate out of ports along the North African coast). Such converts embarked on new lives to which they willingly committed themselves. Slaves, however, mostly converted as a way to liberate themselves from the atrocious conditions of their captivity—as Nicolaus did—clinging secretly to their own religion all the while and telling themselves that their conversion was just for show.

In Nicolaus' case, the ruse worked. As a renegade, he was now eligible to serve aboard corsair ships. He did so, and during one of the cruises he took part in, he managed to desert from his ship and escape.

So Nicolaus returned to Havre-de-Grâce, where he was no doubt greeted with joy by friends and family, and where he took up his former life again. Or he tried to, anyway.

Nicolaus had two problems.

First, he would have had to hide or explain his conversion to Islam. Such conversion—such apostasy—was a very big deal at the time. Spanish ex-slaves returning home had to face the ungentle questioning of the Inquisition. The French had no real equivalent to the Spanish Inquisition, but Nicolaus would nonetheless have had to face a lot of hard questions. Even Inquisitors could sometimes recognize that ex-slaves might still be true Christian at heart despite their apostasy, but turning Turk always counted against you. And if pressed, you could not deny it. All your accusers had to do was yank your trousers down. The fact that you were circumcised would be obvious for all to see. In those days, circumcision was not practised in Europe, and there was only one explanation for why a European Christian would be circumcised: he had converted to Islam (or Judaism).

The second problem Nicolaus faced was more practical in nature: he was a sailor. He tried staying ashore for the better part of two years, but, for whatever reasons, he was unable to make it work. So in order to earn a living, and perhaps to escape from people who knew too much about his past, he signed on as crew aboard a merchant ship and took to the sea once again—after having, no doubt, implored the Blessed Virgin herself to keep him safe.

But Nicolaus was unlucky.

Somewhere off the Atlantic coast of Europe, his ship was surprised by a small fleet of corsairs out of Salé, on the western shore of Morocco. The ship attempted to flee, but the Salé corsairs, whose vessels were notoriously fast, caught up with them easily. After a brief and hopeless struggle, the European ship was overwhelmed.

The first thing corsairs did when they captured a ship was to take inventory—of both cargo and crew. The crew and passengers (if there were any) were immediately stripped of anything valuable they might be wearing, sometimes including their clothing. Then they were examined to see what quality of people they were and so determine what sort of ransom prospects might be expected from each.

Again, Nicolaus was unlucky—very unlucky.

One of the Salé corsairs recognized him as a renegade from Algiers.

During the early 1600s, there was a fair amount of traffic between Algiers and Salé, so it was not unusual for corsairs aboard a Salé ship to have been in Algiers. It was just unfortunate that this one had happened to have been in Algiers when Nicolaus was there.

Nicolaus tried to deny everything, to claim that this was a case of mistaken identity. But there was that simple test to see who was telling the truth: they yanked Nicolaus' trousers down and, sure enough, he was circumcised.

Nicolaus was chained up and thrust down into the ship's hold, along with the rest of the captives, and taken to Salé.

Apostasy was, if anything, a bigger issue for Muslims than for Christians. European Christians were willing, in at least some cases, to acknowledge the terrible stress that slaves were under, to recognize that such converts might still be true Christians at heart, and to offer forgiveness. Muslims were not so lenient.

When they arrived at Salé, Nicolaus' captors took him straightway to the home of a local Muslim magistrate, so that he could be officially judged for his apostasy. On the way there, however, they paraded him through the streets in chains, loudly proclaiming that, having converted to Islam, he had then reneged and become a Christian again. By the time they reached the magistrate's house, they were surrounded by a furious, shrieking mob.

The magistrate attempted to calm everybody down... but failed.

The mob was too worked up. Some of them started punching Nicolaus and kicking him. Tearing him from the hold of the corsairs, they began beating him with sticks. Knives came out. People started throwing stones. The violence grew so hysterical that not only did they kill poor Nicolaus; they built a pyre over his dead body right there on the spot and burned him to ashes.

And so the life of Nicolaus the unlucky ended—snuffed out abruptly in a burst of fanatical mob violence.[1]

In order to survive in the early seventeenth century, you had to be smart, strong, and adaptable—and lucky. Nicolaus clearly had all the former traits. But that was not enough to save him when, against all reasonable odds, he ended up in exactly the wrong place at exactly the wrong time.

When it comes to captives from this period, it is mostly the lucky ones we know about, the ones who escaped and lived to tell their stories. There must have been many Nicolauses, however—on both sides of the Mediterranean, for Europeans enslaved their Muslim captives with just as much vigorous cruelty as Muslims enslaved Christians—whose stories we will never know.

---

1. The outlines of Nicolaus' story can be found in Pierre Dan, *Histoire de Barbarie et de ses corsaires, des royaumes, et des villes d'Alger, de Tunis, de Salé et de Tripoly, (History of the Barbary and its Corsairs and Kingdoms, and of the Cities of Algiers, Tunis, Salé, and Tripoli)*, published in 1649, pp. 364–368.

# Juan Rodelgo: The Tale of a Renegade

Everybody has heard of the Spanish Inquisition and its ruthless use of intimidation and torture. What is less well known is that the Inquisitors' primary responsibility during the sixteenth and seventeenth centuries was to police the spiritual lives not of ordinary Catholic Spaniards but of Jewish and Muslim *conversos* (converts) in order to maintain religious purity and root out heresy among these new Christians. The Inquisitors' purview also included renegades.

As we have seen, it was not uncommon for Christian captives in places like Algiers, Tunis, or Salé to convert to Islam in order to make their lives more bearable. Inevitably, some of these renegades managed to escape and return to their home countries.

For the Inquisitors, repatriated Spanish renegades posed a problem: they had renounced their Catholic faith and embraced damnable heresy. What was to be done with them? In their defence, the returning renegades consistently claimed they had converted only for show, to better the terrible conditions under which they had been living, and that in their hearts they had always remained true Catholics. Even the sternest of Inquisitors had to admit there was some plausibility to this sort of story. Before permitting such lost sheep back into the fold, however, they had to determine not only the truth or untruth of each returning renegade's tale, but also the orthodoxy of his professed Catholic faith.

So all renegades returning to Spanish territories during this period had to face an interrogation/trial by the dreaded Inquisition.

One such renegade was Juan Rodelgo, who found himself before the Inquisition of the Canary Islands in the autumn of 1622.

Juan was a farmer's son in the village of Villacañas in La Mancha (famous homeland of Don Quixote). At the age of twenty (in 1610), he abandoned the tedious labour of the farm and ran off to seek adventure in the wider world. The military offered disaffected young men like him an opportunity not only for adventure but also advancement, both within the military itself and the wider society, as well as the possibility of making his fortune. Juan enrolled in a *tercio*, a military unit composed of swordsmen, pikemen, and musketeers (it is not clear which of these he ended up becoming).

Juan's *tercio* was shipped off to Italy, large parts of which were Spanish/Habsburg possessions in those days. Unfortunately for Juan, he found neither adventure nor fortune in Italy. After spending two uneventful years there, he quit the *tercio* and returned to his family's farm in Villacañas. The laborious life of a farmer still did not suit him, though. Five years later, now twenty-seven years old, he left again, joined up with another *tercio*, and, along with several hundred other new recruits, boarded a flotilla of Dutch ships in Cartagena, bound for Naples.

They never made it.

About 50 kilometres (30 miles) east of Cartagena, they were attacked at sea by a large squadron of Algerine corsairs. A couple of hundred Spanish recruits were killed in the naval battle that ensued, and nearly five hundred were captured, including Juan, who was wounded in the fight. The captive Spaniards were then dragged to Algiers to be auctioned off in the Badestan.

Juan was bought by a local merchant named Yusef, who owned an estate out in the fertile hinterland surrounding Algiers. Yusef immediately put Juan to work tending vineyards and toiling in the fields—a painfully ironic circumstance for a young man who had abandoned the gruelling drudgery of farming for a life of adventure as a soldier. After four years, desperate to escape the grind of farm labour, Juan converted. He took a new Muslim name—Mostafa—and began attending the mosque and receiving religious teachings. Converting did not free Juan/Mostafa from bondage, but it did free him from the farm.

In the summer of 1621, Yusef sent Juan out on his first *corso* expedition, serving as a soldier. Over the next year, Juan took part in three separate expeditions under three different captains: Soliman Reis, a Turk, Calafat Hassan Reis, a Greek renegade, and Mamet Tagarino Reis, a Morisco *expulsado*. Serving on these corsair expeditions would have entitled Juan to a share of the profits, but much of that share went to Yusef, who was still legally his owner. More importantly for Juan, though, being on a *corso* cruise offered something else: the possibly of jumping ship and escaping.

On his third cruise—the one led by Mamet Tagarino—Juan found the opportunity for escape that he had been hoping for.

Mamet Tagarino's expedition (which consisted of twenty-one ships) sailed to the Strait of Gibraltar and split into three squadrons. The squadron Juan was in captured a French vessel. Juan found himself appointed to the crew delegated to take this prize to Tetouan, a corsair port on the Mediterranean coast of Morocco, to sell the booty and French crew there—quicker and simpler than bringing them all the way back to Algiers. Before they could reach Tetouan, however, they were attacked by two European ships. To escape, they ran their own ship aground, leaped ashore, and fled into the Moroccan interior.

Juan managed to give his crewmembers the slip and headed for Tangier, a Spanish presidio (a fortified settlement) on the northwestern tip of Morocco, hoping to enter the presidio and get across the Strait of Gibraltar to Spain.

Walking at night and hiding during the day, he came within half a league of his destination... and then was caught by some local Moriscos, *expulsados* from Spain who by now had been living in Morocco for a decade or so. The Spanish had forcibly expelled upwards of 250,000 Moriscos (Muslims who had been forced to convert to Christianity) in 1609-1614 in a brutal act of ethnic cleansing. Most of these *expulsados* had settled in North Africa, especially Morocco, which was so close to Spain. Juan was dragged before the local Morisco *Caid* (Governor/Chief) for judgement. He managed to convince this man that he was an Andalusian—that is, a former resident of al-Andalus (Muslim Spain)—and a Morisco like themselves, as they could clearly see because he was circumcised, and that he had been separated from the rest of his crew when they were attacked by local Arab brigands.

A significant portion of the crew that leaped overboard from the Algerine corsair ship to safety would have consisted of janissaries. Morocco was not part of the Ottoman Empire, and relations between the crumbling Moroccan royal dynasty and the Ottomans were strained, so a gang of professional Ottoman soldiers wandering the countryside would not have been welcome. It was important for Juan to distance himself from them. Since he was a native Spanish speaker, his story seemed eminently plausible, and the Moriscos let him go.

But Juan then found himself in an untenable position. He had just lied about his identity. Crewmembers of the Algerine ship he had fled from might be picked up at any moment, and they could identify him and ruin his cover story. He might have escaped from Algiers, but there was no way for him to make it to Spain from where he now was. And if he was fingered as a renegade slave attempting to escape, he would be dragged back to Algiers to face brutal punishment.

So close to freedom... but not close enough.

Juan clearly was not ready to give up, though. He decided to quit Tangier and head to Salé, located on the Atlantic coast of Morocco. Salé was a major corsair capital with ties to Algiers, and the only place in Morocco where Juan stood a chance of finding a contact—and patron—in a country where he was a stranger.

To get to Salé, however, he had to trek alone through rough, mountainous country. It was a dangerous journey, for Morocco was suffering a period of bloody civil war, the result of an ongoing struggle between the sons of the deceased sultan for control of the throne. What little 'rule of law' there had once been had collapsed.

Juan hiked the better part of 320 kilometres (200 miles) through country he did not know, all the while avoiding contact with any locals—who would have killed him on sight and never thought twice about it. He also had to avoid being eaten by lions, which freely roamed the wilds of Morocco in those days. The trip must have involved many weeks of tense and gruelling travel, hiding out by day, creeping ahead at night under the uncertain radiance of star- or moonlight, eating whatever scraps he could scrounge along the way.

Somehow... he made it.

The trip came close to killing him, though, and when he arrived in Salé, he was exhausted and ill. Given all that he had endured since his initial capture, it is a testament to Juan's resilience and sheer stubborn will to endure that he made it at all.

Juan's gamble on Salé paid off, for when he arrived there he found a patron: Murad Reis, a Dutch renegade (his Dutch name was Jan Janszoon van Haarlem) who, a couple of years later, would be appointed Harbour Master of Salé by the Moroccan Sultan Moulay Zaydan. Juan's connection to Murad Reis was Calafat Hassan Reis—the second of the three corsair captains Juan had served under in Algiers—for Murad Reis had operated out of Algiers before relocating to Salé, and he and Calafat Hassan Reis knew each other. Thanks to this connection, Murad Reis allowed Juan to stay on board his ship while he convalesced.

Calafat Hassan Reis himself then arrived in town. He had already taken some prizes that season and sent them back to Algiers. In Salé, he purchased a new, relatively small ship, transferred to it some of the cannons from a prize he had taken, and arranged to go out on a *corso* expedition with Murad Reis (corsair captains often teamed up).

By this time, Juan had recovered sufficiently to be able to join the expedition as a soldier aboard Murad Reis's ship.

Leaving Salé, the two ships cruised the waters between the Canary Islands and the Atlantic coasts of Morocco and the Iberian Peninsula—the traditional hunting ground for corsairs operating out of Salé. Murad Reis's ship was not large, having a total crew of sixty-three (a small crew for a corsair ship). Calafat Hassan Reis's ship, smaller than Murad Reis's, had a crew of only forty. Ships like these were fast and manoeuvrable, though, and working in tandem, the two corsair captains quickly captured three vessels: a German ship; a French ship with a crew of thirteen, laden with Spanish wine, which the corsairs took off the coast of Spain; and a caravel with ten men and three women aboard. The passengers aboard the caravel were affluent Canary Islanders, and the expedition's next port of call was Gran Canaria, the largest of the Canary Islands. They went there to ransom these new captives, a procedure that avoided the complications and potential pitfalls of hauling the captives back to Salé and conducting long-distance ransom negotiations.

Before starting the ransoming process, the corsairs first made landfall in a deserted, sheltered bay on Gran Canaria's southwest coast to take on water. When doing this in potentially dangerous territory, corsair captains posted a ring of soldiers armed with spears and scimitars as a security cordon around the area. Juan was part of the force that formed that security perimeter. Finding himself at the far edge of the ring, Juan realized that this was the opportunity he had been waiting for. Driving his spear into the ground so that it would seem like he was still standing there, he took off his shoes and bolted, flinging his scimitar aside too, so that locals would not suspect he was a corsair.

He made it, sprinting away into the hinterland.

After nearly five years of bondage, he became a free man once again.

Despite all that had happened to him—or perhaps in some odd way because of what had happened—Juan was not yet ready to return to his old, dull life as a farmer. Instead, his plan was to blend in with the local population until he could find a ship that was headed to the Spanish territories in the New World and sign on as crew. The island's main port, Las Palmas, had a long history as an important port of call for ships sailing to and from the New World (Christopher Columbus stopped there to have the *Niña*, one of the three ships in his little expedition, refitted), and there was no shortage of such ships. Juan just needed a little time to find one and make arrangements.

Before he could arrange anything, however, Juan was recognized as an escapee by local authorities and brought before the Inquisitional authorities in Las Palmas. During his initial interrogation, Juan lied and claimed he was an escaped Christian slave and not a renegade. As an escaped slave who had stalwartly maintained his Catholic faith throughout his captivity, he would have been accepted by the Inquisitors with little trouble. As an acknowledged renegade, however, he would have been subject to a full Inquisitional trial, since apostasy (renouncing one's faith) was a serious crime. Juan clearly wished to avoid such a trial and the potential for interrogation under torture that went with it, hence his motivation to lie. The Inquisitors believed his story—escaped captives were far from rare on the Canary Islands at this time, and Juan was fully capable of reciting the catechism and other statements of Catholicism, demonstrating that he was a *bona fide* member of the faith—and they let him go. Juan must have been quite convincing, for the Inquisitors did not bother with the formality of checking to see if he had been circumcised.

Juan went back to trying to get a berth aboard a ship bound for the New World.

Before he could manage anything, though, Murad Reis and Calafat Hassan Reis dropped anchor outside Las Palmas and let it be known that they had captives to ransom. The local authorities rowed out and began negotiations. The haggling lasted several days. In the process, the participants ended up talking—gossiping—about a variety of subjects. One of the corsairs mentioned a Spanish renegade who had recently jumped ship while they were taking on water at the south end of the island. Word got around. Murad Reis let it be known that he was willing to trade four Christian captives for this escaped renegade, so that he could hang him publicly from a yardarm.

The Inquisitors heard about all this (the whole town heard about it), and they promptly had Juan arrested and brought before them for a second interrogation. This time, faced not only with a stream of witnesses the Inquisitors brought in to testify but also the direct threat of dire torture, Juan confessed the truth—or whatever version of the truth he thought the Inquisitors wanted to hear.

If the Inquisitors had applied the full rigor of the law, they could have sentenced Juan to be burned at the stake, along with other luckless apostates and heretics, in a public *auto da fé* (act of faith). They did that with fair regularity. In Juan's case, though, they were lenient (even stern-faced Inquisitors could have compassion, it seems). Instead of condemning him to be burned alive, they merely sentenced Juan to several months' penance/religious instruction in a nearby monastery, and then eventually granted him an official pardon and a travel pass and shipped him off back to his home in La Mancha.

So Juan Rodelgo's story ends more happily than others'. Not only did he receive unusual leniency from the Inquisitors; he also freed himself from slavery and evaded the vengeful wrath of Murad Reis. No doubt he returned to his family's farm—one did not dispute the Inquisition's verdicts—but it is unclear if he stayed there, for he disappears from history at this point. Given all that had happened to him, he might well have been past the point where he could settle down into his old life. Did he stay only a little while and then head off again on a vagabond quest for adventure and fortune? Or had he had enough of uncertainty and danger? Perhaps he chose to settle in the familiar land where he had been reared and take up with relief the ordinary, homely life of a farmer. Perhaps he married and had children and grandchildren, whom he held on his lap and told exciting stories to.

If so, somewhere in Spain, today, maybe even in La Mancha, his descendants might still live. In all likelihood—since very few people have ever read the transcript of Juan's Inquisitional trial or know of his story—they are completely unaware of their ancestor's adventures.[1]

---

1. The story of Juan Rodelgo's capture, escape, trial, and eventual return to his home is based on the official transcript of his interrogation penned by an Inquisitional clerk, a nearly 400-year-old document that runs to 92 pages of faded, spidery handwriting. It bears the title *Processo Criminal Contra Juan Rodelgo Natural de Villacañas, en La Mancha* (*Criminal proceedings against Juan Rodelgo, Native of Villacañas in La Mancha*) and is in the collection of the Museo Canario on Las Palmas, on Gran Canaria, in the Canary Islands. I had to tease out from the trial transcript the narrative of Juan Rodelgo's capture and eventual liberation because the story emerges piecemeal in a mosaic of bits and pieces from his own testimony and from the testimonies of a variety of witnesses who were called upon at his trial. I would like to express my profound thanks to David Rodriguez Marín for his invaluable services in transcribing the original Spanish text, and to Jade Carameaux-Jurewicz for help with translation.

# The Travails of Friar Antonio

Once upon a time—back in the 1570s—there was Augustinian friar named Antonio, a Portuguese man living in Spain, who had a big problem: he fell in love with a woman.

This was a problem for him in three ways.

First, and most obviously, Augustinian friars—like all members of the Catholic clergy—were (and are) supposed to be celibate. There were ways around this, of course. Over the centuries, innumerable priests quite successfully kept secret mistresses.

But that brings us to the second way in which this was a problem: it was simply not practical for a man living the communal life of an Augustinian friar to keep a mistress; it was not really practical for him to even be able to see much of the mistress.

And then there was the third aspect of the problem. Back in the sixteenth century, a friar could not leave his order except to join another, stricter order. So Friar Antonio could not simply walk away from the Augustinians. Doing so would have made him officially an apostate, that is, somebody who had renounced his faith. The Holy Office of the Inquisition actively prosecuted apostates of all sorts, including lapsed friars.

So Friar Antonio was faced with a big decision.

One solution, of course, would have been to abandon his mistress. But he clearly loved the woman (whose name has not survived the centuries) and was not willing to live without her. So he was left with only one remaining option: to become a (religious) criminal.

He slipped away from the Augustinians, began a new life as a lay priest (a priest not formally connected with any religious order), took his mistress with him... and lied to everybody about his past and his present situation. In the twenty-first century, this option would have never worked. Today, there are just too many ways to keep digital tabs on a person's identity. The sixteenth century was a looser age, though, and it was neither simple nor easy to keep accurate track of a people's pasts—especially if a person was well connected.

Which Friar Antonio definitely was.

In those days (today too, to some extent), if you had the right connections, you could get away with pretty much anything. Friar Antonio came from an important Portuguese family, was extremely well educated (he had a doctorate in theology and a degree in canon and civil law), and had an extensive network of patronage contacts among the powerful men of the time, including no lesser a personage than King Philip II, the king of Spain himself. Using these contacts, Friar Antonio managed not only to slip away from the Augustinians and become a lay priest, but also to acquire an ecclesiastic position as a Vicar General (essentially an administrative post) on the island of Sicily.

So everything seemed to have worked out. All was in readiness for Friar Antonio—though he was no longer, strictly speaking, a friar—to begin a new life with his mistress. That new life included not only the mistress herself, but also their young son.

In 1577 (when he was just shy of forty years old), Friar Antonio boarded the *San Pablo*, a Maltese galley, in Barcelona. With him were his household retinue: three servants and two people he described as his sister and nephew—the 'sister' and 'nephew' being his mistress and son. Their plan was to take the *San Pablo* to Malta. From there, they would find passage across the relatively short sea distance to Sicily, where they would all take up their new life together. It must have been a supremely exciting moment: their dream was about to come true.

Friar Antonio chose to travel aboard the *San Pablo* for a reason. In those days, the Knights of Malta waged unending war against Ottoman shipping in general and Barbary corsairs in particular, and their galleys were warships with a fearsome reputation. Friar Antonio no doubt figured that travelling on a Maltese galley would be the absolute safest way to cross the Mediterranean— which was infested with Barbary corsairs.

The *San Pablo* left Barcelona at the end of March, travelling in company with two other galleys for safety. At first, all went well. But then a violent storm came up and separated the *San Pablo* from the other ships. To keep afloat, the crew had to throw overboard everything they could, including the ship's cannons, the sails, and even the oars. The vessel survived the storm—just— and, crippled, limped into port on the small island of San Pedro, a few miles off the southwest coast of Sardinia.

There, their luck ran out completely.

On April 1, a fleet of twelve Barbary corsair galliots (slightly smaller versions of a galley) appeared and attacked them. Crippled as it was, and without armament, there was little the *San Pablo* could do to mount a defence.

Friar Antonio, his small family, and his servants were taken captive along with all the rest—almost three hundred unhappy people in total.

The commander of the corsair fleet was Dali Mami Reis, who operated out of Algiers (and who had the singular distinction of being the captain who captured Miguel de Cervantes, author of *Don Quixote*). Dali Mami Reis brought Friar Antonio and his small household retinue to Algiers, where they were all separated from each other and auctioned off in the Badestan.

And so ended Friar Antonio's dream of living happily ever after.

Well… not quite ended entirely.

In Algiers, Friar Antonio was bought by a man named Qaid Muhammad, a renegade Jewish merchant with a complicated past: he had first converted from Judaism to Islam; then, after being held captive for some years in Genoa, he became a Christian; after escaping and returning to Algiers, he resumed life as a Muslim. Qaid Muhammad had risen within the governmental political structure of Algiers to become the Master of the Mint, a position that made him an important and powerful man. He was apparently greedy and corrupt, though, and was accused, among other things, of debasing the city's coinage—that is, of creating coins that were an admixture of silver and other metals and then trying to pass them off as pure silver.

For Qaid Muhammad, Friar Antonio represented a piece of incredibly good fortune. The real profit in the human trafficking that Algiers specialized in, remember, was not simply in selling human beings into slavery or profiting from their forced labour. It was in ransoms. And a man like Friar Antonio—an important ecclesiastic with connections to the very highest levels of power in Spain—would command a *huge* ransom.

Friar Antonio himself, of course, had a new set of problems. He not only had to figure out a way to somehow come up with the enormous sum of money Qaid Muhammad would demand for his own release; he also had to find a way to free his mistress, his son, and his servants.

Qaid Muhammad chained Friar Antonio up in a fetid basement room in his house—not quite an actual dungeon, but close—and handed him pen and paper and told him to start writing people to arrange his ransom. Friar Antonio did just that. The situation was complicated, though. He had been appointed to the position of Vicar General of Sicily, but he had not been able to actually take up the position. The revenues that went along with that position should still have been his, even though he was absent, and he tried to arrange for those revenues to be used to raise the necessary ransom money. In his absence, however, other local Sicilian officials had stepped in and begun acquiring those revenues and were reluctant to part with them. A years-long, acrimonious set of negotiations ensued involving numerous parties, including the Spanish king, Philip II.

Meanwhile, Friar Antonio had to cope with being a captive in Algiers. Most of his time was spent shackled in the 'dungeon' in Qaid Muhammad's basement. Intermittently, though, Qaid Muhammad would send him out on work gangs to do brutally hard manual labour in the hot sun—a tactic employed to encourage Friar Antonio to increase his efforts to acquire the ransom money.

Miserable though much of his time in Algiers was, Friar Antonio had it better than many. Because he was expected to keep up a correspondence regarding his ransom, he was continuously supplied with pen and paper. He also managed to acquire some books (one was the famous *Description of*

*Africa*, by Leo Africanus). So though he endured long days in chains in his cramped cell, he spent much of his time there reading and writing—pursuits that, for an academically-minded man like him, must have been reassuringly familiar and comforting.

He also got to meet a wide variety of people. Qaid Muhammad, being the important man that he was, had many visitors, both official and not. No doubt, Friar Antonio was on display ('Come down into the basement and meet the new Christian priest I've just bought.'), and, as a result, Friar Antonio was able to converse with a wide cross section of Algerine residents: city officials, janissaries, Jews, corsair captains, slaves, other captives. Also, there was a sort of community of scholars among the captives and slaves in Algiers, men from various European nations who all shared one thing in common: an advanced education. These men exchanged resources and ideas and discussed philosophy and scripture—and poetry. One of the friendships Friar Antonio made while in Algiers was with Miguel de Cervantes, author of *Don Quixote*, who was also a captive. The two spent hours discussing poems Cervantes was writing.

Meanwhile, years passed, and Friar Antonio was no nearer to acquiring the ransom he needed.

At some point (it is unclear exactly when), his son died. There is no record of how the boy died, whether by accident, overwork, disease, torture, debilitating despair, or some combination of these. It must have been devastating for Friar Antonio, sitting shackled in his cell, hearing the news of his son's death, helpless to do anything but mourn ineffectually. No doubt he redoubled his efforts to arrange ransom as quickly as possible before his mistress and servants died, too.

It took over four years.

Friar Antonio came to Algiers in April, 1577. He did not manage to leave until July, 1581. His leaving was quite dramatic, though.

When the ransom funds finally arrived, he did not simply hand them over to Qaid Muhammad. Instead, he secretly arranged to have his mistress ransomed. Then, a day or two after she was safely aboard a European ship headed back home, Friar Antonio... disappeared.

Qaid Muhammad was furious. He had every corner of the town searched. He offered a huge reward. He threatened to torture every captive and slave who knew Friar Antonio to force them to reveal his whereabouts. None of it worked. Friar Antonio was gone.

Nobody knows how he managed it.

Every slave and captive in Algiers yearned desperately for freedom. The city authorities were well aware of this and did their very best to shut down potential avenues of escape. All European ships had to surrender their sails and their rudders when they arrived. When it came time to depart, they only got them back after their ship had been thoroughly searched for stowaway slaves.

So Friar Antonio should not have been able to slip away aboard a European ship. He somehow managed it, though. The likeliest explanation is that he used a portion of the ransom funds to buy his mistress's freedom—her ransom would have been less than his—and then employed the remaining money to bribe the port officials who were supposed to be searching ships and to entice some willing ship's captain to smuggle him out of the city.

However he pulled it off, Friar Antonio escaped from Algiers and returned to Spain, where he was finally reunited with his mistress.

After that, the two of them lived happily ever after together.

Well… no. Actually, they did not.

Having returned from Algiers, Friar Antonio tried to take up his old life, or, rather, take up the new life he had been about to embark on before his capture. But there were complications.

Somehow, the fact that he had abandoned the Augustinians in order to cohabit with a mistress came to light. A little over a year after his return, he was officially outed. This, of course, was a very big problem indeed. Among other things, it cost him his chief ally: King Philip II of Spain. It was said of King Philip that 'from his smile to the dagger there was little distance'. That is, he could turn on people in an instant. He turned on Friar Antonio—with, from his point of view, good reason: Friar Antonio had kept a hidden mistress and deceived him. King Philip had pressed to have Friar Antonio's position as Sicilian Vicar General made official and final. He had actively worked towards Friar Antonio's freedom, even contributed money towards his ransom. Now, the king wrote a serious of vitriolic letters denouncing him.

Friar Antonio was not left entirely without allies, though. He turned to no lesser a personage than the Pope.

The Vatican and the Spanish Crown were in the midst of a power struggle at this time, and the Pope likely saw Friar Antonio's case as an opportunity to dispute Philip's authority—to 'pluck his beard' as the saying went (Friar Antonio likely turned to the Pope for aid because he was aware of this power struggle). Whatever his reasons, the Pope officially absolved Friar Antonio of all his sins and reaffirmed him as Vicar General in Sicily.

King Philip was seriously pissed—as the Pope no doubt intended him to be—but there was little the king could do about the situation.

And so Friar Antonio at last made it to Sicily and took up his ecclesiastical position there.

There is no clear record of whether or not his mistress accompanied him. We know nothing about this woman. Her age, her name, her background—all are a mystery. The last thing we know for sure is that Friar Antonio successfully ransomed her. After that... nothing.

After everything that had happened, it seems unlikely that Friar Antonio would have arrived in Sicily with his mistress blatantly in tow. But this was an age, remember, when, if you had powerful enough patronage, you could pretty much get away with anything—as Friar Antonio himself proved with his 'get out of jail' pardon from the Pope.

Friar Antonio's actions over the years seem to indicate that he was devoted to his mistress. So perhaps he did indeed bring her to live with him in Sicily, and perhaps, very circumspectly, the two were able to spend some happy years together there. Perhaps he even ransomed his servants and brought them back from Algiers too, though there is no mention of this. The fate of the poor servants is another mystery.

Friar Antonio served as Vicar General in Sicily for three years before his death in or around 1587, just shy of fifty. The cause of his death is another mystery. He had health problems after his incarceration in Algiers, so perhaps some chronic ailment from that time proved fatal. Of the fate of his mistress, we know nothing at all.

We know the details of Friar Antonio's life because, while he was in Algiers composing ransom-related correspondence, he was also writing a book. Like everything else in his life, though, the story of the book is complicated.

During this period, the Spanish authorities regulated the publishing industry very strictly. The issue was heresy. Ideas are powerful things, and books are a powerful way to disseminate ideas. In Friar Antonio's day, in order for a book to be printed by any Spanish publisher, it first had to be examined by members of the Inquisition and deemed safely non-heretical. Only after it had received this official seal of approval could a book be sent to press. The whole process was taken very seriously: somebody caught publishing an illicit book could be put to death.

It was not just the content of a book that determined its acceptability. It was also the known character of the author. Friar Antonio, with his infamous reputation as a fallen Augustinian friar and a fornicator, would have stood no chance at all of having any book with his name on it published.

So he had to find some other way.

During his years as Vicar General, Friar Antonio served with a bishop named Diego de Haedo. There is no record of what sort of relationship the two men might have had, but we do know this: when the book Friar Antonio wrote was finally published, in 1612, it bore Diego de Haedo's name as the author. Bishop de Haedo had already been dead for four years by that time, and the book was shepherded through the publication process by the bishop's nephew who—confusingly—was also named Diego de Haedo.

It seems that Friar Antonio, knowing he could not get the book accepted if his name was attached to it, gave Bishop de Haedo the manuscript. The bishop, in turn, passed it along to his nephew. The nephew finally acquired permission to publish it twenty-five years after Friar Antonio's death. There is also the possibility, of course, that Bishop de Haedo stole the manuscript upon Friar Antonio's death and passed it off as his own work. There is no way to know for sure.

We do know the book, though. It was a monumental work titled *Topografía e historia general de Argel* (*Topography and General History of Algiers*), and it is one of the most important seventeenth century European works on Algiers. It includes a detailed physical description of the city, equally detailed discussions of the customs, mores, and religion of the inhabitants, plus a history of the rulers of Algiers and a series of dialogues on captivity, religion, and a host of other topics.

The *Topografía* is an absolutely invaluable resource for anybody interested in Algiers in the late sixteenth century.

Only in the past few decades has it been generally accepted that Friar Antonio—whose full name was Antonio de Sosa—was in fact the author of the *Topografía*. For over three centuries, Bishop de Haedo received the credit. Even today, de Haedo is still referred to quite commonly as the author of the *Topografía*.

Antonio de Sosa came from a privileged background. He was intelligent and highly educated, with good connections to the powerful men of his age. He could have had—had clearly been groomed for—a long, comfortable life as a respected and honoured ecclesiastic. For the love of a woman, he walked away from all that. And through all the painful events that followed, it seemed he never abandoned her.

It must have been a great love.

He must have been quite a man.[1]

---

1. In putting together this tale of the tribulations of Friar Antonio, I relied on a variety of sources, including *Topographie et histoire générale d'Alger*, a French rendering of de Sosa's *Topografía*, translated by Dr. Monnereau and A. Berbrugger, originally published in 1870-71 as a series of articles in the *Revue Africaine*, and *An Early Modern Dialogue with Islam: Antonio de Sosa's Topography of Algiers (1612)*, edited by María Antonia Garcés and translated by Diana de Armas Wilson, an English rendering of the first part of the *Topografía*. (If you are interested in reading de Sosa, this is the book to pick up.) Parts of this chapter on Friar Antonio's travails are speculative, but the speculation is, I believe, reasonable and consistent with the documents that have come down to us.

# Vultures and Insatiable Tigers: Father Pierre Dan

European captives enslaved in Algiers dreamed of one thing above all else: being ransomed.

If you were a citizen of a northern Protestant country—England, Holland, the German States, Denmark, Iceland, etc.—and you were not rich, you had two basic options for ransom: private collections raised by individuals (often under the auspices of the church), or funds from the king's or the government's treasury. If you were a citizen of a Catholic country, however, you had a third option: the redemptive friars.

There were two famous Catholic religious orders founded specifically for the redeeming—the ransoming—of captives held in North Africa: the Order of Our Lady of Mercy for the Redemption of Captives (*Ordo Beatae Mariae de Mercede redemptionis captivorum*), known as the Mercedarians, and the Order of the Most Holy Trinity and of the Captives (*Ordo Sanctissimae Trinitatis et captivorum*), known as the Trinitarians. These orders raised large sums of money—from private, corporate, governmental, and royal donors—and then organized ransoming expeditions to various cities in North Africa and bought the freedom of anywhere from a few dozen to several hundred enslaved Catholics at a time.

Such ransoming expeditions were delicate affairs requiring equal amounts of diplomatic tact, hard bargaining, judicious bribery, nerve, and luck. Some expeditions were unqualified successes. For instance, in 1660, 366 Spanish captives were freed during a single expedition to Algiers. Some ransoming expeditions had less success, though.

One such less-than-successful expedition took place in the summer of 1634.

It was a French endeavour, involving both political and humanitarian aims.

The French and the Algerines had entered into a treaty in 1628 that had guaranteed the inviolability of ships and merchandise on both sides. It had not worked out that way. Despite the solemn commitments the treaty contained, both the French and the Algerines had continued to prey on each other's ships, amidst bitter accusations and recriminations—and the virtual collapse of the treaty.

Cardinal Richelieu was the French king Louis XIII's chief minister at the time, and he wanted to stem the haemorrhaging of ships and sailors resulting from the continued depredations of the Algerine corsairs. He sent Sanson Le Page, First Herald of the Armies of France, to Algiers to negotiate a new treaty.

Richelieu also wanted to redeem the hundreds of French slaves in Algiers. To head this aspect of the mission, Father Pierre Dan, a Trinitarian friar, was chosen.

There is no record of how Le Page might have felt about this mission. We do, however, know what Father Dan's reaction was, for he wrote about his experience:

The merit of this endeavour and obedience and charity made me very happy to undertake this journey... Some other of my colleagues were assigned to accompany me, and we were all very glad that we might have such an opportunity to fulfil the goal of our profession, which requires us to expose our lives to all kinds of dangers in order to liberate the poor captives that the infidels have kept in irons in the bondage of their unbearable tyranny.[1]

The mission's objectives were—in principle at least—quite simple: renegotiate the treaty between France and Algiers, ransom the French slaves in Algiers, and return to France triumphant. To help with the second objective, Richelieu had authorized the liberation of Muslim slaves rowing on French galleys (France, like everybody else on the Mediterranean littoral at this time, had a fleet of oared galleys powered by slaves chained to the rowing benches). These Muslim galley slaves could be swapped for French slaves in Algiers.

The ransoming expedition left Marseilles on Wednesday, July 12, 1634. They made the voyage to Algiers in four days—very good time indeed for those days—and arrived on Saturday, July 15. As was the case with all European ships in Algiers, they had to surrender their rudder and sails. They also had to register with the Algerine authorities the amount of ransom funds they had brought with them, pay the required import tax on those funds, hire an interpreter, and arrange a residence for themselves.

Saturday was the day when the Divan—the governing council of Algiers—regularly gathered. So Le Page and Father Dan and the rest were able to meet

---

1. Pierre Dan, *Histoire de Barbarie*, 1649, p. 40.

directly with the Algerine authorities the very day they landed, an auspicious beginning that everybody noted.

There was a problem, though. Algiers was, at least nominally, an Ottoman Regency. That is, it was a province of the sprawling Ottoman Empire, the capital of which was Istanbul. Algiers was governed by the Divan, which was made up of janissary officers. The Pashas were the official Ottoman Governors of the city, though their authority was frequently called into doubt. Pashas took nominal control of Algiers for several years and then were cycled out and replaced by new ones.

As (bad) luck would have it, when La Page and Father Dan and their expedition arrived, the old Pasha had just left, and the new Pasha had not yet shown up from Istanbul.

So they had to wait.

The new Pasha, Yusuf the Second, eventually arrived and received a grand and dramatic welcome. Cannons were fired off to salute him, and a huge parade, including marching bands, poured through the streets. (Father Dan was unimpressed by the music: 'It made such a strange noise that, if it can be called harmony, I must confess it was more capable of producing fright than of giving pleasure.'[2])

The new Pasha greeted the French ransomers shortly after his arrival. They presented him with a series of lavish gifts (as was expected), but he told them he would be far too busy getting adjusted to his new position to have time for them for several weeks.

So they waited some more.

Things look positive enough at this point, though. The Pasha and the Divan had issued a joint decree that all residents of Algiers were to avoid harming the French in any way—'on pain of having no more head.' This, Father Dan noted, was 'the standard phrase they use when they want to threaten people into submission.' There was also another decree: the French slaves employed in the hard labour of hauling stone out to the Mole (the causeway that formed the breakwater that sheltered the Algiers harbour and that required constant upkeep) were relieved of that onerous work. Father Dan observed that:

In the height of incomparable joy, they thanked God for this favour, and prayed for his very Christian Majesty, King Louis XIII, in recognition of the care he had taken to deliver them from this misery, and for the hope that, by the same

---

2. Pierre Dan, *Histoire de Barbarie*, 1649, p. 44.

favour, they would soon be delivered from the shackles and cruel servitude to which they had been miserably reduced by the tyranny of these barbarians.[3]

Unfortunately, this was the high point of the expedition.

When Yusuf Pasha finally found time to see Sanson Le Page and Father Dan, Le Page demanded that the Pasha free all the French slaves and return all the merchandise and the ships that had been taken by Algerine corsairs since 1628, the year the treaty between France and Algiers had been signed. In return, Le Page offered to turn over sixty-eight Muslim galley slaves kept in Marseilles.

The Pasha said this would be very difficult, since returning all those slaves, all the merchandise, and all the ships that had been taken would financially ruin those who had bought and sold them 'in good faith' over the years. Le Page then asked that at least the French slaves be released and that the Algerines undertake not to attack French ships in future. Yusuf Pasha proposed a counteroffer: that the French slaves be put up for ransom and that Father Dan buy them individually from their owners.

Le Page and Father Dan were beginning to grasp the workings of the Algerine system by now, though, and they realized that the Pasha's offer was entirely self-serving, since he personally was entitled to a tax collected on each slave ransomed.

Le Page then changed tactics and attempted to bypass the Pasha by appealing directly to the Divan.

As Le Page launched into his pitch on the floor of the room where the Divan met, however, several women burst into the chamber. According to Father Dan, they were clutching letters in their hands and shouting, 'Charala! Charala!' that is to say, 'God's justice.' The women claimed their husbands had been galley slaves at Marseilles, and that the letters they held proved the French had sold their husbands as slaves to the Knights Hospitaler on Malta. The women demanded that before any French slaves were released, their husbands should first be returned from Malta.

Father Dan was convinced that the women were lying, and that this was all a scheme concocted by Yusuf Pasha. It did not matter. The members of the Divan were outraged. The French were made to appear duplicitous, and negotiations broke down.

Le Page threatened to return immediately to France.

---

3. Pierre Dan, *Histoire de Barbarie*, 1649, p. 43.

In response to this, Yusuf Pasha offered to swap French slaves in Algiers for Muslim galley slaves in Marseilles at a rate of one for one. Le Page stood firm and insisted that he must have all the French slaves in Algiers freed.

At this point, the Pasha came up with a new approach to handling negotiations: if Le Page were to give him a gift of a large amount of gold, he, the Pasha, could arrange matters so that the French slaves could be freed.

Sanson Le Page stomped off in fury.

The negotiations were over.

'After having spent the months of July, August, and September,' Father Dan wrote, 'during the very hottest part of summer, and having suffered an infinity of struggle and labour, we were obliged to leave.'[4] His embittered characterization of all this was that dealing with Algerines was like dealing with 'vultures and insatiable tigers who live on their prey, attacking everywhere, and never return anything.'[5]

To their horror, the French slaves in Algiers were returned to their backbreaking work on the Mole, their dream of liberation shattered. While negotiations had been ongoing, Father Dan had managed to privately ransom some French slaves. These were now prohibited from leaving Algiers until the husbands of the angry wives had been returned from Malta. If Father Dan tried to ransom any more, they too would be consigned to that same limbo—freed men but unable to leave Algiers.

At this point, the Le Page expedition left Algiers, having failed in every way, and returned to Marseilles in disgrace, arriving there in early October.

The Trinitarians were by now desperate to accomplish *something*. They still had most of the funds they had raised for the Algiers expedition, and they cast about for a way to salvage matters. After considerable debate, they decided to go to Tunis.

An expedition was quickly organized, and Father Dan and his brothers set off once again for North Africa. This time they had better luck. After three months of haggling, they managed to ransom forty-two French slaves.

Not what you might call an unmitigated success, but far better than nothing at all.

When Father Dan and the forty-two freed captives arrived at Marseille in early April of 1635, they were greeted by cheers. Monks solemnly sang the *Te Deum* as they disembarked. From there, everybody formed a grand procession and paraded through the town to the Trinitarian monastery, where mass was celebrated.

---

4. Pierre Dan, *Histoire de Barbarie*, 1649, p. 48.

5. Pierre Dan, *Histoire de Barbarie*, 1649, p. 45.

After a short time in Marseilles, Father Dan, his Trinitarian brothers, and the freed captives began a grand procession across France to Paris. At each stop along the way, they performed the same sort of dramatic public pageant they had in Marseilles. Crowds flocked to see them. Solemn masses were performed in each town and fervent sermons delivered—and, one presumes, alms gathered for the multitude of poor captives still enslaved.

Finally, after more than six weeks on the road, the group reached Paris, where they were met by a jubilant crowd of devotees, just as they had been when they came off the ship in Marseilles. They all trooped across the city to the Trinitarian church, where they celebrated the captives' redemption yet again.

The whole thing was a public relations triumph. As an organization, the Trinitarians had been faltering. Father Dan's successful Tunis expedition—and the grand public pageantry staged upon his return—revived their fortunes. And Father Dan himself was elevated to the position of Father Superior at Fontainebleau, the order's headquarters located in the Royal Château just outside Paris.

While he was Father Superior, Father Dan wrote an account of his experiences. Perhaps he started out just intending to create a sort of travel diary. Perhaps not. In any case, he ended up producing one of the major works—some would say *the* major work—of the seventeenth century on North Africa and the Barbary corsairs: *Histoire de Barbarie et de ses corsaires des royaumes, & des villes d'Alger, de Tunis, de Salé, & de Tripoli, divisée en six livres où il est traité de leur gouvernement, de leurs moeurs, de leurs cruautés, de leurs brigandages, de leurs sortilèges, & de plusieurs autres particularités remarquables, ensemble des grandes misères & des cruels tourments qu'endurent les Chrétiens captifs parmi les infidèles* (*History of the Barbary and its Corsairs and Kingdoms, and of the cities of Algiers, Tunis, Sale, and Tripoli, Divided into Six Books where is treated their government, their customs, their cruelties, their robberies, their sorceries, and several other remarkable peculiarities, along with all the great miseries and cruel torments endured by captive Christians among the infidels*).

There is no documentation for exactly how Father Dan put *Histoire de Barbarie* together, but it is not hard to work out what the process must have been. In part, he relied on previously published works dealing with Barbary corsairs and North Africa, like Antonio de Sosa's *Topografía e historia general de Argel* (*Topography and General History of Algiers*). Father Dan also relied on his own experiences in Algiers and Tunis (he periodically mentions how he heard a particular piece of information from somebody he talked with or how he personally saw an event unfolding).

However, the details taken from previously published works and Father Dan's own experiences combined account for only a relatively small portion of the book as a whole. The majority of it seems to have come from reports Father Dan read and from people he interviewed. Just as Father Dan himself had trekked across France to bring his ransomed captives to Fontainebleau, so too would other Trinitarian friars returning from expeditions to North Africa. Once at Fontainebleau, of course, they would have presented themselves before the Father Superior (it is likely that at least some of them had been sent on those very expeditions by Father Dan himself, and that they made formal reports to him). As a result, Father Dan had access to a large number of people—both friars and liberated captives—from whom he could gather information for his book.

The first edition of *History of Barbarie* was published in 1637, two years after Father Dan's return from Tunis. It was an impressive 514 pages long—not counting the Table de Matières (Table of Contents) at the back. A second, revised and enlarged, edition was published in 1649, the year of his death. Both versions of the book have an element of blatant propaganda in them. Father Dan clearly wanted to provide detailed information to his readers about North Africa, but he just as clearly wanted to dramatize the situation, and he focused on the cruelties inflicted upon 'the poor Christian captives' and the heroic and selfless work of his order in liberating them—all in an effort to drum up support, both moral and financial, for the Trinitarian mission. Despite this propaganda element, however, *Histoire de Barbarie* is still a goldmine of information on the geography, history, ethnography, and economics of North Africa. The breadth and scope of material covered results in a book that few others of its time can compete with. It is an encyclopaedic work that generations of readers have consulted.

Unfortunately, *Histoire de Barbarie* has not yet been translated into English. For those who can parse the seventeenth century French, though, it is a fascinating depository of information and well worth the trouble of deciphering.[6]

---

6. The details of Sanson Le Page's and Father Dan's 1634 mission to Algiers are taken from the second edition of Father Dan's *Histoire de Barbarie et de ses corsaires des royaumes, & des villes d'Alger, de Tunis, de Salé, & de Tripoli*, published in 1649 (the year of Father Dan's death), pp. 39-64.

# The Fatima Affair

In the spring of 1609, three Spanish Trinitarian friars sailed to Algiers on a ransom expedition. Their names were Bernardo de Monroy, Juan de Aguila, and Juan de Palacios. The ship carrying them left Spain in March and arrived at Algiers on the first of April.

Once in Algiers, the Trinitarians followed the standard protocol for ransom expeditions like theirs: they registered the amount of ransom funds they had brought with them, paid the requisite tax on those funds, hired an interpreter, arranged a residence for themselves, and reported to the Pasha—and gave him lavish gifts to ensure his cooperation. After that, they began the arduous process of negotiating ransoms.

They were there for a month and a half. During that time, they paid out enough money to free a total of 136 captives. They also celebrated mass regularly in the chapel in what was known as the Grand Bagnio—the prison building that housed captives and slaves in Algiers, which was large enough to hold over a thousand inmates—and also gave religious comfort to the sick and the dying in the infirmary there.

In short, it was an entirely successful expedition. As Father Bernardo de Monroy put it in a letter he sent to his superiors: 'We exhorted the poor Christian slaves we had freed to drop their chains to the ground. They flexed their knees, which had been bent for so long under the torment of their iron fetters, tears in their eyes, sobbing.'[1] With their 136 freed slaves, the three Trinitarian friars boarded their ship and began preparations for departure.

And then the trouble began.

A noisy mob appeared on the docks. A squad of janissaries emerged from the agitated crowd, boarded the ship, placed the three friars and their newly freed captives under arrest, and marched them roughly back into town. The friars had no idea why any of this was happening and vigorously protested

---

1. Henri Ternaux-Compans, *Archives des voyages ; ou, Collection d'anciennes relations inédites ou très-rares, de lettres, mémoires, itinéraires et autres documents relatifs à la géographie et aux voyages* (*Travel Archives; or a Collection of Old Unpublished or Very Rare Reports, Letters, Memoirs, Itineraries, and Other Documents Relating to Geography and Travel*), p. 453.

such ill treatment all the way. It did no good. They and their freed captives—who must have been sick with dismay at this sudden bitter reversal of their fortunes—were thrown into prison.

This unexpected setback had nothing to do with the actions of the members of the expedition. Rather, it resulted from a complicated international situation.

Several months earlier, a ship from Algiers had been captured by the Genoese. A number of children from important families in Algiers were aboard that ship. These children were taken to Livorno, and negotiations were begun to ransom them. Since their parents were influential and wealthy people, the negotiations went fairly smoothly, and a ransom price of about 500 pieces of eight per head—very serious money indeed in those days—was agreed upon and paid. The children were then released and put aboard a ship that sailed for Algiers.

On the journey, however, the ship stopped at a small port on the northwest corner of Corsica. Among the Algerine children was a ten-year-old girl. She is described as one of the most conspicuous among the group of children 'because of her beauty and because she was from a great and noble household.'[2] The girl's name was Fatima.

Exactly what happened is not clear, but somehow Fatima was induced (or forced) to convert to Christianity. The fact that she was singled out for her beauty makes one wonder what the true motivation might have been to separate her from the other children. One contemporary assessment puts it like this: 'Either a secret inspiration from God had enticed her to become a Christian, or her great beauty had made someone delight in her.'[3] Whatever the cause, Fatima left (or was taken from) the ship and did not return to Algiers with the other ransomed children.

It turned out that Fatima was the daughter of the Aga (the Commander in Chief) of the janissaries at Bône (modern Annaba, located on the coast about 400 kilometres/250 miles west of Algiers.) The Aga, a stern man named Mehmet Axá, was in the excited crowd of relived parents and family who met the ship carrying the liberated children when it arrived at the Algiers docks. He was shocked to find that his daughter was not on board the ship. After hearing the story the ship's captain told about her, he stormed off to see the Pasha and demand that Fatima be returned to him at once.

Word quickly got around town that Christians had kidnapped Mehmet Axá's daughter and forced her to convert against her will—she was, after all, only ten years old—and a crowd of angry Algerines converged on the docks, shouting and shaking their fists at the Catholic friars. It was then that the janissaries—

2. Henri Ternaux-Compans, *Archives des voyages*, p. 449.

3. Pierre Dan, *Histoire de Barbarie*, 1649, p. 487.

acting under the Pasha's orders—arrested the Trinitarians and their freed captives and placed them in prison.

The Pasha decided to hold the three Trinitarian friars and their freed captives as hostages to use to negotiate Fatima's release—much to Mehmet Axá's satisfaction no doubt.

At this point, a complicated series of international negotiations began.

The authorities in Corsica claimed that Fatima's conversion was entirely voluntary. This meant that she could not under any circumstances be returned to Algiers. Her father, of course, did not believe any of this and demanded her immediate release. The Corsican authorities, under the auspices of the Duke of Tuscany, the ruler of Livorno, offered a Safe Pass to Mehmet Axá and whoever he might wish to bring with him so that he could travel to Corsica, talk with his daughter, and see for himself that her conversion was indeed voluntary.

Mehmet Axá did not trust the Corsicans and refused the offer. He proposed instead that they meet at a location closer to Algiers. The Corsican authorities did not trust Mehmet Axá and refused his offer.

All this took time—several years in fact. The seventeenth century was a much slower age than ours when it came to communication.

Meanwhile the Trinitarian friars and their once-almost-freed captives were kept as hostages in the prison in Algiers.

Negotiations continued, and more parties became involved.

In 1612, no lesser a dignitary than the Ottoman Sultan himself issued an official order for the release of the Trinitarians. Algiers was technically a regency of the Ottoman Empire, so the order should have been obeyed. Algiers' fealty, however, was more theoretical than actual, and the Algerine authorities refused to budge. They were determined that they would release the Trinitarians only after Fatima was freed, and they defied the Sultan's order.

In 1613, the Governor of Oran, which was then a Spanish outpost, devised a scheme to smuggle Father de Monroy out of prison. The attempt failed.

In 1614 the situation was complicated by a new development.

The Bey (the Governor) of Alexandria, a man named Muhammad, was captured by a European ship. A deal was put together to swap him for the Trinitarians. The Ottoman Sultan favoured this arrangement and gave it his full support.

But...

Back in 1609—the year the Algerine children had been captured and ransomed—a young man named Diego de Pacheco, the son of the Marquis of Villena, a Spanish nobleman of very high rank, was seized by corsairs from Algiers and sold into slavery in that city. The Marquis was desperate to free his son. He was such an important and influential figure that he succeeded in scuppering the deal to swap the Bey of Alexandria for the Trinitarians and tried to exchange his son for the Bey instead. He failed, and his son remained a slave.

In 1617, the new Pasha of Algiers—the Algiers Pashas served three-year terms—brought with him a second order from the Ottoman Sultan to release the Trinitarians. The Algerine authorities ignored this order as they had the first.

Negotiations dragged on with no noticeable success.

Then, in 1618, an event occurred that further complicated matters. News arrived that Fatima, who was now nineteen years old and known as Madalena, had married a Christian.

In 1621, the Governor of Oran offered a massive ransom for Father de Monroy. The Algerine authorities refused the offer.

In the end, nothing was ever resolved.

Diego de Pacheco, the son of the Marquis of Villena, ended up in Istanbul, where he converted to Islam. He died there in 1619.

Juan de Aguila (one of the three Trinitarian friars) died in prison in Algiers in 1613.

Muhammad, the Bey of Alexandria, died in prison in Sicily in 1616.

Juan de Palacios (another of the three Trinitarian friars) died in prison in Algiers in 1616.

Bernardo de Monroy (the last of the three Trinitarian friars) died in prison in Algiers in 1622.

And that was the end of it.

There is no record of what happened to the 136 ransomed captives and no further details about Fatima/Madalena.

Not all ransoms were this pitilessly complicated, of course, but the story of Fatima serves as an example of just how complex the ransom process could be, for it included not just the immediate people involved—the captives and those endeavouring to free them—but also the tangled web of international politics and influence.

In some ways, not so very different from our own times, really.

# CORSAIR CAPTAINS

# Simon Danseker: The Devil Captain

Barbary corsairs were Muslims operating out of North African ports, but they were not all North Africans. Quite a number of them were renegades. That is, quite a number of them were European Christians who had renounced their own religion and converted to Islam—'turned Turk' as the expression was.

North African Muslims eagerly welcomed European converts to their religion. More importantly, once such new converts had adopted Islam, they became fully accepted members of the Muslim community. In Europe, renegades were universally detested as traitors to the true faith. Nonetheless, many Europeans did convert and made new and successful lives for themselves, plying their trades, marrying, and raising families, often becoming important and respected—and completely accepted—members of their communities in the process.

Some of these European renegades no doubt became Muslims because they underwent a true transformation of faith, but others seem to have switched religions for more pragmatic reasons. Slaves who converted could find a pathway to freedom, or at least to less onerous conditions. Captives who converted quickly enough could sometimes avoid slavery entirely. One sub-group of Europeans seemed especially prone to pragmatic conversion: pirates. In the uncertain times of the early seventeenth century, numerous European pirates settled in North African ports, where many of them became renegades and were welcomed.

In fact, European pirate captains did not necessarily even have to become renegades. Just the mere possibility that one day they might convert was sometimes enough for them to be welcomed—as long as they were bringing in sufficient loot.

One of the most famous of these non-renegade pirate-turned-corsair captains was Simon Danseker.

Simon Danseker was a Dutchman, likely born in Dordrecht, in the Netherlands, around 1570. By his thirties, he had become a privateer captain. Such privateers received official letters of marque from the States General—the governing body of the Republic of the Netherlands—authorizing them to harass Spanish shipping (the Republic of the Netherlands fought its own war for independence, against the Spanish, two centuries before the Americans fought theirs against the English). Each privateer expedition was financed by private backers who invested in the expedition in hopes of making a profit on the sale of any booty the privateer ship managed to acquire. The government also took a share, in return for issuing the original letter of marque and so turning what was essentially a pirate expedition into a legally sanctioned enterprise. So privateers were employed by the States General for a political end—helping to win the war of independence against Spain—but they were also a species of entrepreneurial businessmen out to make their (and their backers') fortune.

Simon Danseker was a particularly successful privateer captain. He picked up the name Danseker (which is a Dutch version of 'Dancer'), so the story goes, because he reliably returned to his home port at the end of each expedition (loaded with booty), and that sort of cruise—out and back again to the same port—was commonly referred to as a round dance.

That 'round dance' reliability did not last, though. In the middle of what appears to have been a successful career as a privateer captain, Simon Danseker abruptly changed course.

Sometime around 1605-06, he wound up in Marseilles. Exactly what he was doing there is not clear. He might have had a letter of marque authorizing him to hunt in the Mediterranean, but he might simply have taken off on his own, for if the stories about his actions in Marseilles are true, he certainly did not behave like an honest privateer. In fact, it looks like he might have intended to abandon privateering entirely.

Perhaps it was for love. One version of his story has him marrying the daughter of the 'Governor' of Marseilles. Things did not go well, though. He quarrelled bitterly with the city authorities (and thus also with his new father-in-law) and accumulated ruinous gambling debts, as a result of which he lost his ship (perhaps the debt and the quarrel with the authorities were connected). Whatever the case, the new life he had tried to make for himself in Marseilles disintegrated quite spectacularly.

In desperation, he stole a fishing boat from out of the Marseilles harbour and fled the city.

Danseker must have been a charismatic character, for he was able to entice a crew—perhaps members of his privateering crew—to help him steal the fishing boat and follow him out of Marseilles into the unknown.

Using that stolen Marseilles boat, Danseker and his men captured a large merchant ship (some sources say it was English). They then sailed both vessels to Algiers, where, as Dutchmen and thus fellow enemies of Spain (the Algerines were perennially at war with Spain), they were allowed to land and sell their booty.

Danseker then proceeded to launch an astonishingly successful career as a corsair operating out of Algiers—without converting to Islam. At some point, he fell in with Captain John Ward, an English renegade captain based in Tunis (see the chapter on Captain John Ward below), and for some time (until they had a falling out), the two of them ravaged the Mediterranean with a fleet of ships. Danseker became known as the *Dali Rais*—the Devil Captain—partly because of his fearless daring and ruthlessness, but also because he refused to convert to Islam and so, from the Muslim perspective, was indeed a kind of devil incarnate.

Danseker liked to sail in large ships, one of which was described as being equipped with 55 cannons and a crew of 400. His crews were composed of both Europeans (mainly Dutchmen) and North African Muslims. During the time he operated out of Algiers, he captured an average of something like fifteen European ships a year and sank an untold number of others, a success rate that enabled him to amass a huge fortune and live in an opulent mansion in Algiers when he was ashore.

Danseker and Ward not only enjoyed successful careers as corsair captains; they also had an important influence on their hosts. They are credited with being the men who began the process of teaching the Barbary corsairs how to build and sail European-style, square-rigged sailing ships—Danseker in Algiers and Ward in Tunis.

Danseker's corsair career was spectacularly successful, but it only lasted three years. By that time, he seems to have had enough of piracy (or had amassed enough wealth) to consider quitting the game. He also began to develop enemies in Algiers, and his continual refusal to convert was becoming a provocation. Perhaps all along he had planned to spend only a few years as a North African corsair.

Whatever his motivation, he began negotiations with several European powers for a pardon.

When all else failed, European monarchs and governments dealt with well-known pirate captains by granting them an official pardon for their piratical deeds and providing them with a new place of residence. It might not have been actual justice, but providing pirates with legal amnesty and a haven where they could settle down unmolested with their loot effectively took them out of commission and so made the seas a little safer.

Danseker managed to arrange a pardon from the French King Henry IV.

At first, this was a great success all around. King Henry rid the seas of a notorious pirate (and incidentally received a handsome gratuity from a grateful Danseker as well), and Danseker settled down peacefully in Marseille.

And lived happily ever after.

Well… not quite.

Simon Danseker planned his new life as a retired ex-pirate carefully.

Having arranged his pardon from the French king in secret while he was still in Algiers, he bought three ships that had been brought into the harbour there as corsair prizes, acting as if he were merely purchasing them as an investment. At a given signal, however, the Muslim crews of these ships were killed outright, tossed overboard, or taken captive. Danseker's new fleet of four ships then sailed out of the Algiers harbour, taking with them to freedom a large number of European slaves, the merchandise the ships contained, and two cannons Danseker had earlier 'borrowed' from the Pasha of Algiers. Some versions of the story claim that, on his way to Marseilles to take up his pardon, Danseker captured one of the great Spanish galleons and came away with treasure worth half a million pieces of eight.

His arrival at Marseille created quite a stir, since he came sailing grandly in at the head of a flotilla of ships heavily laden with a huge mass of booty, a crowd of liberated slaves, and gangs of Muslim captives.

As an ex-pirate, Danseker was—not surprisingly—a notorious figure, respected and admired by some, loathed by others. He made the pilgrimage to Paris and met there with King Henry IV, giving His Majesty a generous gift of treasure (to ensure the permanency of his pardon). He spread his money around in Marseilles, too, trying to buy allies. He still had to employ bodyguards all the time he was there, though.

The stories about him are not clear, but perhaps he chose Marseilles as his new home so that he could return to his French wife. Whatever the case, he spent five years there in relative peace.

It did not last.

Danseker had too valuable a skill set to let him retire, and the French authorities decided to employ him in their dealings with the Ottoman Regencies. First, he played a role in an expedition to Algiers. He was then sent to Tunis as part of a mission to negotiate the ransom of French captives there.

Initially, things in Tunis went well. The Dey (the ruler) of Tunis himself came out to the ship Danseker was using—an extraordinary gesture of courtesy—and the two men spent a pleasant afternoon together, so pleasant that the Dey invited Danseker to his palace the next day. Danseker accepted. The following morning, he came ashore accompanied by twelve men—his usual contingent of bodyguards—and walked to the Dey's palace. As he approached the entrance gate, an honour guard of janissary soldiers opened the doors for him and ushered him through.

And then slammed the doors shut before the bodyguards could follow.

It turned out that Danseker's absconding from Algiers and taking the French king's pardon had made him enemies—implacable enemies—not only in Algiers itself but all across North Africa. He was brought before the Dey of Tunis in chains and beheaded on the spot.

And that was the end—sudden and messy—of Simon Danseker.

Ironically enough, it was the two cannons he had taken out of Algiers that formed Danseker's most lasting legacy in the Muslim world. Year after year, the Algerine authorities irately demanded their return. Finally, as one of the prerequisites to signing a treaty with the French, the Algerines succeeded in repatriating their guns.

For decades, the Algerines proudly displayed the two cannons on the Mole, the breakwater that protected the Algiers harbour, as an example of the might of the city and of how the *Dali Rais*—the Devil Captain—had been brought low.

Such was the life of a pirate.[1]

---

1. In putting together the story of Simon Dancer, I relied on four sources: Andrew Barker, *A true and certaine report of the beginning, proceedings, ouerthrowes, and now present estate of Captaine Ward and Danseker, the two late famous pirates*, published in 1609; Anthony Nixon, *News from Sea of two notorious Pyrates, Ward the Englishman, and Danseker the Dutchman*, published in 1609; the chapter titled 'Les deux canons de Simon Dansa (1606-1628)' in Henri Delmas de Grammont, *Relations entre la France & la régence d'Alger au XVIIe siècle*, première partie (*Relations Between France and the Regency of Algiers*, Part 1), published in 1879; and Horatio F. Brown, ed., *Calendar of State Papers and Manuscripts Relating to English Affairs Existing in the Archives and Collections of Venice, and in Other Libraries of Northern Italy*, Vol. XI, 1607-1610, published in 1904.

# Calafat Hassan Reis: The Sorcerer

During the age of the Barbary corsairs, successful corsair captains were not only wealthy and important men; they were folk heroes. Tales were told of their daring exploits and of how they bravely met their end: one captain's legs were blown away by a chance cannon ball during an attack; another suffered fatal musket wounds but insisted on having a chair brought to him and sat in it shouting clear orders to his men to the last; a third escaped capture by beaching his ship and marching away inland with his crew, only to succumb to wounds received while battling a local militia.

The *corso* was a violent, dangerous business, and few captains died peacefully in their beds. But the stories kept being told—and kept the names of renowned corsair captains alive even after the captains themselves were long gone.

One of the names that have come down to us is that of Calafat Hassan Reis.

We have already encountered him in the story of Juan Rodelgo: he partnered with Murad Reis on the expedition to the Canary islands. He will show up again in the account of João De Carvalho Mascarenhas in the *Narrative Tales* section of this book. It is no coincidence that Calafat Hassan Reis keeps cropping up. In his heyday in the 1620s, he was one of the most successful (and infamous) corsair captains of Algiers.

Born into a poor family in Greece, he was likely captured in a corsair raid and became a renegade—like so many others of his generation. Before he began his career as a corsair, he worked as a caulker, somebody who filled in the gaps between the planks of a ship's hull to make them watertight. One of the words for a caulker is 'calfateur', and the story is that he kept this name as a sort of ironic homage to his past.

Calafat Hassan Reis was wildly brave and wildly successful; he was also reputed to be a sorcerer of great power. Despite all this, however, he—like so many other corsair captains—did not end up enjoying a peaceful retirement. In fact, his end was quite... Shakespearean.

This chapter recounts the story.

In the summer of 1626, Calafat Hassan Reis was hunting in the waters along the southern coast of Italy and on into the eastern Mediterranean, leading a fleet of seven heavily armed, square-rigged sailing ships and several oared galleys (Algerine corsairs, like corsairs in general, often hunted in packs during this period).

Things began well in a modest way, and they took several small prizes. Then, one morning, they spotted a large Venetian merchant ship. Calafat Hassan Reis sent four of his galleys and his lightest, fastest sailing ship to chase after the Venetian. The wind was light, and the galleys—which relied on manpower at the oars rather than the wind—quickly overhauled their prey.

The plan of attack in a situation like this was a standard one: the galleys would fire a few shots from their bow cannons as they drew near to intimidate the crew of the Venetian ship. If such intimidation did not succeed, the galleys would crash up against the ship's hull and the janissary soldiers crowded onto the galleys' decks would swarm the ship, shrieking and shouting, brandishing scimitars and pikes and pistols.

This time, it did not work out that way.

In a situation like this, many European vessels would have simply surrendered. The Venetian ship did not. Instead, it loosed off volley after volley of witheringly effective cannon fire and drove the galleys back. Eventually, it took Calafat Hassan Reis's entire fleet to overcome the Venetian. It was not until they had reduced the merchant ship to a wreck—the masts shattered, the sails ripped to shreds by cannon balls, dead men littering the deck—that the corsairs were finally able to board it. The corsairs lost a lot of men. No more than a couple of dozen remained alive aboard the Venetian vessel.

At first, Calafat Hassan Reis was furious. The paltry gain of a single ship was not worth the men he had lost or the damage his fleet had sustained. But then he discovered that there were three Capuchin friars aboard the Venetian vessel, passengers on their way to the Holy Land. This was good news indeed, for Catholic priests could often be ransomed for very high prices. They alone made this capture worth the effort.

The friars were transferred to Calafat Hassan Reis's ship and chained up in the hold, and the fleet moved on in search of new prey.

After taking a further couple of small prizes, they stopped at the port of Modon (modern Methoni, located on the southwest corner of the Peloponnese Peninsula; Greece was part of the Ottoman Empire at this time) to refit and revictual. Calafat Hassan Reis was in the process of selling the three Capuchin friars locally—selling them to a local dealer who could then negotiate the ransoms for them was faster and easier than hauling them all the way back to Algiers. As he was in the midst of negotiations, though, word came of a large merchant ship out at sea passing nearby. He grabbed up the friars, had them flung back into the hold of his ship, and launched his entire fleet as quickly as possible.

The large merchant ship turned out to be French, large indeed, and loaded down with valuable cargo. Like the venetians, the French refused to be intimidated and fought back, but there was little they could do to prevent the inevitable. Calafat Hassan Reis's fleet overwhelmed them, taking the ship, all the men aboard, and all the cargo.

This was the beginning of six weeks of continued and astonishing successes. The corsair flotilla raided along the coast of Sicily, making incursions inland to abduct people—men, women, and children—from towns and villages near the coast. They went on to take several more merchant ships at sea. At one point, they encountered a Dutch ship. The Republic of the Netherlands had a treaty with Algiers at this time, so Algerine corsairs were supposed to leave Dutch shipping alone. Calafat Hassan Reis hailed the Dutch captain and went aboard his ship, where the two men talked quite amicably—the Dutchman had no reason to suspect that Calafat Hassan Reis would breach the treaty. While they talked, however, Calafat Hassan Reis's men quietly boarded the Dutch ship and overwhelmed the crew. Calafat Hassan Reis claimed that the cargo the ship carried was from Naples, and since Naples had not signed any treaty with Algiers, the cargo was his to take—which he did.

By the time the summer season began to turn, Calafat Hassan Reis's ships were stuffed with captives and booty—including the three Capuchin friars still chained up in the hold of Calafat Hassan Reis's ship.

It was time to consider returning to Algiers.

Calafat Hassan Reis did not make such decisions lightly. In fact, he did not really make them at all. Rather, he let them be made for him through the divinatory properties of what one European chronicler refers to as his 'magic book'. He was not alone in this. Most Barbary corsair captains indulged in some sort of divinatory practice.

It is not clear exactly what Calafat Hassan Reis's 'magic book' might have been, but perhaps it was a version of a book mentioned by Antonio de Sousa:

Wherever and whenever corsairs head for Christian lands, before making any move they first consult their Book of Omens, searching for clues as to where they should go, and under no conditions do they do other than what their book and predictions tell them. They give such credit to these predictions that before they set sail, or disembark, or battle some Christian vessel, or sack some region... in fact, before they do anything during the time of their corsair activities, they first cast lots and consult the Book of Omens.

If before their very eyes there should appear a clear and manifest chance for great gain or booty, should the Book of Omens and its predictions not reveal the same, under no conditions will they attempt the enterprise or move one step in its direction. On the other hand, there is no adventure so arduous or difficult, no danger so manifest into which they will not plunge if their Book of Omens foretells their success. They may find themselves deceived an infinite number of times, and yet they still believe in the Book of Omens, no less than in their Koran.[1]

Calafat Hassan Reis's practice of divination gave him a reputation as a powerful sorcerer among North Africans and Europeans alike. We moderns—like Friar Antonio—tend to be sceptical about such things. There was no denying, however, that Calafat Hassan Reis was spectacularly successful at taking booty and captives, and it seems that he himself attributed this success to his sorcerous, divinatory practices. So faced with a decision about whether or not to end his corsairing for the season, he consulted his 'magic book'. The result was clear: it was not yet time to return to Algiers.

So Calafat Hassan Reis ordered his fleet northwestwards, towards the southern coast of Sardinia, to do a last series of raids there before returning in triumph to Algiers.

What Calafat Hassan Reis did not know, however, was that his summer of spectacularly effective raiding provoked several European powers into doing something they rarely did: cooperate.

Pope Urban VIII, King Philip IV of Spain, and Ferdinando II, Grand Duke of Tuscany, organized a joint expedition to hunt down and destroy Calafat Hassan Reis and his fleet and to liberate the captives and booty he had taken. The Pope contributed three galleys, the Spanish king eight, the Tuscan duke three.

After casting about for some time and following rumours, they eventually heard a report that Calafat Hassan Reis and his fleet were anchored near the island of San Pietro, off the southwest tip of Sardinia. They headed there with all the speed they could muster.

Calafat Hassan Reis was caught completely by surprise by the unexpected arrival of this formidable galley fleet.

The first thing he did was consult his 'magic book'. This time, he performed a specific ritual. Placing two arrows in the hands of one of his crew, one arrow

---

1. María Antonia Garcés, ed., Diana de Armas Wilson, trans., *An Early Modern Dialogue with Islam: Antonio de Sosa's Topography of Algiers (1612)*, p. 155.

representing the European forces, the other his own, he intoned certain words from his book. From the movement of the arrows, it became clear that he should fight, for the ritual of the arrows predicted that he would not be killed, nor his ship taken.

Reassured, Calafat Hassan Reis prepared his fleet to resist the attacking galleys.

Calafat Hassan Reis's ship was the largest square-rigged vessel in his fleet, 150 feet long, armed with no less than 46 large and six medium-sized cannons, with a crew of 300. One of the Tuscan galleys headed straight for this ship, followed by eight others. The rest of the galleys spread out to attack other ships in the fleet, firing their bow cannons, loaded with grapeshot and chain-shot, to clear their adversaries' decks and rip through the rigging, and then jointly assailing individual corsair ships.

At first, the corsairs more than held their own, but then the wind dropped, leaving their square-rigged ships unable to manoeuvre. The attacking galleys had no such problem and used their advantage to the fullest, nimbly avoiding the corsair ships' broadsides, and then swarming the ships. There were not nearly enough corsair galleys to beat them back, and after two hours of vicious battle, the European galleys had taken two of the square-rigged corsair ships and were closing in on the others. Several of the corsair galleys fled, abandoning their companions.

Seeing all this, Calafat Hassan Reis, whose ship still held out, decided it was time to stage a strategic retreat.

There remained the matter of the wind, though.

He resorted to ritual sacrifice for salvation.

A ram was brought out—all corsair ships had aboard them a group of rams for this very purpose—and the animal was cut into four quarters. Crying out the ritual words, Calafat Hassan Reis then threw each of these quarters into the sea, in the four directions, in hopes of calling up a favourable wind. This sort of ceremonial sacrifice was standard Barbary corsair practice. They employed it whenever they needed a wind (like when they were passing through the Strait of Gibraltar, where a good following wind meant they could escape pursuit by the Spanish warships that patrolled there), or when they needed to calm the wind (if they were caught in a sudden storm).

The sacrifice did not work. No wind came.

The attacking galleys closed in for the kill.

In a fury, Calafat Hassan Reis fetched some of the treasure he had acquired and began casting it into the sea so that his attackers could not take it, hastily dumping the mass of flashing silver and gold coins into the waves. Then he set fire to his ship, so they could not take it either. Blinded by rage at this unlooked-for and ignominious end to a summer that had otherwise been so spectacularly successful, he threw into the flames a young European girl—a girl of 'rare beauty' whom he had previously taken captive and forced to be his concubine—and dove over the ship's gunwale into the sea.

Men from the galleys scrambled aboard Calafat Hassan Reis's burning ship, killing the last of the corsairs they found aboard, hoping to douse the flames and save the ship. The fire had advanced too far, though. The ship was doomed. The men who had come aboard began to abandon the vessel. But then, from belowdecks, they heard the cries of the European captives still chained up in the hold.

A few sprinted down into the burning, smoke-filled hold and freed as many of the captives as they could, hacking through their chains and hauling them up the gangways. They could not save them all, though. Many died screaming and choking as the flames engulfed the ship. All who could—men from the galleys and newly freed captives alike—leaped overboard into the sea.

Among the captives saved were the three Capuchin friars whom Calafat Hassan Reis had captured at the beginning of the summer. They were provided with free passage to Rome, where they were given an audience with the Pope. After that, they continued their voyage to the Holy land and back—without incident.

Calafat Hassan Reis was fished out of the sea, singed by the flames, half drowned, fuming and enraged, but very much alive. The prophecy of the arrows had been fulfilled: he had not been killed, and his ship had not been taken.

They took him to Naples and threw him into a dungeon.

The story does not end there, though.

News of Calafat Hassan Reis's capture and subsequent imprisonment in Naples soon reached Algiers.

When Calafat Hassan Reis's wife heard what had happened to her husband, she went straight to the Divan—the ruling council of Algiers—and demanded that they find a captive in Algiers of sufficient rank and importance so that he could be exchanged for her husband. Since Calafat Hassan Reis was one of the foremost corsair captains in Algiers at this time, the Divan readily agreed.

The captive they settled on was Don Pedro de Carvajal, a Spanish gentleman of high rank who had been taken by Algerine corsairs while sailing from Spain to Oran. Naples was a Spanish possession at this time, so choosing a high-ranking Spanish captive made perfect sense.

Negotiations were begun to swap Don Pedro for Calafat Hassan Reis.

Things progressed slowly, though—very slowly—and after four years there was still no resolution. Calafat Hassan Reis remained chained up in the Naples dungeon; Don Pedro remained a slave in Algiers.

And then a report arrived in Algiers that Calafat Hassan Reis had been executed in Naples by being burned alive at the stake. The news spread quickly throughout Algiers, causing widespread fury. Calafat Hassan Reis's wife, along with her parents, marched to the Divan at the head of an angry mob to demand justice. Since Calafat Hassan Reis had been burned at the stake, they said, Don Pedro must also suffer the same fate.

The members of the Divan agreed to their demand. Moreover, they offered up a second Spanish Gentleman—a man named Don Juan—as well. It was a way to send a message to their Spanish enemy: if the Spanish dared to roast an Algerine corsair alive, the authorities in Algiers would roast two Spanish gentlemen in return. Don Pedro and Don Juan were immediately seized and imprisoned in preparation for their execution.

As all this was playing out, however, the parents of Calafat Hassan Reis's wife began hatching a scheme of their own.

Don Pedro was a wealthy, educated man from a powerful family. The widow's parents persuaded themselves that if they could convince him to convert and become a renegade, he would naturally become an important man in Algiers and so make a suitable husband for their now-widowed daughter. They visited Don Pedro in prison and made the offer to him: die a fiery, agonizing death, or convert, marry our daughter, and begin a new life in Algiers. This is not as odd an offer as it might seem. Algerine society at this time was remarkably fluid, and there were many European renegades in positions of importance. Becoming Muslim wiped the slate clean, and a man could begin anew.

Not only did Don Pedro decline their offer; he ridiculed it and said that he would rather stay true to the faith of his fathers and die than live as an apostate.

Don Pedro and Don Juan were taken from their prison and hauled through the streets in chains to the place of their execution. A great crowd followed, shouting angrily.

They burned Don Pedro first, shackling him to an upright stake and heaping deadwood around him. As the wood was set ablaze, the crowd pressed forward, shouting taunts and insults. Don Pedro held his head high and loudly recited his prayers—until the flames and the smoke stifled him.

Then it was Don Juan's turn.

Don Juan, however, had seen enough. He cried out and raised his finger theatrically towards heaven—the recognized symbol that a person wished to become a Muslim. He was immediately freed of his chains and paraded back through the city streets to the palace of the Pasha. To general applause, the Pasha issued Don Juan new clothing and enrolled him among the janissaries, so that he would draw pay as they did.

And so Don Juan became a renegade and took up a new life in Algiers.

A report of the burning of Don Pedro soon reached Naples. The news spread quickly throughout the city, causing widespread fury, and an angry mob filled the streets, demanding justice. The city authorities needed little encouragement for they were as outraged as the ordinary citizens.

For Calafat Hassan Reis had *not* been burned at the stake. He had remained in the Naples dungeon all this time.

The false report of his execution had been spread about in Algiers by a corsair captain who loved Calafat Hassan Reis's wife. He had hoped that news of her husband's death would make her more inclined to accept him. Perhaps it did; perhaps it did not. There is no way for us to know.

It did have one clear effect, though.

Calafat Hassan Reis was hauled from his dungeon and through the streets in chains to the place of his execution. A great crowd followed, shouting angrily. They shackled him to an upright stake and stacked a pile of deadwood around him. As the wood was set ablaze, the crowd pressed forward, taunting him. He died with his jaw clamped, staring straight ahead, as if indifferent to them all.

The story of Calafat Hassan Reis comes from two works by Pierre Dan, the Trinitarian friar who was in Algiers in the summer of 1634 as part of an unsuccessful ransoming expedition.[2] He records in *Histoire de Barbarie* that while in Algiers he heard that Don Juan suffered acutely from remorse for having abandoned the religion of his birth.

Maybe. Maybe not. It is what Father Dan would have wanted to hear, after all. Don Juan was, perhaps, a practical man who valued being alive more than being religiously faithful. There were more than a few men like that.

Such were the times in which they lived.

---

2. The details of Calafat Hassan Reis's summer of plunder and eventual capture come from Pierre Dan's *Les plus illustres captifs: recueil des actions héroïques d'un grand nombre de guerriers et autres chrétiens réduits en esclavage par les mahométans* (*The Most Illustrious Captives: a Collection of the Heroic Actions of a Large Number of Warriors and other Christians Enslaved by Muslims*), Volume 2, edited by Le R. P. Calixte, pp. 323-330. The details of Don Pedro's execution, Don Juan's conversion, and Calafat Hassan Reis's death come from Pierre Dan's *Histoire de Barbarie*, 1649, pp. 444-446.

# Captain John Ward: The Archpirate

John Ward (sometimes known as Jack) was born in the early 1550s into a poor family of fisherfolk in Kent. Fishing was a hard life without much recompense, and for an ambitious young man it had precious little to offer in the way of a better future. At some point, when he was perhaps in his mid-thirties, Ward abandoned fishing and joined the Elizabethan Sea Dogs—the English privateers employed against the Spanish—in hopes of bettering his lot. England's conflict with Spain lasted almost twenty years (1585-1604), and though details of Ward's early life are scanty, it is likely that he served as a privateer for much of that time.

And then, after James I came to the throne, peace was declared with Spain, the Sea Dogs were disbanded, and Ward—like hundreds of other ex-privateers—found himself unemployed. He fetched up in Plymouth, where he had a wife and likely some children (though this is not clear). For lack of better employment, he entered the King's Navy and became a crewman aboard a ship named *The Lion's Whelp*. He found serving aboard a navy ship entirely unsatisfactory. He was fiftyish by now, forced by poverty to serve as a lowly crewmember—no doubt the oldest crewmember—aboard a ship which, by rights, he felt he should have been commanding. And there were no better prospects for him in sight.

When he was not required to be on duty aboard *The Lion's Whelp*, which at that time was moored in the harbour for refitting, he spent his off hours in the town's taverns drowning his sorrows and frustrations. One source describes him as follows:

All day you should hardly fail but find him in an alehouse. Oaths were almost as ordinary with him as words, so that he seldom spoke a sentence, but one was a syllable. He would sit melancholy, speak doggedly, curse the times, repine at other men's good fortunes, and complain of the hard crosses that attended his own. He was welcomed into any taphouse more for love of his coin than love of his company, and all the reputation that his own crew held of him was but this, that he was a mad rascal.[1]

❀

Ward was typical of hundreds of English ex-privateers, who had spent years leading an exciting life, being lauded by all as patriotic heroes, and making good money while doing it, but who now found themselves deprived of what they had considered their legitimate livelihood and facing a bleak future—and moreover feeling themselves discarded and belittled. Ward, however, in his capacity as a 'mad rascal,' determined to do something about his situation.

The plan—not surprisingly, perhaps—was conceived in a tavern.

Sitting drinking with some of the crew of *The Lion's Whelp*—men equally as disgruntled as he—Ward heard about a 'Papist' who had loaded a treasure of gold aboard a local merchant ship and was preparing to flee the country with it (England at this time was not a country in which Catholics felt comfortable). It took several drinking sessions, but Ward eventually convinced a group of a dozen or more well-lubricated men that the solution to their situation was simple: they just needed to steal the vessel containing the Papist's gold, a small merchant ship which lay anchored in the harbour in preparation to depart in a day or two, and flee with it—and live happily (and rich) ever after. It was the sort of plan that sober men would have scoffed at. Fuelled by equal parts alcohol and desperation, though, Ward and his inebriated, ragtag crew screwed up their courage and set off to do the deed.

Creeping down to the docks in the black of night, they rowed out in a purloined boat to the little merchant ship, climbed aboard, overpowered the two crewmembers left as a night watch, and then slipped out of the harbour on the tide—no doubt jubilant at the complete and stunning success of their plan.

A few hours later, safely distant from Plymouth, they dragged the two nightwatchmen up from the hold where they had been imprisoned and demanded to know where the Papist's treasure was hidden, threatening dire violence if the nightwatchmen did not immediately cough up the location. The two men's stuttering response was not what they expected.

Taverns are public places, and Ward and his men had been drunkenly plotting their piratical exploit for a couple of days. A relative of the Papist had overheard them and, on the off chance that their plans turned out to be

---

1. Andrew Barker, *A true and Certaine Report of the Beginning, Proceedings, Ouerthrowes, and now Present Estate of Captaine Ward and Danseker the two Late Famous Pirates: from their first Setting Forth to this Present Time*, pages 2 & 3 of the narrative (the pages are unnumbered). I have lightly edited Barker's original text.

more than just alcohol-sodden fantasies, had warned the Papist that he should remove his treasure from the merchant ship and store it safely ashore before sailing.

So there was no treasure aboard the ship.

This was devastating news. Ward and his gang had just committed piracy—a hanging offense—and there was now no going back for them. But they had got nothing for their pains except a small merchant ship and two frightened captives they now had somehow to dispose of. In desperation, they searched the ship, hoping to find some portion of the treasure that might have been left behind. There was none. They did, however, discover a store of fresh food—including a stock of venison pasties—and, more to their liking, a case of good wine. Here is a description of what happened next:

At sight of the wine, Ward raps out oaths like pellets out of a piece that fly as swiftly as they can pass, one after another, and calls, 'Come, let's be merrie, my hearts. Though the birds be flown, and we have found nothing but the empty nest, yet come, let's be merrie and freely fat ourselves with their fodder. Here is good cheer provided for us. An ounce of sorrow will not pay a penny debt! It is bootless in these days to lie in a dich and cry for help, and therefore, my hearts, let us live in hope that our fortunes will be better. What say you, my bloods? Who would be aboard *The Lion's Whelp*, with bare and hungry allowance of cold fish and naked cheese, when we may thrust our arms up to the elbow in a venison pastie?' Breaking open the case of wine, he cries, 'Here, my mates, is a health to our good fortunes, and a pox on the hangman! We know the worst, and let's therefore now hope for the best. We'll be merry tonight with wine and venison, and tomorrow we can take counsel what's best to be done.'[2]

The next morning—no doubt nursing aching heads—they passed Land's End and approached the Isles of Scilly. As they continued onwards, they spotted a French merchant ship, larger than their own—but not too large. Ward immediately organized his men, sent most of them below decks, and began to sidle up to the French vessel. From the Frenchman's point of view, Ward's small ship, with only a couple of men on deck, presented no threat, especially since the French vessel was equipped with six cannons for defence. Ward drew

---

2. Andrew Barker, *A true and Certaine Report*, pages 6 & 7.

close and engaged the French captain in innocent conversation. Their talk went on for some time—while Ward stealthily eased his ship nearer and nearer.

When the two vessels were finally close enough, Ward shoved his rudder hard, crashed into the French ship's side, and ordered his men to swarm aboard. They surged up from belowdecks and overpowered the French crew before they knew what was happening.

Ward put the Frenchmen in their ship's boat and left them to the mercy of the sea. Then he headed back towards Plymouth and moored his two ships— the original small merchant ship and the new French prize—discreetly in a sheltered bay some distance from the town. Slipping ashore, Ward collected a new batch of volunteers from the local taverns in the area, his negotiations with them no doubt facilitated by liberal quantities of alcohol and enticing promises of the untold riches awaiting them.

With his two ships now adequately manned—and the nightwatchmen from the merchant ship deposited onshore—he set sail for the coast of Spain.

These early exploits of Ward's reveal the traits that made him such a successful pirate captain. He was a risk taker, a man who could unflinchingly face danger and uncertainty. He was also a hugely experienced sailor, having learned the ways of the sea both during his fishing days and his time as a privateer (he had known the rhythm of the tide well enough to use it to float the merchant ship quietly out of Plymouth harbour). As his encounter with the French ship shows, he was also well versed in the tricks and strategies of privateering. And he was a highly persuasive man when he wished to be and could effectively inspire and control usually unruly seamen men both on land and at sea. Above all, perhaps, he could be fearlessly, unhesitatingly aggressive when the moment called for it, triumphing over seemingly insurmountable odds and inspiring his men to acts of bravery they would otherwise never have contemplated.

This was a skill set that served him well in the years to come.

Under Ward's leadership, his two ships cruised the waters off the coast of Spain and quickly captured a fluyt, a type of Dutch merchant ship, considerably larger than the French vessel they had taken in the Channel. With this new ship in his possession, Ward no longer needed the original small merchant ship he and his men had stolen in Plymouth, so he put the fluyt's Dutch crew in it and sent them packing. The next ship he encountered was a settee, a smallish, highly manoeuvrable ship with lateen sails—just the sort of ship a pirate could make good use of. He captured the settee in short order and added it to his growing fleet.

It was now decision time.

Ward had ships and men, and he had loot taken from both the French vessel and the Dutch fluyt. He now needed a place to sell the booty, refit his ships, and give his men some shore time to keep them happy. Since he was an outlaw pirate, European ports were closed to him. The obvious choice left was North Africa, and the obvious choice of North African ports was Algiers. This was risky, but Algiers had a reputation at the time for welcoming pretty much anybody who had sufficient cash to pay the required port taxes (and bribes). So Ward took the risk.

Under ordinary circumstances, things would likely have worked out just fine. The circumstances in Algiers just then, however, were not ordinary. A short time before, an Englishman in the service of the Duke of Florence had led a madcap mission to set all the ships in the Algiers harbour ablaze. In the event, he failed to do much damage, and the only lasting effect was to provoke the Algiers Pasha into declaring a vendetta against the English. For starters, the Pasha had a dozen Englishmen who were then in Algiers publicly tortured to death.

It was at this point that Ward and his crew sailed—all unknowing—into the Algiers harbour. They were promptly arrested, and their ships impounded. The Pasha declared that they too would be made to pay for the perfidious Englishman's despicable act.

As we have seen, Ward could be a persuasive man. He also seems to have been the sort of captain who stood by his men. Somehow, he managed to work out an arrangement with the Pasha to ransom his crew: Ward would go out on a pirate cruise, capture as many ships as possible, and then return and hand over the booty to the Pasha in exchange for his men's freedom. Since Ward's crew were to stay imprisoned, he was provided with a new crew composed of local sailors and a contingent of janissaries.

So off Ward went, in his old ships but with a new crew unknown to him. There must have been frictions and uncertainties, for janissaries were notoriously haughty, particularly with unbelievers, and overcoming the language barrier would have been challenging (especially during battles at sea). But the new arrangement apparently worked well, for not only was Ward able to gain sufficient booty to free his men; he also acquired a respect for janissaries that lasted much of his career, and he used them regularly among his crews after this.

Back in Algiers, Ward paid off the Pasha, pried his crew out of the Algiers dungeons, and then quit the city as quickly as he could.

He still had the same problem, though: he needed a safe harbour somewhere in North Africa that he could use as a base of operations. This time, he chose Tunis.

On his way there, he captured several European ships and amassed a pile of treasure. As his little flotilla approached the vicinity of Tunis, however, they encountered a Maltese war galley. Such galleys were large, formidable vessels, rowed by slaves—mostly captured Muslims—chained to the oarbenches, and manned by the Knights of Malta, a militant, quasi-religious organization dedicated to the destruction—and looting—of Muslim shipping. Most Barbary corsairs fled the approach of a Maltese galley wherever they could. Not Ward. As one contemporary account puts it:

Understanding there was a Man of War of Malta set forth on purpose to take him, Ward began to bestir himself, for his desires admitted no limitation, nor could he persuade his mind to submit his neck to any servile yoke. 'The law of nature' (quoth he) 'allows every man to defend himself when assailed and to withstand force by force!' In that resolution, he opposed himself against the force of his enemy. Many assaults were made, and several showers of shot sent forth on both sides, yet the forces of Ward did so far disanimate the Maltese that the edge of their courage was clean taken away, and they were forced to submit themselves to the mercy of their enemy. By this victory, Ward did add much power to his former strength. Sailing from thence, he bended his course to Tunis.[3]

Like Algiers, Tunis was an Ottoman possession, and so there were ruling Pashas there, rotated regularly by the Ottoman Sultan in Istanbul. In Algiers, the janissaries and the Pashas vied with each other for power. In Tunis, the janissaries had by this time staged a successful coup and taken over control of the city. Tunis still remained nominally loyal to the Ottoman Sultan, and Pashas continued to be sent out to rule, but they served as mere figureheads. The real power lay with the janissaries, and the man who wielded that power on a day-to-day basis was the head of the janissaries: Uthman Dey.

Having learned his lesson in Algiers, Ward prepared carefully for his entry into Tunis. The first thing he did upon arriving was to dole out portions of the treasure he had acquired in the form of 'gifts' (bribes) to port officials. He then started working his way up the hierarchy of power, dispensing larger and more extravagant gifts.

---

3. Anthony Nixon, *News from Sea of two notorious Pyrates, Ward the Englishman, and Danseker the Dutchman,* published in 1609, page 3 of the narrative (there are no page numbers). The authorship of *News from Sea,* which was a pamphlet rather than a book, is uncertain. It is traditionally attributed to Anthony Nixon, but this is far from certain. I have lightly edited the original.

Ward had 'street smarts' in abundance. He was also a quick study and able to adapt rapidly to new circumstances. He figured out that Uthman Dey was, in fact, the man to deal with in Tunis, and so he sidestepped the Pasha and made Uthman Dey a proposition. It is unlikely that alcohol was involved this time (though with Ward, one is never sure). The scheme Ward presented was so radical, though, that it may very well have emerged from a drinking session between the two men.

Ward suggested that Uthman Dey make him an official member of the Tunis corsair community. More than this, Ward also wanted to include janissaries as regular members of his crew (having clearly been impressed by them). This may not at first seem like such a revolutionary idea, but Ward, remember, was still (nominally) a Christian, and the corsairs of Tunis were all Muslims. Allowing an unbeliever into their ranks and giving him command over Muslims was unthinkable. Ward offered Uthman Dey an irresistible enticement, though (the same enticement he had no doubt offered his crew-to-be in the Plymouth taverns): money. Ward convinced Uthman Dey that he would become rich—very, very rich.

Uthman Dey went for it.

It was a scheme that benefited both sides. Uthman Dey (and a fair portion of Tunis) benefited not only from the booty Ward brought in but also from his years of experience and his expertise, for he taught the Tunis corsairs how to build, sail, and navigate European-style square rigged ships, and so kickstarted the process that led the Barbary corsairs to abandon their oared gallies for sailing ships, allowing them to enlarge the scope of their operations and escape the confines of the Mediterranean. Ward, in turn, gained not only a safe harbour but also acquired guaranteed rights as a legitimate corsair captain along with connections to the highest places of power in Tunis—and so could avoid the sort of nasty surprise he had received upon his arrival in Algiers.

The next few years were very good for Ward (and Uthman Dey). Ward went out with a small fleet of well-armed, well-manned ships and took prize after prize, hauling the booty and captives back to Tunis and divvying up the profits, and he became one of the mainstays of the Tunis corsair enterprise. Few eye-witness descriptions of corsair captains exist, but there is the following brief but revealing portrait of Ward from about this time, given in a report tendered to the English Ambassador in Venice:

John Ward, commonly called Captain Ward, is about 55 years of age. Very short, with little hair, and that quite white; bald in front; swarthy face and beard. Speaks little, and almost always swearing. Drunk from morn till night. Most prodigal and plucky. Sleeps a great deal and is often on board when in port. The habits of a thorough 'salt.' A fool and an idiot out of his trade.[4]

This less-than-flattering portrait of Ward was probably quite accurate. It certainly fits with what is known of the man: a drunken reprobate, but also a bold, skilled pirate captain. Given the wild life that pirates tended to lead, this blend of drunkenness, boldness, and hard-learned expertise was likely not uncommon—in fact, in some cases the drunkenness might have led to the boldness. It was certainly a combination that worked for Ward, and for some considerable time, he operated out of Tunis with spectacular success. At one point (as we saw above), he teamed up with Simon Danseker, and the joint fleet of these two notorious non-Muslim corsair captains terrorized the Mediterranean—until Ward and Danseker quarrelled over the distribution of booty and parted company.

So Ward went back to operating on his own.

And then an event happened that changed everything.

On one of his pirate cruises, the small fleet of ships Ward was leading was scattered by a storm. Only his own and one other ship remained. A little after this, the two ships encountered a 'great Argosy'—a massive Venetian merchant ship named the *Reniera e Soderna*, laden with goods valued in the millions of ducats. The Venetians built such behemoths not only to carry vast amounts of cargo, but also as protection against pirate attacks. In Venice, the *Reniera e Soderna* was considered invulnerable.

Taking such a large ship was no easy task, for not only did it dwarf Ward's smaller (though more manoeuvrable) vessels; it was also well armed with cannons, and its captain was under orders to vigorously defend his ship and its valuable cargo. In the seemingly one-sided encounter, Ward's leadership proved a deciding factor. Here is a contemporary account of what happened:

Ward is grown the most absolute, the most resolute, and the most undaunted man in a fight that ever any heart did accompany at sea. In the battle to take the great Argosy, he did in the deadly conflict so undauntedly bear himself that it was as if he had courage to outbrave death and the spirit to outface danger, bastinadoing the Turks out of his ship into the Venetians' and pricking others

---

4. Horatio F. Brown, ed., *Calendar of State Papers and Manuscripts Relating to English Affairs Existing in the Archives and Collections of Venice, and in Other Libraries of Northern Italy,* Vol. XI, 1607-1610, pp. 140-41.

on even with the point of his poniard, so his resolution alone was the cause of the victory, and his forwardness made even cowards venturous.

At last, having seized the Argosy for his own and brought her into the Bay of Tunis, he discharged and unladed her goods, dividing the spoils with the Turks, to the great enriching of the whole country, and to the advancing of his own pride.[5]

Ward's daring and determination undoubtedly played a crucial role in this encounter, but something else did as well: luck. The day was relatively calm, leaving the massive bulk of the *Reniera e Soderna* stranded helplessly in the water, while the sails of Ward's smaller ships caught just enough of a breeze to be able to manoeuvre. Ward, experienced seaman that he was, made good use of this advantage, gliding his ships past the *Reniera e Soderna,* delivering withering broadsides, and then gliding away again. Ward also had another piece of luck. The *Reniera e Soderna* was supposed to carry a full complement of soldiers in order to repel any pirates audacious enough to attempt boarding it. The ship's captain, however, had left most of the soldiers behind and replaced them with paying passengers—in an attempt to increase profits. So when Ward and his men finally swarmed up the larger ship's steep sides, they met with little resistance.

The taking of the *Reniera e Soderna* cemented Ward's reputation as the most important, most successful pirate captain in Tunis. It also made Ward, Uthman Dey, and everybody else who had invested in Ward's expedition fabulously rich. As the quote above suggests, though, it had another effect as well: it enflamed Ward's ambition. He took the *Reniera e Soderna* as his own flagship and had it fitted out for corsairing, sawing ports in the hull and installing no less than sixty cannons. When the refit was completed, the ship became one of the largest corsair vessels ever to operate out of a North African port, carrying a crew of four hundred: a hundred and fifty Englishmen and two hundred and fifty janissaries.

While this was all going on, though, Ward was pursuing another strategy—a secret strategy.

With the capture of the *Reniera e Soderna*, Ward now had enough wealth to retire, and he started covert negotiations for a pardon from James I, the English king. As we saw in the case of Simon Danseker, European monarchs and governments could sometimes be persuaded to grant official pardons to pirate captains, providing them with legal forgiveness and a haven where they could settle down unmolested with their loot—and so take them out of commission

---

5. Andrew Barker, *A true and Certaine Report*, pages 11 & 12.

and make the seas safer. Ward sent emissaries (and generous bribes) to England to begin the process.

He ran into a problem, though.

King James saw himself as *Rex Pacificus*—the King of Peace. This was in large part his motivation for ending hostilities with Spain when he assumed the English throne. He worked hard at forming peaceful relations with other European powers as well, including Venice—especially Venice, which seems to have had a particular importance for him—and he went out of his way to maintain good relations with the Serene Republic.

Ward had taken numerous Venetian ships over the years, which was bad enough. But his capture of the 'invincible' *Reniera e Soderna* was more than the Venetian authorities could endure. When sounding the waters for possible allies in the matter of Ward's pardon, one of his emissaries approached the Venetian ambassador in London. Here is the ambassador's report on the matter to the Doge and the Venetian Senate:

I am in duty bound in the interests of the owners of the ship *Reniera e Soderna*, which was captured by the pirate Ward, who has his headquarters in Tunis, to inform your Serenity of representations made to me by an English merchant who, on leaving Venice, touched at Tunis this last August and is now arrived here. This person tells me, in the name of Ward, that Ward and all his followers, who number about 800, offer to give up their piratical career and to return to England if they can obtain the king's pardon. They know that this they can never obtain without the consent of your Serenity because of the many injuries they have inflicted upon your subjects. Ward therefore offers to restore all that those subjects have a right to and that he now holds, namely, three ships with all their guns and armament and goods to the value of thirty or forty thousand crowns in silk, indigo and other merchandise. My informant declares that he himself had seen these people, and that Ward would give even more. He pointed out how important it was to remove from his nest a pirate with so large a following, and, as far as England was concerned, this would mean the cessation of piracy in those waters. He begged me to keep this offer secret, for if the Turks came to hear of it, it was likely they would hinder the design on account of the profits they now draw. He also begged for an early answer so that long delay might not imperil the success of the plan.[6]

---

6. Horatio F. Brown, ed., *Calendar of State Papers*, Vol. XI, 1607-1610, p. 49.

The venetian Ambassador did not provide an early answer. In fact, he worked hard behind the scenes to thwart Ward's pardon—so successfully that he was able to announce in another report that, 'The King declared he would never pardon Ward without the assent of the Republic [of Venice], although Ward is spending large sums to obtain it.'[7]

So Ward's attempt at a pardon failed. The Venetians were too implacably set against him, and King James wanted good relations with Venice too much to go against their wishes in the matter.

By this point, Ward's wealth was financing a lavish lifestyle in Tunis. Here is a description:

Ward lives there in Tunis in a most princely and magnificent state, his apparel both curious and costly, his diet sumptuous, and his followers seriously observing and obeying his will. He hath two cooks that dress and prepare his diet for him, and his taster before he eats. I do not know any Peer in England that bears up his port in more dignity, nor hath his attendants more obsequious unto him.[8]

Such luxury did not keep Ward in port, though. The newly refitted *Reniera e Soderna* beckoned, and he set out in it, along with several other, smaller ships, for yet another corsair cruise—fully expecting, no doubt, to continue his long string of triumphs.

The cruise was not blessed with luck. Strife erupted aboard the *Reniera e Soderna* between the English renegade crew and the janissaries. Ward knocked some heads but then got fed up and left the ship to take command of one of the smaller vessels. This proved to be his one stroke of good fortune.

Before the flotilla of corsair ships—the massive *Reniera e Soderna* trailed by the smaller vessels—could encounter any suitable prey, they were struck by a violent story and scattered. The cutting of so many new gunports into the hull of the *Reniera e Soderna*, it turned out, had fatally damaged the integrity of the ship's timbers, and the ship came apart in the storm. All but a handful of those aboard perished.

This was disaster on a grand scale.

---

7. Horatio F. Brown, ed., *Calendar of State Papers*, Vol. XI, p. 95.

8. Andrew Barker, *A true and Certaine Report*, page 13.

When Ward and what was left of his flotilla limped into Tunis, word spread quickly of what had occurred. The friends and families of the 250 drowned janissaries were wild with grief and fury. Only the power and influence of Uthman Dey saved Ward from a very public, very painful death at the hands of an enraged mob.

Ward holed up in Tunis for a time, sending out several of his captains on corsair cruises to try to recoup some of his losses. The Venetians, however, had ramped up the number of warships they had on patrol and put all the resources they had into hunting down and exterminating Ward and his confederates. Ward's captains fell victim to several of these Venetian warships, and the situation went from bad to worse. At this point, Ward seems to have entered into an arrangement with Uthman Dey rather like the one he had negotiated with the Pasha of Algiers. Uthman Dey had lost money on the *Reniera e Soderna*, and he wanted to recoup his losses. Ward's ploy of sending out his lieutenants had failed. Now he would have to do it himself. Like the Algiers Pasha, though, Uthman Dey sent him off with a janissary crew to make sure he stuck to the plan.

Ward did. Hunting in the western rather than the eastern Mediterranean—to avoid the Venetian warships that were seeking him—he captured a number of ships and hauled them back to Algiers. Ward was now an official member of the Tunis corsair community, so he was welcomed in Algiers and had no difficulties conducting business there. It took some time, but eventually he paid Uthman Dey off, got his English crews back, and regained some of the wealth he had lost. Thanks to the Venetians, though, the Mediterranean was still a dangerous place for him.

So he slipped away—right out of the Mediterranean entirely. With several ships, he began hunting the Atlantic littoral of Europe, using Irish ports as a base. One of the English administrators assigned the task of keeping Ireland clear of pirates was arrested for 'having given shelter to Ward the pirate.' The man pleaded that 'the pirate was far stronger than himself and had seven hundred men against his own three hundred.'[9] Even if this estimate of Ward's forces was exaggerated, it gives a sense of the resources Ward could still draw on, even at this low point in his career.

Ward's presence in European waters and, more particularly, his haunting the English Channel and using Irish ports, set off a political firestorm. By this point, Ward had become the most infamous English pirate of the age, feared and hated for the damage he had caused to English shipping. The authorities could not just stand by while he continued to prey on English shipping. So the

---

9. Horatio F. Brown, ed., *Calendar of State Papers*, Vol XI, p. 189.

A view of Algiers from the sea

A view of the Algiers harbour

A view of the city of Algiers

*Above*: A depiction of a bagnio (a slave prison) in Algiers

*Left*: A depiction of an Algiers Pasha

*Below*: Slaves arriving in Algiers

*Top*: Slaves in the Badestan (the slave market) in Algiers

*Above*: Slaves in chains

*Right*: A depiction of Ouda Bachi Topeclaure, René du Chastelet des Boys' owner, in full janissary regalia

*Above*: A depiction of Friar Antonio in Qaid Muhammad's 'dungeon'

*Below*: Salé seen from the sea

*Right*: A ship
approaching Salé

*Below*: A view of
Tetouan

*Above*: A view of Tangier

*Below left*: A depiction of Simon Danseker (drawing by Arne Zuidhoek)

*Below right*: A depiction of Calafate Hassan Reis (drawing by Arne Zuidhoek)

*Above left*: A depiction of Captain John Ward (drawing by Arne Zuidhoek)

*Above right*: A depiction of Claes Compaen (drawing by Arne Zuidhoek)

*Below left*: A depiction of Captain John Smith

*Below right*: A depiction of Captain Henry Mainwaring

A depiction of João De Carvalho Mascarenhas

A depiction of Father Pierre Dan

The cover of Father Pierre Dan's
*Histoire de Barbarie*

Trinitarian friars ransoming
slaves in Algiers

*Above left*: Filippo Pananti

*Above right*: A depiction of René Du Chastelet des Boys

*Below*: A depiction of Elizabeth Marsh

*Above*: A woman travelling through the Moroccan countryside by donkey, encased in the sort of contraption Elizabeth Marsh used

*Below*: Europeans arriving at the gates of Marrakesh

*Above*: A depiction of Elizabeth Marsh confronting the Sultan

*Below left*: A depiction of Moulay Ismail Ibn Sharif

*Below right*: A depiction of a Barbary corsair captain

*Right*: A Barbary corsair wielding
a stick

*Below*: A Dutch privateer ship

*Above*: A Dutch fluyt, showing the distinctive lack of stern and bow castles.

*Below*: A carrack

*Above*: A Barbary corsair galley

*Below*: A European ship fleeing corsairs

*Above*: A corsair galley attack

*Below*: The devastating effect of a broadside

Royal Navy was mobilized, laws promulgated, Irish ports closed, and their waters patrolled. As a result, Ward was faced with the same problem he had encountered when he first left Plymouth on the stolen merchant ship: there were no safe harbours for him. Once again, he was driven to North Africa.

Out of options, Ward settled in Tunis once again. For a brief time, there was the possibility of a pardon offered by the Duke of Tuscany, but that never worked out. Ward was pushing sixty by this point—an old man, both by the standards of the time and, especially, by the standards of his profession. He was ready to quit the sea. There were difficulties with him settling permanently in Tunis, however. The relatives of the men who had drowned aboard the *Reniera e Soderna* still had not forgotten and yearned for vengeance, and Ward, still a Christian, was looked upon as an outsider. There was one clear solution to the problem: he converted to Islam, took the name Yusuf, and became a full-fledged member of the Muslim community.

At this point in his life, Ward had a visitor, a Scot name William Lithgow who had travelled, mostly on foot, across Europe, down the Italian peninsula, across to Sicily, and from there to Tunis, where he met Ward. Lithgow wanted a 'safe-passage' to Algiers—the equivalent of a travel visa—and he went to Ward in hopes that the ex-corsair captain might be able to help him acquire one. Here is Lithgow's description of his visit with Ward:

In Tunis I met with an English Captain, General Ward, once a great pirate and commander at sea who, being denied acceptance in England, had turned Turk and built there a fair palace, beautified with rich marble and alabaster stones. With him were some fifteen circumcised English renegades whose lives and countenances were all alike, desperate and disdainful. Yet old Ward, their master, was placable enough and provided me with a safe-passage to Algiers. On diverse times in my ten days staying there, I dined and supped with him.[10]

So Ward seems to have achieved what every pirate captain dreamed of but few achieved: a comfortable, peaceful retirement in his old age, surrounded by the luxuries his wealth could provide.

It did not last, though.

---

10. William Lithgow, *The Totall Discourse of the Rare Adventures and Painefull Peregrinations of Long Nineteene Years Travayles*, 1632, reprinted 1906, p. 315.

When Ward was close to seventy, an outbreak of Bubonic plague—the Black Death—burned through Tunis. Thousands of people perished, among them Yusuf Reis, aka Captain John Ward.

It could not have been a pleasant death, but Ward did expire in his bed as an old man rather than on the heaving deck of a ship, or in a cold stone dungeon, or burnt at the stake in a public spectacle—like so many of his contemporaries.

Captain John Ward was the most notorious English pirate of his day. A successful play was written about him ('A Christian turned Turk: Or, The Tragicall Lives and Deaths of the two Famous Pirates, Ward and Dansiker'). Pamphlets were published and widely disseminated describing his adventures and depredations. He became known as the Archpirate Ward—a pirate above all others in daring and cruelty.

The English—and the other European powers, especially Venice—greeted the news of his death with a collective sigh of relief.

# Claes Compaen: Every Pirate's Dream

Claes Compaen was a Dutchman. Like his compatriot Simon Danseker, he began his piratical career as a licensed privateer attacking—and looting—Spanish shipping but then turned pirate. It was not peace with Spain that turned him, as it did other Dutch (and English) privateers. With Compaen, it was personal.

Compaen was born in Oostzaan (then a village north of Amsterdam) in 1587. As many young men did, he went to sea, trading in far-off places like Guinea, on the west coast of Africa. He must have been a canny trader, for he prospered. By the early 1620s, when he was in his mid-thirties, he had amassed considerable capital and was a captain in the Dutch merchant marine. The Twelve Years' Truce with Spain ended about this time (in the spring of 1621). With the renewal of war, privateering was looked upon as a patriotic duty. It was also, of course, profitable—at least potentially. Compaen decided to sink his capital into a privateering expedition.

After going through the necessary first step of registering as an official government sponsored privateer with the appropriate authorities, Compaen received a letter of marque legally sanctioning him to attack and loot Spanish shipping. He equipped his ship, acquired a crew, and set out.

He was apparently as successful at privateering as he had been at trading, for he consistently returned with sizeable loads of booty. He encountered a problem, though. It is unclear exactly what happened, but, one way or another, Compaen was denied what he considered to be a proper share of the profits from his privateering expeditions.

The legality of prizes brought in by Dutch privateer captains was adjudicated by a handful of local Admiralties. These Admiralties were also involved in the sale of the booty, however. It is possible that some of the men of the Admiralty that assessed Compaen's booty were corrupt. Privateering could generate a lot of money, and where there is a lot of money available, there are, inevitably, crowds of people squabbling to get access to it. Much of the profit that privateering generated went to the investors, men who were already wealthy and influential, leaving the sailors who did the actual privateering with relatively little to show for their efforts—though that little could still be significant, and certainly amounted to more than an ordinary sailor's wages.

Dutch privateer captains typically received about 1 per cent of the total profit, plus various other perks. Compaen seems to have been denied even that. He himself once claimed that the final reason he turned against the Admiralty was a large cargo of sugar he had brought in that the Admiralty confiscated, refusing to allow him any share of the profits of its sale.

Whether it was the purloined sugar or something else, the Admiralty's actions outraged Compaen, and he decided to strike out on his own.

Compaen was clearly very astute, though, for he knew better than to openly contest the wealthy and influential men of the Admiralty. Instead, he set about organizing a new privateering expedition, for which he received the Admiralty's official blessing and a letter of marque. He then bought a ship from the widow of a dead captain. The ship—the *Walte*—was 200 tons, 25 metres (80 feet) long, and armed with 17 cannons. This was just the right size for a privateering/ pirate vessel: small enough to be nimble and manoeuvrable, but large enough and well-armed enough to be a serious threat. Compaen hired a crew of 80 to man it. One version of the story has it that he had run out of funds by this time, and that he used his reputation as a successful privateer captain to borrow 8,000 guilders (a sizeable sum of money) from local financial backers, including men from the Admiralty. As a final gesture, he invited these backers to a celebratory dinner onboard his new ship.

It was an opulent occasion, with generous quantities of food and drink— and contented smiles all around, one imagines. At the end of it, Compaen presented his backers with the bill for the meal, claiming he had spent the last of his money to equip the expedition. His backers paid up. Compaen no doubt seemed to them to be exactly the kind of captain they wished to cultivate: effective at sea, but a man who did not complain or dispute their judgement about how to apportion the booty he brought in.

The next day, Compaen and his eighty men set sail in the *Walte*.

The first thing they did was accost a herring buss, one of the large fishing fleet plying the waters off the Dutch coast in the North Sea. After transferring a sizeable portion of the herring buss's load of fish to his own ship (partly to serve as food for his crew and partly to sell for ready cash), Compaen presented the buss's captain with an official looking but entirely bogus IOU from the Admiralty and sailed away. (The Admiralty never honoured the IOU, and the fishermen were never reimbursed their loss.)

After that, Compaen took his first prize as an outright pirate. Since he no longer had to return to his home port to have the booty assessed and portioned out, he split the profits evenly among his crew. This was a fairly radical approach to things, but it naturally made him popular.

It is not clear whether his crew knew all along that they had signed on for a pirate cruise, or if Compaen's generosity won them over. One version of the story depicts him heaving both the ship's Bible and the ship's Log—both representing the legality of the privateering enterprise— over the ship's side and into the sea to demonstrate the seriousness of his intentions. Whatever the case, his crew committed themselves to a life of piracy with him.

A short while later, a storm forced the *Walte* to shelter in the harbour at Vlissingen. The crew waited out the storm in the local taverns, where they no doubt spent much of their recently acquired loot. Word got around that Compaen shared booty evenly with his crew. As a result, when the storm subsided and the *Walte* took to the sea once more, fifty of the local men went eagerly along, swelling the size of the crew to 130.

Compaen launched his career as a pirate by hunting the waters in and around the English Channel, taking whatever ships he could, from Spain, Portugal, France, even the Netherlands. He was hugely successful, making use of a combination of artful deviousness backed up by violence where necessary—an approach that he had no doubt perfected in his days as a privateer. He left English shipping alone, though, for he needed ports out of which he could operate, and he had found those ports in Ireland, at least for a time. He established commercial relations with the local English overlords there and sold them his pirate booty at discounted prices. This cozy relationship ended when he took some ships containing English cargo. The resulting fracas permanently closed Irish ports to him, and he had to look elsewhere for a home base.

Like others before him, he realized there was only one place to go: North Africa.

By 1624, he had established himself at the port of Saint Croix (modern Agadir, about 800-kilometres/500-miles south of the Strait of Gibraltar, and about 550-kilometres/340-miles south of Salé). He began things there by paying the local Alcaide (the Governor of the town) a hefty bribe of more than 1,500 Moorish ducats (the currency used along that coast) for the right to be able to provision and refit his ships. By this time, he had begun to collect followers and was head of a fleet of half a dozen ships. He had also swapped the *Walte* for a larger vessel, close to 40 metres (130 feet) long, armed with twenty-six cannons and an unspecified number of *pattareroes*, (swivel guns that fired stone shot instead of iron), with a crew of 100.

Leading this fleet in his new, larger flagship, Compaen raided a vast expanse of water, ranging from the west coast of equatorial Africa all the way up to the English Channel. He was astonishingly successful—and seemingly unstoppable. The States General tried sending out fleets of warship against him, but with no result. They also wrote Moulay Zaydan, the Sultan of Morocco at that time, requesting to have Compaen arrested and detained if he put into any Moroccan port, but this too proved fruitless.

Compaen himself estimated that he (and his fleet) had captured a total of more than 350 ships during his pirate career. With this sort of volume, he used several ports along the Moroccan coast to sell his booty, including Mogador (modern Essaouira), Safi, and Salé. In Salé, he employed Simon Danseker the Younger—the son of Simon Danseker—to market his booty. Danseker the Younger seems to have been ruthlessly self-serving, though, so much so that he and Compaen had a falling out that ended in a skirmish between their ships, both firing broadsides at each other. Danseker lost and had to flee Salé, for his reputation there was ruined. (Danseker the Younger eventually negotiated a pardon with the States General and became a legal Dutch privateer.)

With Danseker gone, Compaen needed a new fence. The man who stepped up was a Dutch renegade named Murad Reis (aka Jan Janszoon van Haarlem, the renegade corsair captain from whose ship Juan Rodelgo escaped). As he had with the Alcaide of Saint Croix, Compaen began his business relationship with Murad Reis by giving him an initial bonus payment, this one of 1,000 guilders. The two men worked successfully together for some considerable time, both growing rich in the process.

Despite his success, Compaen apparently grew tired of the pirate's life. Before their quarrel, he told Simon Danseker the Younger that he intended to keep attacking as many ships as he could, from whatever country, until he had amassed sufficient wealth. Then he would try to negotiate a pardon with some European Government—preferably the Netherlands—and live out the rest of his life in peace.

As we saw above with both Simon Danseker (the Elder) and John Ward, pardons were an effective method for ridding the seas of particularly troublesome pirates. Compaen was, technically speaking, a Barbary corsair in that he operated out of North African ports. Unlike many of his privateer-turned-pirate countrymen, however, he never converted to Islam. This crucial factor made him eligible (as it had both Danseker and Ward) for a pardon.

Compaen sent out feelers via intermediaries and, in the spring of 1627, when he returned to Salé from a pirate cruise, he received notification of a pardon not only from the Netherlands but also from England. The Dutch pardon had been brought to him by his half-brother, who spent the better part of six months living in Murad Reis's house in Salé waiting for Compaen to show up. The English pardon was brought to him by an agent of the English king, Charles I. Compaen politely declined the English pardon and took the Dutch one. There was a time limit on this pardon, though. That time limit had already been extended once (Compaen was a hard man to track down), and he needed to get back to the Netherlands before it expired.

Leaving Salé, he sailed northwards, making the best time he could. Before reaching the Netherlands, though, he did make a stop: at an Irish port, where he and his men had a last wild fling with the local whores. After that, he sailed straight for the Netherlands, arriving just before the pardon expired.

Compaen made his obeisance to the Stadtholder, Frederick Hendrik, Prince of Orange, and spread a considerable portion of his wealth around to facilitate his acceptance. After that, he settled down peacefully in the village of Oostzaan, where he had been born, and lived the rest of his life there until he died peaceably in his bed in 1660 at the age of seventy-three—the fulfilment of every pirate's dream.

Claes Compaen is unique among seventeenth-century privateers/pirates in that a biography was written about him while he was still alive. This biography, first published in 1659 and written by 'the Schoolmaster of Oostzaan' (that is all we know about him), provides us with considerable detail about Compaen's life—though some of the details are questionable because the Schoolmaster was clearly intent on presenting Compaen as an example of how people are ultimately, and justly, punished for their misdeeds.

According to him, Compaen's wealth evaporated over the years, and he died in dire poverty. Since the Schoolmaster tried to depict Compaen's life as an exemplar of the old adage that crime does not pay, Compaen dying a pauper seems a bit too convenient. In Compaen's case, it looks like 'crime' did pay, and that he managed to fulfil the dream of every pirate captain (and most ordinary people): a comfortable, peaceful, respected old age.

Compaen's pirate career was astonishingly successful—he took over 350 ships, remember. This number is even more impressive when one considers that Compaen was a pirate for only about four years, from 1623 to 1627. The amount of wealth he amassed from the loot taken from so many ships must have been huge. And he had been a successful trader in the earlier part of his career at sea, so he knew how to manage his business affairs. Other than a pious wish for justice to be done, there is no compelling reason to believe that Compaen ran out of money as he aged. He likely lived out his life in Oostzaan quietly, spending his days fishing in the canals and drinking sedately in the local taverns.

In the early 1930s, a Dutch clairvoyant claimed she had learned by occult means that Compaen had indeed died a wealthy man, and that he had buried the remains of his treasure at Zaandam (the next village over from Oostzaan). Treasure hunters dug about for several years but found nothing much. Perhaps Compaen's treasure is still there somewhere, buried in an iron-bound oaken chest, black with age, hidden in some nook or corner, or under the floorboards of an old church building, waiting to be found.

Then again, perhaps not.[1]

---

1. The details of Claes Compaen's life and career as a pirate come from the Schoolmaster's biography of him: *'t Begin, midden en eynde der zee-roovereyen van den alderfamieusten zee-roover Claes G. Compaen van Oostzanen in Kennemer-landt: vervattende sijn wonderlijcke, vreemde en landts-schadelijcke drijf-tochten: waer in verthoont wordt, hoe hy met weynigh schepen de zee onveyligh ghemaeckt, een ongelooffelijcken buyt, en groot getal van schepen van alle landen gheroost, en afgeloopen heest* (*The beginning, middle, and end of the pirate Claes G. Compaen from Oostzaan in Kennemerland, encompassing his wonderful, strange, and destructive travels, wherein it is shown how he sailed the sea in many ships, acquiring an unbelievable amount of booty, and capturing a great number of ships from many lands*), first published in 1659. My thanks go to Joris van Os for his invaluable help with the Dutch text.

# NARRATIVE TEXTS

# Captain John Smith on Pirates and Renegades

As we have seen, Barbary corsairs were not just Muslims from North Africa. Their ranks were swelled by a flood of Christian renegades, men who 'turned Turk'(converted to Islam) and became Barbary pirates themselves. So why did so many Europeans desert their homelands, convert, and attack European shipping? One answer to this question comes to us from Captain John Smith.

John Smith is best known for his involvement with the Jamestown colony (and Pocahontas), but in his early life he adventured in Eastern Europe. On his way there, he was shipwrecked and ended up for a time as a crewmember aboard a French pirate ship in the Mediterranean. After that, while fighting against Ottoman Turkish forces in Hungary, he was captured, enslaved, and taken to Istanbul. He escaped by killing his owner and then travelled through Germany, France, Spain, and Morocco before eventually making his way back to England.

All of this means that he could speak with some authority regarding European pirates and their connections with Barbary corsairs. In the excerpt below, he explains why English (and, by extension, other European) pirates became renegades and Barbary corsairs.

After the death of our most gracious Queen Elizabeth, of blessed memory, our royal King James, who from his Infancy had reigned in peace with all nations, considered he had no further employment for men of war [King James I concluded a peace treaty with Spain in 1604 and so put English privateers out of work]. Those [privateers] who were rich rested with that they had; those who were poor, and had nothing but from hand to mouth, turned pirate: some because they felt slighted by those for whom they had got much wealth; some because they could not get their due; some that had lived bravely would not abase themselves to poverty; some vainly, only to get a name; others for revenge, covetousness, or other ill motives.

As they found themselves more and more oppressed, their passions increasing with discontent. This made them turn pirates.

Now because they grew hateful to all Christian princes, they retired to Barbary, where although there be not many good harbours but Tunis, Algiers, Salé, Marmora, and Tetouan, there are many convenient roads, or the open sea, which is their chief lordship. For the best harbours within the Straits of Gibraltar—Alcazarquivir, Oran, Melilla, Tangier, and Ceuta—are all possessed by the Spaniards. Beyond the Straits, they have also Arzilla and Mazagan. Marmora they have likewise lately taken and fortified. Captain Ward, an Englishman, and Captain Dansker, a Dutchman, first made their markets in North Africa to sell booty when the Moors knew scarce how to sail a ship. Captain Bishop was ancient and did little hurt, but Captain Easton got so much he made himself a Marquis in Savoy, and Ward lived like a Pasha in Barbary. Those were the first that taught the Moors to be men of war.

Many times the English pirates had very good ships, and well manned, but they were commonly so fractious amongst themselves, and so riotous, quarrelsome, treacherous, blasphemous and villainous that it is more than a wonder that they could so long continue to do so much mischief. And everything they got, they basely consumed amongst Jews, Turks, Moors, and whores.

They would seldom go to sea, as long as they could possibly live on shore. Being mixed in with the French and the Dutch (but with very few Spaniards or Italians), commonly running one from another, they became so disjointed, disordered, debauched, and miserable that the Turks and Moors began to command them as slaves and force them to instruct them in their best skill, which many an accursed *renegado*, or Christian turned Turk, did, till they made those Sallymen [the corsairs of Salé] or Moors of Barbary as powerful as they be, to the terror of all the Straits. Many times they take purchase in the Atlantic and, yes, sometimes even in the English Channel. They are the most cruel villains in Turkey or Barbary.[1]

---

1. This description of how European pirates became Barbary corsairs is taken from Chapter XXVIII, 'The bad Life, Qualities and Conditions of Pirates; and how they taught the Turks and Moors to become men of War,' in John Smith, *The True travels, Adventures and Observations of Captain John Smith into Europe, Asia, Africa, and America, from Ann. Dom. 1593 to 1629*, originally published in 1629. I have lightly abridged the original, modernized the spelling, and replaced some of the archaic phraseology to make the text more accessible.

So there you have it. According to John Smith, it was King James' peace treaty with the Spanish that drove the English pirates to North Africa and debauchery that allowed the North Africans to eventually gain the upper hand. More than this, it was expat English (and other European) pirates who taught the North African corsairs how to use European style square-rigged sailing ships and so enabled them to abandon their oared galleys and burst out of the confines of the Mediterranean and launch a new era of Atlantic raiding.

A fine example indeed of the law of unintended consequences.

# Captain Henry Mainwaring on the Suppression of Piracy

Henry Mainwaring was born in 1586 into a wealthy and influential English family (his maternal grandfather had been Vice-Admiral of Sussex and a favourite of Queen Elizabeth I). As a young man, he was educated at Oxford, became a lawyer, and then started a nautical career, serving as a pirate hunter in the service of King James I. He soon turned pirate himself, however, and though his career as a pirate captain was short—1612-1615—it was extraordinarily successful, especially considering that he was only 26 when he began it.

After three years of vigorous and highly profitable piracy, Mainwaring negotiated a royal pardon, eventually ending up a knight and a Gentleman of the Royal Bedchamber. In later years, he served in a number of official posts, including Lieutenant of Dover Castle and Deputy Warden of the Cinque Ports. He also served as Surveyor of the Navy and sat in the House of Commons for a year (1621-1622). He was a royalist during the English Civil War. As a result, he ended up in exile in France, where, for the first time in his life, he apparently ran out of options and died in poverty.

Mainwaring was not, technically speaking, a Barbary corsair. He never converted to Islam, and he never received legal authorization from any North African city state to support his piratical activities (legally speaking, remember, Barbary corsairs were not pirates; they were privateers acting under the lawful authorization of the authorities in their home ports, just as English privateers like Sir Francis Drake or Walter Raleigh did). Mainwaring operated out of North African ports, though, and was on friendly terms with both the Sultan of Morocco and the Dey of Tunis. So though he may technically have been more pirate than corsair, he was definitely a part of the larger Barbary corsair enterprise.

Mainwaring made two decisions that proved crucial to his career. First, he focused on French and Spanish shipping and avoided attacking English ships. Second, he did not convert to Islam.

Once a European pirate captain converted to Islam and became a renegade, he crossed a line, and his chances of ever receiving a pardon by a European monarch were vanishingly slim. This mattered, because, as we have seen, the issuing of royal pardons was a fairly common way of clearing the seas of particularly troublesome pirates. A royal pardon was the dream of many an expat pirate—after he had first accrued a sufficiently large fortune, of course.

Since Mainwaring had never bothered English ships and had not converted, and since he was an irritating thorn in the sides of the French and the Spanish monarchies, both of whom complained bitterly to the English King James I about him, King James saw fit to offer Mainwaring a royal pardon in 1615.

Mainwaring was just about to turn thirty at the time.

There is no doubt that Mainwaring gained his pardon and the various offices and ranks he held in large part because of his family connections. He was also, however, an obviously intelligent, capable man. And he could write. He is perhaps best known now for his discourse on English piracy: *Of the Beginnings, Practices, and Suppression of Pirates*. Completed around 1617, it was never actually published in book form in Mainwaring's day. Instead, Mainwaring presented a handwritten copy to King James I.

*Of the Beginnings, Practices, and Suppression of Pirates* is relatively short— only 40 printed pages—but it covers considerable ground: the origins of post-Elizabethan English piracy, the reasons men became pirates, the methods such pirates used at sea, details about the ports and harbours around the world used by pirates, and how to suppress and prevent piracy. Mainwaring—recipient of a royal pardon as he was—is renowned for the ironic fact that his advice for how to stop piracy was to not grant pardons to pirates. He did indeed argue this, but it was part of a larger, more nuanced proposal.

Here are Mainwaring's thoughts on how to suppress piracy.

I think the best and surest way, and that which might much advance the wealth and glory of our State, would be to devise some more universal employment than now we have, by which men of that spirit [i.e., ex-privateers] might not complain, as they now do, that they are forced for lack of convenient employment to enter into such unlawful courses [as piracy]. The proof of this is plain, for since your Highness' reign there have been more pirates by ten to one than there were in the whole reign of the last Queen.

There are now no voyages to speak of but to Newfoundland, which they [the ex-privateers] hold too toilsome, or to Newcastle, which many hold too base, or to the East Indies, which most hold dangerous and tedious. As for your Highness' ships [i.e., the Royal Navy], the entertainment is so small, and the pay so bad that they hold it a kind of slavery to serve in them. I speak of the private sailor, not the officer. In this I must say to myself *Ne sutor ultra Crepidam* [Let not the cobbler judge beyond his last] and leave the project to your Highness' singular judgment, only I must emphasize this, that it is an ill policy which provides more for the punishing than the preventing of offenders.

Next, to take away their hopes and encouragements, your Highness must put on a constant immutable resolution never to grant any pardon, and for those that are or may be taken, to put them all to death, or make slaves of them, for if your Highness should ask me when those men would cease offending, I might answer, as a wise favourite did the late Queen who demanded of him when he would cease begging. He answered, when she would cease giving. So say I, such men will cease offending when your Highness ceases pardoning. And in the little observation I could make in my small travels, I have noted those countries best governed are where the laws are most severely executed; as for instance in Tunis, where no offence is ever remitted, but is instead strictly punished according to their customs and laws.[1]

*Of the Beginnings, Practices, and Suppression of Pirates* is a fascinating little piece in a number of ways. The brief argument Mainwaring presents above—that the king should first ensure a decent livelihood for privateers who, put out of work by his peace treaty with Spain, would otherwise be drawn to a life of piracy because they had few other options, and that only after such employment was readily available should those who still chose to become pirates be punished—shows a remarkably practical and commonsense approach: address the cause of the problem rather than the effects. Unfortunately, his advice went unheeded.

---

1. G. E. Manwaring and W. G. Perrin, eds. *Publications of the Navy Records Society: The Life and Works of Sir Henry Mainwaring*, Volume 2. pp. 41-42.

# The Narrative of João De Carvalho Mascarenhas: Captured at Sea by Algerine Corsairs

Barbary corsairs conducted land raids, but they took most of their captives at sea. One of the most complete—and most dramatic—narratives of a violent corsair attack at sea is that written by João de Carvalho Mascarenhas who endured five years as a slave in Algiers in the first quarter of the seventeenth century. Like a number of other European captives who survived enslavement and managed eventually to return home, Mascarenhas wrote a book describing his experiences: *Memorável relaçam da perda da Nao Conceição que os Turcos queymárão à vista da barra de Lisboa* (*Memorable Account of the Loss of the Ship Conceição that the Turks Burned in Sight of the Bar of Lisbon*).

João Mascarenhas served as a soldier for the Portuguese crown in a wide variety of locations. By his own account, before he had reached the age of thirty, he had been to Brazil, Mozambique, various places along the east coast of Africa as far north as the shores of the Red Sea, the Middle East (where he saw the waters of the Tigris and the Euphrates rivers), Persia, Mongolia, and India, where, among other places, he visited the Ganges.

In March of 1621, after completing a tour in the Portuguese controlled territory in India, Mascarenhas embarked from Goa (the Portuguese enclave on India's west coast) on the *Nossa Senhora da Conceição* (*Our Lady of Conception*), a large carrack that was returning to Portugal.

Carracks were, for the time, very large ships—sort of the seventeenth century equivalent of a container ship. They had high 'castles' at the bow and stern, three or four masts, and capacious holds (in order to carry the various sorts of treasure the Portuguese had looted from the Indian subcontinent and the Spice Islands further east). The voyage between India and Portugal was notoriously dangerous, for not only were the ships that attempted it threatened by storms *en route*, but since they were crammed with expensive merchandise—spices, silks, treasure of many sorts—they were the target of all manner of pirates as well. Some estimates are that ten to twenty per cent of the Portuguese carracks that left India never made it to Portugal.

Conditions aboard the *Conceição* were atrocious. Not only was the ship crammed with treasure; it was crammed with people as well. The vessel was perhaps 45 metres (150 feet) long by something like 9 metres (30 feet) wide (though it is hard to know for sure, since Mascarenhas did not provide us with exact dimensions). Into this rather modest-sized vessel (by modern standards), somewhere between six and eight hundred people—sailors, soldiers, and passengers—were packed. The voyage lasted slightly over seven months, during which time bad food, bad water, overcrowding, and disease took a ruthless toll.

Despite the dangers and adverse conditions aboard, the *Conceição* made the voyage successfully, and Mascarenhas managed to survive it.

The route back to Portugal took the *Conceição* across the Arabian Sea, down the east coast of Africa, and round the Cape of Good Hope on Africa's southern tip. From there, forced to follow the prevailing winds, it ended up at the island of Saint Helena (the place where Napoleon was incarcerated and died), where it stopped to replenish water and supplies and to make repairs. Following the winds again, the *Conceição* headed for the Azores. There, the ship's captain received a letter informing him that a fleet of Algerine corsair ships was cruising the Portuguese coast, but that a squadron of Portuguese ships, under the command of Dom Antonio de Ataíde, was in position to escort the *Conceição* safely into Lisbon harbour.

After receiving this reassuring bit of news, the *Conceição* left the Azores and sailed to the Portuguese coast, arriving in the waters near Lisbon in early October. They saw no sign of the Portuguese fleet. The wind was weak and contrary, and they struggled to make headway. Just before dawn, they heard the sound of voices ahead in the darkness along with the creaking of ships and decided to furl their sails and wait for daylight, hoping to see the Portuguese fleet.

The grey radiance of morning, however, revealed a nasty surprise.

At this point, it is best to let João de Carvalho Mascarenhas tell the story himself.

To my knowledge, the *Memorável relaçam da perda da Nao Conceição* has never been translated into English before.

So here, for the very first time in English, is the story of João de Carvalho Mascarenhas.

By midnight, we were close to Lisbon, and towards the end of the second watch [i.e., close to 4:00 AM] we heard the sound of people talking ahead, as if our ship had been anchored in a city harbour. Believing that they were in the middle of Dom Antonio de Ataíde's fleet, the *Conceição*'s crew joyfully set about preparing the ship to drop anchor at Lisbon.

As day broke, we discovered seventeen large ships of thirty to forty guns each. Though we saw clearly that they did not belong to our fleet, we imagined that they were ships laden with salt which had come from Setubal [located about 80 kilometres/50 miles south of Lisbon].

These ships, however, were Turkish [i.e., they were Barbary corsair ships].

As soon as the Turks were informed by the Christian sailors they had with them that this ship that had so suddenly appeared was a carrack from India, they held a council, put their boats in the sea to warn each other, deployed their battle flags, and, protected by their shields, formed themselves into battle order.

In our naivety, since we had not yet fully grasped what was happening, we kept our illusions—because we could not believe that there could be so many enemies so close to home. Our ship's captain ordered the flag lowered, but it was quickly hoisted up again when it was understood from their insolence that these ships were enemies.

We fired on their flagship, and the captain of that ship, as soon as he saw that we had no intention of surrendering, took in his mainsails and reefed his spritsails, keeping only the topsails and the mizzen sails. The other ships made the same arrangements, with the intention of attacking our ship and boarding it.

Our ship was in the worst possible state. During the seven days it had taken us to sail from the Azores, we had done nothing but carry luggage and bundles up on deck from below. Passengers from India typically fit what they have brought with them into light luggage. In order to avoid paying the excessive duties that are charged on anything transported belowdecks, they insist that their baggage be brought up on deck towards the end of the voyage. The crew were thus weary from the exertion of carrying so many pieces of luggage, and the ship's deck was clogged and crowded with baggage and cluttered with mooring lines that had been pulled out in preparation for anchoring at Cascais.

Despite everything, however, our men acted with so much courage and ardour that in less than a quarter of an hour they had cleared the bridge and cleaned it with large tubs of water, carried the passengers' luggage back down belowdecks, and set up protective rope nets and shields.

By then, our men were armed and at their posts. The armament was very poor, though—for it had been several years since the ship had first left for India, and it had passed through two severe monsoon seasons. The men's muskets were barely serviceable, and the lances were all rotten. The courage of the men, however, compensated for the defects of their weapons.

Gunners were assigned at the rate of one for every two guns, though it would have taken at least two for each gun to operate them effectively. But the men behaved like old soldiers. Our captain, Dom Luis de Sousa, placed himself in the middle of the bridge, a steel shield on his arm and a naked sword in his hand, waiting bravely for the cannonade of the enemy.

Our ship remained motionless in a light wind.

On their guard, and in good combat formation, the enemy approached us, all at the same time, from all sides and with all their ships. They injured and killed many of our people. One of their first cannon balls carried away the leg of the master gunner, who died immediately. It was a heavy loss, for he was very brave and very proficient when it came to artillery. A splinter struck and badly wounded a young man who was on the bridge and who had been an officer aboard a galley. Since he could no longer move, he was later burned alive when our ship was set on fire.

There were by then more than twenty-five victims, dead and wounded combined. One of them was the captain. A musket ball broke his sword in two and struck him on his right leg, where the garter was—not a serious injury. But immediately after, another bullet struck him, hitting his leg a span higher and passing through the muscle. As he was greatly weakened and unable to remain upright, he lay down on a crate at the mouth of a hatch, and from there he gave his orders.

The enemy, among whom our artillery had wreaked havoc with chain-shot and bar-shot, withdrew, most of their ships damaged by the fighting, and also because of the resulting danger from the proximity of our ship, for when it rolled, because of its great size, it would tear away the spars and bowsprits, along with the rigging, of the corsair ships alongside it.

One of these corsair ships, the largest, with more than forty guns, was captained by Calafate Hassan Reis, the bravest Turk in Algiers, and well known as such. Seeing that his ship was lost, demolished by our bar-shot, and ready to sink under the effect of the many cannonballs it had received, he made a virtue of necessity (though this did not diminish his act of courage), and, abandoning his ship and brandishing a red flag which he had snatched from the stern, he leapt onto our ship and entrenched himself in the forecastle with four hundred Turks and Moors whom he had brought with him. These were the bravest of Algiers, the elite, and for the most part renegades like him.

He fastened his flag to the foremast, and he and his people launched a volley of arrows and musket shot, followed by many others, causing us great harm.

During this fight, with our men holding the midship deck and the stern, and they the bow, a renegade from Setubal climbed the foremast, and, with a hatchet, began to cut as much of the rigging as he could. Addressing his fellows, calling them each by name, he urged them to join him, or he would do it all by himself with his hatchet. He cut the stays of the foreyard, which fell suddenly with such violence that all the Turks below it were killed.

Our enemies were so numerous and so closely packed together that all our musket balls hit them. Two of these Turks came out boldly from the forecastle, swinging their scimitars and shouting. One of them scrambled up the mainmast ratlines and was already near the top when he was hit by a bullet and fell dead. The other passed to the stern and reached the compass, where he was killed by a sword thrust.

In the middle of this tight fight, a black Javanese cook who was among us ran amok—such is the custom of their country when a man decides to kill his enemy or to die trying. Alone, with a bare sword in his hand, he rushed towards all the Turks on the forecastle. But he received so many bullets and arrows that he could not carry out his plan and was immediately killed.

The moment after this, a soldier told Pero Mendes de Vasconcelos, who was travelling with his wife and children and carrying forty thousand cruzados, to step aside a little because of two Turks. One was aiming at him with a musket. Another aimed at the soldier himself with an arrow. No sooner had the soldier said these words than Pero Mendes received a bullet in his chest from which he subsequently died, but the arrow lost its force as it glanced off a rope, and its feather merely brushed the eyes of the soldier without doing him any harm.

In this combat, the ship's chaplain, Brother Gregorio, a Franciscan, conducted himself with great bravery. He ran from place to place, a crucifix in his hand, to confess and encourage men, so that it is impossible to properly describe his bravery and holy zeal (though this was very little compared to what he did afterwards in Algiers, on the occasion of the plague that struck that city).

Father Manuel Mendes, who was travelling to Rome as Procurator General of the Jesuits in India, also behaved in an excellent and admirable way. During the whole trip he never stopped teaching and preaching. But it was especially during this fight that he behaved with the bravery of a young man, though he was already very old. He confessed the wounded, exhorted able-bodied men, and encouraged everybody by his example. Several times the captain told him to take refuge belowdecks, for there he could confess the wounded and avoid many risks. But he replied that he considered his life less valuable than that of those doing the fighting, that there were wounded who could not get below, and that he would therefore remain on deck. This he did until the ship was set on fire.

His companion, Father Mota, a lay brother, behaved like an old soldier, helping in every way he could to care for and comfort the wounded and to cover the dead, so that the living would not lose heart at the sight of them. He did all this with great Christian zeal, a zeal which he would later show in captivity by caring for the plague-stricken, until he himself died of that illness.

There were also two clerks aboard our ship. One, called Dom Patricio, was Castilian, and he came from the Philippines, bearing letters for His Majesty. Both behaved like excellent priests. I remember Dom Patricio with sorrow, though, for afterwards he died in Algiers, burned alive by the Turks, those savage scoundrels, for defending the Catholic faith.

The fight continued throughout the day, with many dead and wounded on our side. The Turks who had boarded our ship began to regret their rash action and abandoned hope of accomplishing anything which was to their advantage. Most of them were already dead, and their ship was lost. They therefore began to make signals to ask the other corsair ships to come to their aid or to send them reinforcements. These ships, cruising past us, continued to fire—and to receive—numerous broadsides. The corsairs who were aboard our ship called out to them, but they never dared draw too close to us. They sent out ship's boats and prepared to pick up those who leapt overboard.

Our men understood their plan, however, and did not want to let an enemy leave so easily. So they attacked the corsairs with a wild cry of 'Santiago!'— attacking with such fury that, in spite of resistance, they managed to successfully mount the ship's forecastle. The corsairs, however, using the tridents of our fishermen which they found there, and the points of the spears which remained to them, repelled our men three times. Finally, our men overwhelmed the corsairs, throwing into the sea those they did not kill, and so made themselves not only masters of the forecastle but of the whole ship. They finished off those who had leaped into the sea by throwing pieces of wood, stones, even sacks of rice at them from above, and they left onboard only one alive, who surrendered to the captain.

So we had victory that day, at the end of a fight that had lasted from seven in the morning until six in the evening. We had more than thirty dead and wounded, among whom were killed seven cannoneers. There was not a ship among the enemy, however, that did not have at least ten dead and wounded. Of the Turks who had boarded us, no more than eight escaped—among them that traitorous dog Calafate Hassan Reis, who made it to the flagship of Tabaco Reis, Commander-in-Chief of the corsair fleet.

Our battle that day against the Algerine corsairs was one of the most remarkable fights of our time. If the participants had been other than Portuguese, books would have been written and stories told about it that would have spread throughout the world, and there would be no province, however remote, where people did not know of it.

That a single ship, with only twenty-two cannons, fought for a whole day, without receiving help and without surrendering, against seventeen large corsair vessels, each armed with thirty-five to forty guns... I do not know if this has ever happened. And that such a small number of soldiers, passengers, sailors, and cabin boys, exhausted by an eight-month sea voyage, fought against five thousand Turks, fearless shooters all, who had left Algiers only fourteen days before... Never to my knowledge, in ancient or modern times, has anything like this happened to any nation.

The fight that day only ended when the darkness of night fell. The enemy gathered their ships together and moved away from ours until they were at a distance of more than a cannon shot. Some engaged in laying planking over the holes our cannon balls had made in their hulls (and those holes were not small); others repaired the yards and the bowsprits that had been broken during their attempts at boarding us; others lashed their masts together where they and the rigging had been damaged by our bar- and chain-shot.

Our ship offered the most astonishing spectacle. The numerous discharges of artillery and musketry had torn the sails to shreds, and there was hardly the space of a handspan that had not received a projectile. Nor was there any rigging, pulley, or rope that was not dislocated, broken, or torn. The stern looked ready to crumble away, and, seen from a distance, the ship appeared to be sheathed with cannonballs, for few of them had managed to smash through the hull, and they remained stuck in the planking.

During the night, we threw our dead into the sea and treated the wounded. But the men who were unwounded had no time to rest, for they immediately had to put the ship back in order: installing new sails, repairing the rigging, re-setting the foresail, which had fallen to the deck, and adjusting the forestay, which was broken. Everything had to be repaired, and we found the work of that night more difficult than the struggle of the day. We spent the entire night completely repairing the ship, so that it looked as if it had just left the port of Goa. The next day, the enemy, seeing our ship so different from the state in which they had left it at nightfall, were so amazed that they wondered if indeed it was the same ship.

As soon as our ship was repaired, a little favourable wind arose, but so light that it served no purpose. Everything ended in a great calm and a painful heaviness that lasted well into morning.

When it was light, the sailors scanned the sea from the ship's gunwales and from the top of the mainmast without discovering any sails. Our ship could not go to Cascais [a headland a little under 20 kilometres/12 miles west of Lisbon] because, when the wind began to blow, it immediately became contrary. Near Ericeira [a stretch of sandy coastline about 40 kilometres/25 miles north of Cascais] we could see a small, sandy beach where there seemed to be a good anchorage. After consulting, we decided to go and anchor there in six or seven fathoms of water, for the enemy, if he reappeared, would not attack us so close to land, and if he did, our ship would not fail to be rescued.

Because we had so few uninjured men, it seemed impossible for us to support another day of combat. The principal officers were all wounded, and of the fourteen cannoneers, seven had been killed and four wounded, so that only three remained. Close to land like this, we reasoned we were well placed to receive reinforcements to help us fight off the corsairs' attacks.

This plan seemed good to us, and we put it into practice. We were prepared to go as far as Peniche [a headland 40 kilometres/25 miles north of Ericeira] if the wind allowed it.

We were letting out the mooring lines, within cannon shot of Ericeira, when we saw a sail coming towards us from the shore. We thought this ship was bringing us reinforcements or ammunition, but when it approached nearer, we saw it contained only three crewmen. One of them shouted to us in a loud voice that someone—I cannot recall who—was asking us to go back to sea immediately, for the coast could be dangerous in this season, and the ship might easily be lost. We should search out the fleet of Dom Antonio de Ataíde, he told us, which was awaiting us out at sea.

Our people asked this boat to take the women and children and all the others unfit for the combat, along with all the jewels, because the enemy could not be far away, since they had not had enough wind to move off. The boatman luffed as much as he could and said with an expression of the greatest fear in the world that he had orders not to approach our ship on pain of his life, and that he therefore could do nothing to help us.

The captain then told the pilot to take the ship in the direction of the open sea—as we had been directed—which the pilot did immediately.

Would to God that the captain had acted differently, and that this boat had never come to us from the shore. It was the damnation of our ship, and those who followed this direction committed a serious fault, because on the injunction of a simple boatman, and without having received a letter ordering it expressly, they were not obliged to act against their original intention.

And so our ship sailed out into the open sea—heading straight for the enemy.

We encountered them around eight o'clock in the morning, when we no longer had the possibility of returning to land, for the opposing ships were very light and fast, and they would have easily caught up with ours before we could reach the coast. We therefore preferred to continue in the same direction, to show that they were not afraid, and because, sailing thus, we hoped we might come within sight of Dom Antonio de Ataíde's fleet.

We had our artillery and men ready for the fight, under the same conditions as the day before, and with the same assurance, but we had many wounded and suffered from the depletion of our crew, especially the cannoneers.

The enemy drew near.

As soon as we saw them and realized they were intent on attacking us, the Captain summoned the captive Turk whom he had in his power since the day before and who was still alive. He told this Turk that he was personally going to pay for the harm that his people intended to do us.

This was, in truth, a cruel gesture, for after a fight, and in a war where there are prisoners on both sides, you do not kill anyone in cold blood.

Summoning a Pole whom he had brought with him from Hormuz, and who had been many years a prisoner of the Turks, the Captain handed the Turk over to him and told him to kill him before the ships of his people reached ours. The Pole immediately tied the Turk's hands behind his back, and, taking up a scimitar, he told the Turk to come forward because, on the Captain's order, he was going to cut off his head.

The Turk answered not a word. No sadness appeared on his face. Moving forward with the assurance and courage of a brave soldier (Turkish men are extremely brave), he went to sit near the gunwale, his face turned towards the sea, and, so that the scimitar could reach him more easily, he lowered his head without a word, and without it being necessary to say anything to him, as if he were indifferent to death and did not regret life.

The Pole gave him two blows with the scimitar, which completely tore off his head and made it fall into the sea. His headless body remained there for a moment, but the Pole gave this body a kick which made it take the path of the head.

The Turks learned, after they captured our ship, that the Pole had cut off the head of this man, and yet they did him no harm.

The enemy ships advanced in single file, one behind the other, following their flagship, all sails out, with their battle flags showing. Only the flagship flew white flags. As soon as he was within cannon range, he fired a blank shot, which meant, like the white flags, that we should surrender.

However, we were not in a mood to give ourselves over to him, and so we responded with a salvo of cannon balls. When the enemy understood our determination, they first sailed in the same direction. Then, turning towards us, they took down the white flags, replacing them with red flags, and they furled their lower sails as well as their spritsails. All the other ships did the same, and they passed in front of our ship at a distance, firing cannons and muskets at us.

We attached less importance to such an attack than on the day before. The first cannonballs of a battle are indeed those that one fears the most, and as we were no longer so afraid, we responded to their attack so forcefully that they were obliged to move off from us.

They regrouped around their flagship about a league from us. That flagship was a very large vessel. Its Reis (that is what they call the Captain) was Cara Mostafa. They immediately held a council. There, as we learned later, Tabaco Reis, the Captain-General of the squadron, said that he wanted nothing to do with our ship, and intended to return to Algiers. He was content with the nineteen English vessels he had already taken, all captured in one morning, and which had cost him only one cannon shot, after which all had lowered their flags. He took most of the English with him and had sent their captured ships ahead two days earlier.

However, that dog Calafate Hassan Reis—he who had escaped our ship by swimming—responded that he had lost his vessel, that four hundred Turks and Moors he had brought with him had perished, and that it was not honourable for the Turks of Algiers, or for himself, to return having lost a ship and all it contained, and to have suffered so many casualties, without having taken such a valuable prize, or at least having set it afire and sunk it. It was, he argued, only one ship, and they had sixteen. 'Give me command of a ship,' he declared, 'and if that Portuguese ship, after a new assault, refuses to surrender, I will set it on fire!'

The words of this renegade Greek prompted another man of the same nation, his comrade Abibi Reis, who was one of the bravest men in Algiers, to persuade all the others that they must attack, and that he alone would set fire to our ship or die in the attempt.

Very reluctantly—for he is better known for his luck than for his courage—Tabaco Reis had his squadron assume the same formation as before, and in the same order. They again raised their colours and passed us within cannon range, though without a single shot being fired from any of the ships.

After passing by our ship with their red banners waving and with numerous bastard trumpets blaring, they saw that the courage of our people did not weaken, and they then accepted the inevitable.

Their flagship came towards us, and the others followed in the same order, approaching so close that their spars and ours almost touched. Each of them, one after the other and without stopping, fired a broadside, and, finally, the ship commanded by Abibi Reis approached very close to our stern with the intention of setting our ship on fire. When he was near our stern gallery, which, according to custom, was covered, because of the rains, with a tarpaulin, he took off his turban, tore a length from it, and broke a flask of brandy over it. This brandy had been mixed with linseed oil, sulphur, and gunpowder, a mixture that, when it catches fire, can only be extinguished with vinegar.

He then bound a strip of his turban, soaked with the brandy mixture and set afire, at the end of an arrow which he fired into the tarpaulin of our gallery. The fire caught easily and became so violent that it was no use pouring water on it. Our carpenters had no trouble breaking the railing of the gallery apart with their axes and heaving the burning tarpaulin into the sea, but it was impossible to beat the fire back.

This pirate dog made his ship advance until it was side to side with ours. He then set fire to the main deck. At the same time, in the forecastle, which was very well defended, for we did not want it to be taken again as it had been the day before, somebody fired a musket at Abibi Reis. The ball took him in the chest and laid him on the stern deck of his ship. He only had time to swear that he would let all the Christians aboard our own ship burn to death, since he himself was dying. Upon this, his cursed soul sank away to Hell. He may have burned our ship, but he lost his own vessel, and he lost his life as well.

Our cannons fired so furiously against Abibi Reis's ship that it was shot to pieces and most of the Turks aboard it killed. In an effort to get away from this ship, we veered downwind. But as the fire had already taken hold on our ship's stern, and the wind blew the flames inside the gallery and into the Captain's cabin, which caused the ship to burst into flames with the greatest violence, exploding what we thought were sacks of clovers but in fact contained gunpowder. It is thus with everything transported by a ship like ours: drugs, fabrics, cinnamon, pepper... What are they but fuel for fire?

By now, our people had abandoned their weapons and rushed towards the fire, though without any real hope of being able to extinguish it. As the flames reached the mainmast, some Turks abandoned their own vessel, which was drifting, shattered and dismasted, close to our ship. Brandishing scimitars and hatchets, they swarmed aboard our ship to pillage it.

We now faced a terrible choice, caught as we were between three cruel enemies: the fire, the water, and the Turks. Finally, considering the Turks to be the most inclined to pity, our people began to scramble aboard the corsair ship still drifting alongside ours. If that ship had not been there, none of us would have survived. The Turks of the other ships came immediately with longboats, pulling us out of the crippled corsair ship and transporting us to other ships. They also rushed to try to save some of the cargo in our vessel, but they could not take even a single piece of cloth.

Escaping to the nearby corsair ship was how most of our people managed to save themselves. The seriously wounded, however, remained behind and were burnt alive—and they received a better reward in heaven than that which, in this realm, awaited the survivors.

A few of the Turks were also burned. Their greed drove them to go belowdecks in our ship searching for loot. When they tried to climb back up, the fire blocked their way, opening for them the road to Hell—where they will stay forever.

Finally, in hardly an hour, the richest ship that had left India in many years was set ablaze and sank without leaving a trace. In pepper alone, our ship transported six thousand eight hundred quintals.[1] The hold and the decks were crammed with boxes and bales, and a lavish and extravagant present which the king of Persia was offering to His Majesty was stowed aboard as well. The ship also transported Captain Luis de Sousa, who had just commanded the fortress of Ormuz, in India, who had on him two hundred thousand cruzados.[2] There were also other extremely wealthy passengers. Moreover, our ship carried a very large quantity of diamonds.

This battle caused many deaths. A soldier named Antonio Caldeira, who had been in charge of the port deck cannons, and who had behaved valiantly that day and the day before, had the misfortune to be killed, by the last musket ball that penetrated into the ship, while he stood in the middle of his battery. He died like a brave and loyal soldier at the post entrusted to him.

When the Turks boarded our ship, they found the quartermaster on board with a steel shield on his arm that had belonged to the captain and his bare

---

1. A quintal was roughly 100 pounds (45 kilos). So 6,800 quintals was equivalent to 308,440 kilos (680,000 pounds), which in turn is equivalent to about 308 metric tons/300 Imperial tons/340 US tons. In other words, a *lot* of pepper.

2. One Portuguese cruzado was equal to roughly ten Spanish pieces of eight (the famous coin all pirates lusted after). So the Captain de Sousa was transporting the equivalent of two million pieces of eight—a mind-numbingly colossal sum in those days.

sword in his hand. He had not thrown down his arms, as is customary when a ship is captured. Two Turks approached him from the front and another from behind. They sliced off his head with their scimitars. This man, from the first moment to the last, had fought with a bravery that is impossible to surpass.

I do not intend to celebrate any further the survivors, for an action so well known as ours, and which took place so close to our kingdom, speaks for itself. Neither will I speak further of those who behaved with especial bravely, since it is public knowledge, and I would risk favouring some rather than others. Suffice it to say that all stayed at their posts and behaved excellently.

For two whole days, seventeen large corsair ships, with five thousand combatants and more than five hundred pieces of artillery, were unable to reduce one lone ship that had only twenty-two cannons and a hundred and some men, weakened and sick after eight months at sea. If the fire had not consumed our ship, the corsairs would not have conquered it, for they had already lost two of their own ships and many men, while our men retained all their ardour for battle, happy to show the Turks of Africa how the Portuguese can fight.

After the fire of our ship and the losses of theirs, our surviving people were all transported to the Turkish ships. It was done in an hour, on Monday, October 11, 1621.

From the morning we awoke to find ourselves in the midst of the Turkish fleet until the day they set fire to our ship, there had been a great calm and the world seemed to be all ablaze with heat. But as soon as our ship was burned and our people transferred to the enemy vessels, a westerly wind arose, so strong that it was impossible to sail with the topsails unfurled. If we had had that wind two hours earlier, the Turks would not have taken us, and we would certainly have got home that day.

No one, however, can escape the will of Heaven.[3]

---

3. The narrative of João de Carvalho Mascarenhas can be found in *Memorável relaçam da perda da Nao Conceição que os Turcos queymárão à vista da barra de Lisboa vários sucessos das pessoas, que nella cativarão, E descripção nova da Cidade de Argel & de seu governo & cousas muy notáveis acontecidas nestes ultimos annos de 1621 atè 1626. (Memorable Account of the Loss of the Ship Conceição that the Turks Burned in Sight of the Bar of Lisbon; Including the Successes of Several People Who Were Captured, Plus a New Description of the City of Algiers and of its Government and a Description of the Very Remarkable Things that Happened Between the Years 1621 and 1626*), first published in Lisbon in 1627. It also exists in a French version, titled *Esclave à Alger: Récit de captivité de Joao Mascarenhas (1621-1626)* (*A Slave in Algiers: The Story of the Captivity of Joao Mascarenhas*), translated by Paul Teyssier, published in 1993. The translated text comes from Chapters III – VII. I relied mostly on the French text.

# Father Pierre Dan on the Slave Market in Algiers

Father Pierre Dan, the Trinitarian friar who appeared in the *Vultures and Insatiable Tigers* chapter in the *Captives* section above, was in Algiers in the summer of 1634. As ransom negotiations wore on fruitlessly, he must have had considerable time to wander the city, for *Histoire de Barbarie*, the book he wrote, contains quite a few details of events he claims to have witnessed personally or to have heard about directly.

Father Dan was a religious man, and a man of his age, fervent in his belief in the wickedness of North African corsairs and of Islam itself, and this colours his narrative. He was *there*, though. He witnessed events firsthand, and he presents the kinds of details that can only come from direct eye-witness testimony.

Except for snippets here and there, *Histoire de Barbarie* has never been translated into English before. So what follows is available to English readers for the first time.

Here is Father Dan on the slave market of Algiers.

The place where this infamous and accursed commerce in people is ordinarily conducted in Algiers is in the middle of the city. It is named the Badestan, or the Souk, and is a square marketplace with galleries on all four sides, all uncovered. It is the custom in Tunis, Salé, Tripoli, and other cities of Barbary to assemble and conduct business in markets like this. As in all of Turkey, it is in public places like these where captives are sold.

Here is how it is done.

Soon after the captives have been taken, the jailer—known as the *Bâchidu*—of the Bagnio [the prison] in which captives are kept under guard brings them to the Badestan in the presence of the Reis, or Captain, and other officers of the vessel which captured them, who go along in order to determine how much the captives will be sold for. For purposes of the sale, there are brokers, rather like horse traders, who, well versed in this business, walk through the market along with the chained captives, shouting as loudly as they can: 'Who wants to buy? Who wants to buy?' This is a thing I have seen many times in Barbary—with so much sorrow that I must admit that it brought tears to my eyes and made my heart turn cold.

It must be said here that, while Christians receive returns from their investments by lending their money at interest or by receiving annuities, in corsair cities, the barbarians invest their money in the purchase of captive Christians. They use these captives to plough their lands, cultivate their gardens, and tend the cattle in the pastures of their *masseries* [farms], or they send them to sea, or employ them in some other kind of work—all of which generates a profit for the owners. They do all this not only in the hope that they will profit from the purchase of such slaves, but that they will also be able to ransom their slaves for much more than they paid for them. The owners promise themselves that, with time, they will receive six times more than it cost to maintain their slaves, or they will sell them at whatever price they can get, trading them like horses.

To better sell these slaves, the brokers portray them as being far more robust and in much better condition than they actually are, so that the buyers will buy them more willingly.

Those buyers look carefully at these poor Christians, who are displayed naked, or however the sellers may see fit, without any consideration of the captives' shame. The captives must quickly obey any orders given to them. If they do not, they are beaten with sticks, which these inhuman barbarians are always quick to use. The buyers then look closely at whether the captives are strong or weak, healthy or sick, and whether they have any sores, or some incapacitating disease that might prevent them from working.

Next, they make the captives walk, jump, and caper about, goading them with sticks, to ensure that they do not have any ailments. They also examine the captives' teeth, not to know their age, but to learn if they are subject to catarrhs and fluxes which could inconvenience them and render them less useful. Moreover, they look into the captives' eyes, and even study their physiognomy and their appearance in order to draw conclusions about whether their temperament is good or bad.

But they look most carefully at the captives' hands. They do this for two reasons. Firstly, they wish to see whether the hands are soft or calloused, to determine who among them are working men. Secondly, and principally, they examine the captives' hands to indulge in the practice of palmistry, to which they are addicted, even though such a practice is vain and ridiculous. They believe that they can recognize, by the lines and the signs that they observe, whether potential slaves will live long, whether they have signs of hidden sickness, are dangerous, or are malcontents. They even believe they can see if escape is prefigured on the captives' palms. They so depend on these prognostications that they employ them in order to decide whether or not to risk their money in the purchase of a particular captive.

The souls of these barbarian tyrants are possessed by greed more completely than any other men's in the world.[1]

---

1. Pierre Dan, *Histoire de Barbarie, et de ses corsaires, des royaumes, et des villes d'Alger, de Tunis, de Salé, et de Tripoly*, 1649, pp. 392-393.

# Filippo Pananti: Narrative of a Residence in Algiers

The following narrative comes from a book, published in the early nineteenth century, in which the author narrates his experience of being captured by corsairs from Algiers and of being taken to that city.

The nineteenth century is right at the end of the period of corsair dominance (the French overran Algiers in 1830, putting a final end to the Algerine corsair enterprise), and a work from that period might at first seem a bit out of place, considering that most everything else in this book comes from the sixteenth and seventeenth centuries. Algiers, however, was an odd place, and though it was a desperately turbulent city in many ways, it also managed to maintain an almost supernatural constancy in terms of basic functional tasks. If you were a captive brought to Algiers in 1605, 1705, or 1805, the experience was essentially the same. And the city itself was essentially the same as well—as if it existed in some sort of weird time stasis.

So a captivity narrative from the nineteenth century is very much like a captivity narrative from the seventeenth century in terms of the activities and places described. What differs is the type of description. Early nineteenth century writing is much closer in form to the writing we are familiar with today: it evokes a sense of time and place through the use of vivid descriptions in a way that feels familiar and natural to us. As a result, this nineteenth century narrative makes Algiers come alive more than earlier narratives do.

This chapter contains a series of excerpts taken from a book, published in 1818, titled *Narrative of a Residence in Algiers.* This is an English rendering of a book written by an Italian poet named Filippo Pananti and published originally in Italy, in 1817, under the title *Avventure e osservazioni sopra le coste di Barberia* (*Adventures and Observations on the Barbary Coast*).

Born in Tuscany in northern Italy around 1776, Pananti was forced to flee his homeland because, as a newly minted university graduate, he championed liberal republican views that were considered dangerously radical at the time by the local authorities. As a result, in 1799 he went into exile in England. Some years later, as he was on his way back to Italy, Algerine corsairs captured the ship he was on as it approached the Italian shore, and he was taken to Algiers.

Nineteenth century narratives may in some ways feel natural to us, but the English rendering is a little too formal and flowery for modern tastes, and I have simplified some of the original text. So what follows is a gently edited version. Pananti has a tendency towards melodrama, particularly at the end of the extract. This does not, however, negate the fact that his description of conditions in Algiers is still basically accurate.

Here, then, is the early nineteenth century English translation (slightly abridged and lightly edited) of Filippo Pananti's account of his adventures in Algiers. We begin *in medias res*, just after Pananti's ship has been taken by Algerine corsairs.

The squadron of corsairs that had attacked and captured us then set sail, steering along the coast.

Some days later, several white specks began to rise in the western horizon, and a fine breeze soon brought us within sight of that great centre of piracy— Algiers. An extensive semi-circle of hills rises in amphitheatric beauty round the city, many of them studded with country houses. The view is exceedingly interesting and picturesque as seen from the sea, and the numerous vineyards and the orange and olive groves which surround the town show great marks of industry and cultivation that does not bear much analogy to the fierce character and vagrant life of these African tyrants.

As we approached our anchorage, a shout of joy ran through the ship we were on, marking the satisfaction of the barbarians. Nor had we any reason to be other than joyful ourselves at the idea of having finally ended our tedious sea voyage, embittered as it was by our misfortunes. So perfectly comparative are our notions of happiness that the prospect of landing at Algiers, which, under any other circumstances, would have created the utmost horror, was, in the present instance, hailed with a strong degree of joy. Like the patient, who, rather than bear the agony arising from his wounds, submits to a painful operation, we flattered ourselves that the end of the cruise would also be the end of our sufferings.

No sooner had the corsair ships anchored than preparations were made to go ashore. Hamida Reis, the commander of the corsair squadron, with a stern voice inspired no less by his natural ferocity than a consciousness of having us now completely in his power, ordered the sailors he had captured into the longboat, under charge of the Aga, the Captain of the janissaries. We captive passengers were destined to grace Hamida Reis's own splendid triumph, and he ordered us into the pinnace appointed to convey us to shore, towards which we directed our course.

Upon our landing, he immediately ordered us to form a procession behind him. He then moved on with colossal self-importance. An immense concourse had collected to welcome with acclamations the triumphant return of the pirates. We were, however, neither plundered nor insulted, a treatment which many Christian slaves are said to have met with upon disembarking at this inhospitable place. In the manner of the Roman ovation, we made a long circuit, arriving eventually at the place destined for holding examinations of captives and the assessing of captured prizes.

Hamida Reis entered the building that was our destination, while we remained outside the door until called for. A large awning shaded the entrance, and under this we eventually passed to confront the members of the regency, in barbarous pomp and horrid majesty, seated before us, accompanied by the Ulemas, or expounders of the law, and the principal Agas of the Divan.

We were then, without farther ceremony or preamble, asked for our papers, which were duly examined, nor was that canting gravity wanting, on this occasion, which is usually assumed to justify acts of rapine and plunder. Our collected papers were presented to the English Consul, whose presence is always required on these examinations, to verify any claim he may have to make. This gentleman soon saw the insufficiency of our documents, but, stimulated by the goodness of his heart and sentiments of pity for persons in our unhappy condition, he made every possible exertion to extricate us from the appalling dilemma with which we were now threatened.

The circumstance of some of the party, being natives of a country united to the dominion of France, did not restrain the Consul's generous efforts: we were unfortunate, and that was sufficient to ensure the protection of an Englishman. But Hamida Reis boldly sustained the remorseless laws of piracy. Drawing the finest distinctions imaginable between domiciliation and nationality, he proved himself a most able lawyer—according, at least, to the African code of public laws. [1]

'A good prize! Prisoners! Slaves!' was now murmured throughout the council, and soon communicated to the crowd assembled without, which, by its cries, seemed to demand such a decision.

The British Consul then formally demanded the English lady who was among us, along with her two children. Upon this being accorded, the Chevalier Rossi, her husband, advanced a few steps and, with dignified courage, supported his claim to liberation on the principle of having married an English woman and of also being the father of two British subjects, his children. This application being successful, he soon rejoined his anxious wife and children.

---

1. At various times, Algiers signed peace treaties with European nations, and the major European powers had maintained Consuls in Algiers from the end of the sixteenth century onwards. When Pananti was captured, Algiers and England had an arrangement to respect each other's ships and nationals. That agreement, however, did not necessarily protect non-English nationals travelling aboard English ships—like Pananti and the French citizens he mentions.

This was followed by a general cry in the hall of 'Schiavi! Schiavi!'— 'Slaves! Slaves!' —which horrible word was echoed by the multitude.

The members of the council then rose, and, on the assembly being dissolved, the English Consul and his attendants, together with the Chevalier Rossi and family, departed, leaving us, the victims of slavery, in a state of shocked insensibility.

Before we had recovered from our stupor, we were led away across a considerable part of the city, accompanied by a great number of spectators. It being Friday, the Moorish Sabbath, hundreds of the infidels, in coming from the mosques, were soon attracted from every direction to enjoy this new spectacle of degraded Christianity.

When we arrived at the palace of the Pasha, inhabited at present by the Dey, the first objects that struck our eyes were six bleeding heads ranged before the entrance. And as if this dreadful sight was not sufficient of itself to harrow up the soul, it was still farther aggravated by the necessity of our stepping over them in order to pass into the court. They were the heads of some rebellious Agas, who had dared to murmur against the Dey's authority, but our fears naturally represented them as having been severed from the bodies of Christians and purposely placed there to terrify new inmates of this fatal region.[2]

A dead silence reigned within the walls of the building. We were ordered to range ourselves before the Dey's window, so that the despot could feast his eyes upon us. Soon, he approached, looking at us with a mingled smile of exultation and contempt. Then, after he made a sign with his hand, we were ordered to depart. After a third circuit of the town, we arrived before a large dark looking building. Entering into it, we stumbled, as if by an involuntary impulse.

This was the Great Bagnio, or house of reception for Christian slaves, which, without gilding the pill quite so much, may be plainly rendered by a simpler word—prison. Every fibre trembled, and our limbs tottered under us as we were forced to enter that horrid receptacle. The first words which escaped the keeper after our entrance were, 'Whoever is brought into this house becomes a slave!'

He might well have added: Lasciate ogni speranza, voi, che 'ntrate! [The famous warning at the entrance to Hell in Dante's *Divine Comedy*: 'Abandon all hope, ye who enter here'].

---

2. From the mid-1500s to the late 1600s, Algiers was administered by Pashas, Governors sent by the Ottoman Sultan in Istanbul to rule the city in his name. By the late seventeenth century, Algiers had achieved virtual independence and was ruled by Deys, who were elected/appointed by the janissaries who by then controlled the city. Pananti was captured in 1813. The Dey of Algiers at that time was Haji Ali ben Khrelil, who held that office from 1809 to 1815 (when he was assassinated). Haji Ali had a reputation for ruthlessness.

In passing through the dark and filthy courtyard, we were surrounded by a multitude of slaves, bearing about them all the signs of abandoned sufferers. They were ragged, lank, and haggard, with heads drooping, eyes sunk and distorted, cheeks imprinted by the furrows of a protracted wretchedness which seemed to have withered their souls, and, by destroying the finer impulses of their nature, left no trace of pity for the sufferings of others. We passed them by without the slightest manifestation from them of that sympathy so naturally expected in such a situation. Exhausted by long confinement, and wrapped up in a sense of their own melancholy fate, they viewed our appearance with a stupid indifference unaccompanied by any fellow feeling at all.

Our ascent up the prison staircase was not unlike that of a malefactor when mounting the scaffold to a gallows. However, as some indulgence is generally granted to condemned criminals, the keeper treated us during that first day with particular attention and respect, inviting us into his own apartment and insisting that we should partake of his dinner, thus making up for the anxiety and fasting of the preceding day.

The following day was occupied in communicating with the English Consul and other friends in the city, together with the principal Jews who were likely to be most useful in forwarding the work of our liberation.[3] For my own part, I began to view things in a somewhat more favourable light: my excellent friends, the Chevalier and Madame Rossi, warmly interested themselves with the Consul on my behalf, while that worthy and philanthropic minister did everything in his power to extricate me from the horrid situation in which I was placed.

It was whispered in the Bagnio that my freedom had been formally demanded from the ministers of his excellency the Dey, but that they had refused—or, rather, they had agreed, but upon one condition: my paying down three thousand sequins in gold. This, they said, was because they knew I was a great poet wallowing in riches! Poetry and riches is indeed a strange association of ideas. Little did my new masters know the value of poets in Europe.

It was further said that it was his excellency the Dey's intention to avail himself of my wonderful talents in affairs of great importance. What on earth could he have done with me? Poet laureate? Virtuoso of the bedchamber? Musician extraordinary to his Highness the Pasha? None of these brilliant appointments would have turned my brain, for to me chains are not the more acceptable for being made of gold.

While these various speculations were current, the Guardian Pasha, or principal keeper of the Bagnio, took me by the arm and commenced a grave

---

3. Jewish merchants in Algiers had business contacts with their brethren in European cities like Livorno and Marseilles, and they often managed the ransoming process for captured Europeans.

sermon on the flattering prospects that seemed to await me. 'Surely,' said he, 'fortune has now evidently taken you under her peculiar protection. For you arrive a slave in Algiers, and the next day you are considered for a post which others do not attain in a hundred years! You should leap for joy.'

'Have I not,' said I, 'every reason to be afflicted? What consolation can there be for him who is in chains?'

'Oh, the weakness of human nature!' replied the Guardian Pasha. 'Slavery is the natural state of man. All...'—these were his exact words—'...all depends on the law of the strongest, on circumstances, and on necessity. We are all the slaves of custom, of the passions, of disease, and of death. But those who rise to power are no longer slaves. And thus you may have slaves at your nod, and by obeying one, command a thousand.'

'You have a good head,' he continued, 'can speak well, and are a great acquisition to us. When once you are interpreter and secretary to the Dey, you will swim in gold, become the lamp of knowledge, and possess gardens of voluptuousness. You will be a great personage, and all will bow before you!'

'Too much honour,' I answered. 'I do not merit it.'

Then, 'By what accident,' I asked, 'has the Dey condescended to cast his eyes on me?'

'Why,' said the Guardian Pasha, 'it has always been customary for the Dey to have a slave for his secretary. One of these infidel dogs having betrayed his trust, however, the Dey had his head struck off. Another came, but this rogue used to carry news to the European Consuls, and so he was condemned to die under the *bastinado*. A Jew was next taken into the service of his Highness, but as he only thought of making money, his treasures were seized and himself burnt. A Moor and Arab were successively tried without effect, and after being removed had their heads taken off, to avoid telling tales.'

The Guardian Pasha paused, and then said. 'The Dey, having once more determined to try a Christian, you are the happy man upon whom he has fixed his choice.'

'Tell me,' said I, 'How long did the two Christians, Jew, Moor, and Arab remain in office?'

'Some continued three, six, and ten months. But none reached a year's servitude. All had a short life and a merry one.'

'These honours,' I said then, 'very wonderful as they may be, appear to involve too much responsibility. A thousand thanks, therefore, for the interest you so kindly take in my advancement, but I fear your Deys are too easily disgusted with their followers and begin to play the tyrant rather early.'

After the above conversations, I naturally began to reflect on the good fortune which these folks were desirous of heaping on me. If left to my own inclination, I determined I would prefer to take the course of the disappointed candidate for a public employment in London who, after many fruitless applications, one day called on his expected patron, and told him he had a length procured a post. After congratulating him on his success, the patron ventured to ask what his new post might be. He replied that it was a place in the Shrewsbury coach, which should, that very night, convey him far from a town where he was heartily tired of listening to the flattering and unmeaning promises of his patrons.

As I had been engaged in conversing with the Guardian Pasha regarding my future, we passed to and fro amongst the dark corridors of the Bagnio, where the victims of servitude lay huddled in groups, stretched along the bare earth with nothing but a little covering of straw.

Then the English Vice-Consul appeared, he who had kindly recommended us to the Grande Scrivano and Guardian Pasha. He came to inform me of the steps which had been taken by his generous principal, the Consul, in my favour with the Dey. The Grande Scrivano, however, determined to destroy the slight rays of hope shed by the Vice-Consul's visit, informed me that I should now consider my fate as finally decided, for though the Consul's eloquence and credit might prevail with his master, yet the negative once being given, my future doom became irrevocable, and the exertions made for my liberation, when unsuccessful, would only render my case more hopeless.

As may be easily conceived, I passed a sleepless night, embittered by the most painful apprehensions.

The first rays of light had not yet dawned, nor had either men or animals had time to recover from the preceding day's labour when the turnkey, with a hoarse and stentorian accent, exclaimed, 'A trabajo cornutos!' ('To work, cuckolds!'). This was followed by the application of a cudgel to the shoulders of those who manifested the smallest disinclination to obey the summons in double-quick time.

Before we left our prison, the Aga made his appearance, bringing with him numerous iron rings, to be riveted onto our left ankles, there to remain in perpetuity as a sign of our bondage. The horrible weight of these rings can only be known to those who have worn them.

Having successively applied them to the legs of my companions, the Aga put one into my hand, saying that his excellency the Dey, as a mark of most particular favour, would allow me the distinguished honour of putting on my own ring. This is not unlike the fatal privilege, granted to the viziers of the Porte, of strangling themselves with the cord sent for that purpose by their master.

With similar feelings did I put on this dreadful emblem of my servitude. A cold sweat covered my forehead, my heart throbbed with anguish, my eyes no longer saw my surroundings. I attempted to speak, but could not articulate. Looking downwards, I caught sight of the degrading badge, and, with a deathlike silence, I yielded to my fate.

The number of new victims of different nations mustered on this occasion, and all captured during the last cruise of the barbarians, amounted to two hundred. Being ordered to proceed to the scene of our labours, a mournful silence marked our progress, which was attended by guards both in front and rear, armed with whips, who frequently repeated, 'A trabajo cornutos! Can d'infidel, a trabajo!' ('To work cuckolds! Dog of an infidel, to work!'). Thus escorted, we arrived at the public ovens, where two rusks of black bread were thrown to each of us, as if to mere dogs. I observed that the old captives, who had arrived on the ground long before our party, greedily snatched them up and soon dispatched both with a frightful avidity.

After this, we arrived at the great Hall of the Marine. Seated there, in all the pride of their tyrannical power, were the various members of the executive government, including the Agas of the militia, the grand Admiral, first Captain of the squadron, the Cadi, the Mufti, and the Ulemas and judges according to the Koran. We were then ranged along in regular succession, selected, numbered, and looked at with particular attention. We stood as we were, our hearts beating agitatedly, waiting for whatever might come next.

A profound silence reigned throughout the hall.

Then it was broken by the Minister of Marine, first Secretary of State, who called out my name.

I was ordered to advance. Various interrogatories were put to me, relative to my occupations in England and other relations with that country. I answered them all in the best way I could.

The Minister paused, regarding me.

Then he pronounced the talismanic words I so yearned to hear: 'Ti star franco!' ('You are free!').

We are told that the most agreeable tones heard by human ears are those of well-earned praise, or the most treasured sounds of those expressed by a beloved. No! The sweetest voice which can possibly vibrate through the heart of a man is that which restores him to liberty!

To form an adequate idea of what I felt on this unforeseen and happy change of circumstances, it will be necessary for the reader to conceive of a victim with the bandage on his eyes, the fatal axe uplifted, whose ears are suddenly astounded to hear a pronouncement of grace and mercy!

A case like mine was absolutely unique in the annals of Algiers, there being no example of another slave's liberation so immediately after his captivity without ransom, since the decrees of those barbarians are usually of inexorable fatality.

A soldier was ordered to knock off my irons. This done, he, in his turn, desired me to go and thank the Minister. This dignitary then shook me by the hand, adding many expressions of civility and, finally, ordered the Dragoman [the Interpreter] to conduct me to the house of his Britannic Majesty's Consul.

The first impulse of joy had fairly inundated my heart and, when once at liberty, I could move my limbs with some facility. But the next thought was for my unhappy companions, who, on the strength of my unexpected liberation, were induced to flatter themselves with the wild hope of being treated in a like manner. Next to my own safety, nothing on Earth could at that awful moment have afforded me such heartfelt satisfaction.

Departing slowly with my new guide, I stopped repeatedly, and looking back with wistful eyes, vainly anticipating the pleasure of seeing them follow. But the order was already given to conduct them all to labour, and their respective occupations were even pointed out. I saw them hang down their heads, eyes suffused with tears. They advanced a few steps towards me, pressed my hands, sobbed adieu... and disappeared.

Those who have never been to Algiers and witnessed the fate to which captives falling into the hands of these barbarians are condemned cannot form any true idea of the greatness of the calamity which fortune has in store for them, or into what an abyss of sorrow and wretchedness they have been plunged. Even I, who experienced it to a certain degree in my own person, am at a loss for language equal to a description of what such captives feel and suffer when precipitated into this dreadful situation.

No sooner is anyone declared a slave, than he is instantly stripped of his clothes and covered with a species of sackcloth. He is also generally left without shoes or stockings, and often obliged to work bareheaded in the scorching rays of an African sun. Many suffer their beard to grow, as a sign of mourning and desolation. Their general state of filth is not to be conceived.

Some of these wretched beings are destined to make ropes and sails for the squadrons of corsairs. These are constantly superintended by keepers who carry whips—and frequently extort money from their victims as the price of somewhat less rigor in the execution of their duty. Other slaves belong to the Dey's household. Many are employed by the rich Moors, who bought them at market, in the lowest drudgery of domestic employment. Some, like beasts of burden, are employed in carrying stones and wood for any public buildings that may be going on. These are usually in chains, and they are justly considered as the worst off among their oppressed brethren.

What a perpetuity of terrors, anguish, and monotonous days they suffer without a proper bed to lie on, proper raiment to cover them, or proper food to support nature. Two cakes of black bread, like those already alluded to, thrown down as if intended for dogs, is their principal daily sustenance. Had it not been for the charity of a rich Moor, who left a legacy for that purpose, Friday, the only day they are exempted from work, would have seen them without any allowance whatever.

Shut up at night in the prison, like so many malefactors, they are obliged to sleep in the open corridors, exposed to all the inclemency of the seasons. In the country they are frequently forced to lie in the open air or, like the troglodytes of old, shelter themselves in caves. Awakened at daylight, they are sent to work with the most abusive threats, and thus employed, become shortly exhausted under the weight and severity of their keepers' whips.

Those destined to sink wells and clear sewers are for whole weeks obliged to be up to their middle in water, respiring a mephitic atmosphere. Others employed in quarries are threatened with constant destruction. Some, attached to the harness in which beasts of the field are also yoked, are obliged to draw nearly all the load, and never fail to receive more blows than their more favoured companions, the ass or the mule. Some are crushed under the falling of buildings, while others perish in the pits into which they are sent to be got rid of. It is usual for one or two hundred slaves to drop off in the year for want of food, medical attendance, and other necessaries.

And woe be to those who remain if they attempt to heave a sigh or complain in the hearing of their inexorable masters. The slightest offense or indiscretion is punished with two hundred blows on the soles of the feet, or over the back.

Whenever a captive is taken ill in Algiers, motives of self-interest call upon the Moorish proprietor for a little indulgence, but were it not for the benign charity of Spain, which has established a small fund to support a hospital for the reception of slaves, the latter, when overcome with disease, would be left to perish in the streets. By means of the above benevolent institution, they may at least hope to die in peace.

Although a price is set on each captive, which may encourage a hope of freedom, yet, from the peculiar mode in which their liberation must be effected, this hope is almost always unavailing. If, after having obtained leave to exercise their trade, they acquire any property, they are not allowed to pay it for their ransom. Offers of this kind have always been rejected, on the grounds of the Dey being legal heir to all the property of his slaves. Frequently, in order to get possession of it a little sooner, the owner is dispatched.

Captivity is thus surrounded with aggravated cruelties, which seem to have no end. It is not enough that these poor slaves should groan under excessive labour and multiplied blows, but derision, abuse, and contempt must be added, and this species of suffering is, if possible, more acutely felt than the former. 'Faithless Christian dog!' is the ordinary mode of addressing a slave, and this degrading epithet is invariably accompanied with the most insulting gesture and sometimes by personal violence.

On one memorable evening towards dark, as I was walking the streets, a hoarse voice called out to me. On drawing nearer, I beheld an unhappy being stretched on the ground, foaming at the mouth, and with the blood bursting from his nose and eyes. I had scarcely stopped, struck with horror and apprehension, when, in a faint voice, the man said, 'For Heaven's sake have pity on my sufferings, and terminate an existence which I can no longer support!'

'Who are you?' I asked.

'I am a slave,' said the poor creature. 'An Oldak of the militia who was passing this way and happening to be near me at the time shouted at me, 'Dog of a Christian! How dare you stop in the road when one of the faithful passes?' This was followed by a blow and a kick which threw me down a height of several feet and has left me in this condition.'

On another occasion, the situation of a still more unfortunate slave was equally calculated to excite my indignation and sympathy. He was sorrowfully seated under an old wall. At his feet there lay an immense load, under which he seemed to have sunk. His visage was pallid and meagre, his eyes fixed on the ground, all expressing strong signs of premature age brought on by grief and suffering.

'What can be the matter, my friend?' said I, addressing myself to this unfortunate wretch.

'Poor slaves!' he replied. 'There is no help for us in this world, and our groans are not heard in Heaven. I was born in Naples, but what country have I now? There is nobody to assist me. I am forgotten by all. I was a noble, a rich and illustrious man in the place of my birth. See how wretchedness and slavery have changed me. It is now eleven years since my suffering began. During that time, I have in vain solicited the assistance of relatives and fellow creatures, but all to no purpose. There is no longer anyone on whom I can place hope or reliance. What have I done to deserve so much oppression and suffering?'

After he had given vent to his feelings, I did my best to recommend patience, resignation, and hope. I also touched on the promises of eternal reward to those who suffer here below with becoming fortitude. All this was answered only by a forced smile, accompanied by a look which spoke volumes.

Having endeavoured to communicate a limited notion of its physical effects, I feel I ought also to make a few remarks on the moral tendency of slavery. All agree that loss of liberty is the greatest misfortune which can possibly befall a human being. Without any of those consolations which generally accompany other griefs, it does not give rise to any of those impulses which are calculated to support the mind in adversity.

All our other sorrows awaken feelings of tenderness and sympathy in generous minds and inspire respect. Thus, if not relieved, they are, at least, blest with commiseration. The prisoners who have been shut up in the Bastille, the fortresses of Spandau, Olmutz, Magdeburg, Stetin, and the Tower of Oblivion in Persia displeased the great, and may perhaps have deserved incarceration, but they were regarded as important, as men of no common characters. When the exiles of Siberia passed, they were followed by a sympathetic look of pity not unmixed with admiration. People sighing, exclaimed: 'There goes an exile!'

As to slavery, you cannot divest it of a certain opprobrium, and servile baseness that freezes the heart, disgusts the sight, and repels sympathy. There is an unconscious horror created in the mind towards this most unnatural state, and we proscribe the slave, as the Hindus do the member of a cast who may have violated the precepts of their religion. Even the captive himself, when long accustomed to be thus regarded, begins seriously to think his nature has experienced a change, and in that state of mind, considers himself as degraded as he is unhappy. Chains, while they are thought disgraceful by the free, depreciate the wearer in his own esteem until his soul is deprived of all the salutary influence of liberty, and he is at last persuaded to look upon himself as inferior, and the man who was born free, to direct his piercing eye and noble front towards Heaven, sinks to the degrading alternative of forgetting the original intentions of nature.

The soul is often purified in the crucible of adversity, but in a state of slavery, there is something so abject and forlorn that it destroys the courage and quenches all the fire of generous sentiments, depriving its victim at once of mind and dignity, and he who suffers enslavement feels that the streams of pity are dried up within him, while the flame which animated his heart in better days is extinguished. Another of slavery's evils, and by far the worst, is that virtue—which teaches us to vanquish every grief, or render them sources of utility—is generally weakened and often altogether extinguished in a mind habituated to slavery. Sorrow vitiates the heart and breaks the spirit. Virtue springs from great and generous souls, while vice is the offspring of meanness. Religion too, that column of Heaven, to which we cling when all around us totters, ceases to afford consolation to the heart that is ulcerated. Those who are taught to regard themselves as entirely abandoned on Earth no longer look to Heaven for support.

To conclude this melancholy subject, of all human sufferers, I believe the Christian slaves of Barbary are the most pitiable, being in that dreadful state when deep and long continued sorrow has absorbed every pleasurable emotion, leaving behind a sentiment of sadness and despair, a situation in which life seems embittered by an envenomed dart. Under the rod which smites them, they cannot any longer raise their heads, and they perforce fall oppressed and cast down by the weight of their sufferings.

Thus do these poor souls live and die in Algiers.[4]

---

4. Filippo Pananti, *Narrative of a Residence in Algiers*, pp. 64-95.

# The Odyssey of René Du Chastelet des Boys

René du Chastelet des Boys was a member of the French aristocracy. He came from La Flèche, a town about 225 kilometres (140 miles) southwest of Paris, where his family was among the local *noblesse de robe* (nobles of the robe), lesser French aristocrats whose rank derived from their service in administrative and judicial posts (those employed in such positions wore traditional robes of office, hence the name). Des Boys' family were magistrates, and since his parents intended that he should follow in that venerable calling, when he came of age, they packed him off to the Université d'Orléans to study law.

The Université d'Orléans was a prestigious school. Its alumni included men like Jean Calvin (John Calvin), the controversial Protestant reformer and founder of Calvinism, Molière, the famous playwright and actor, and Charles Perrault, whose *Histoires ou contes du temps passé* (*Stories or Tales of Times Gone By*) contained the originals of many of our best-known fairy tales. Des Boys, however, did not thrive there, and he abandoned his studies and joined the army. In the summer of 1640, when he was about twenty, he took part in the successful siege of the town of Arras, in what was then the Spanish Netherlands but is now in the region of Artois, in northwest France. It is not clear what soldierly role des Boys played in the siege, but it did not involve the use of muskets (as is made clear below in part of his narrative). After the siege, he managed to use his family position to get discharged from the army and, after a debilitating bout of dysentery, returned to his studies at the Université d'Orléans.

Things did not go well there, for he fell in with the wrong sort of company and spent too much time drinking, gambling, and womanizing. His family would not—or could not—provide him with more than the bare minimum of financial support, and he ended up in debt and in legal difficulties. He also lost his only coat in a gambling game, and since he had no money to buy a new one and winter was coming on, he returned to his family home in La Flèche—in disgrace.

Things did not go well in La Flèche either. His family were furious with him, the other local aristocrats sneered at him, and he was ostracized. As a result, he decided to flee his home and seek a new life for himself.

Des Boys chose Portugal as his destination. At this time, Portugal had just wrenched itself from Spanish control (it had been a possession of Spain from 1580-1640), and King John IV had assumed the Portuguese throne. Portugal and France shared a common enemy—Spain—and King John, who was sometimes referred to as John the Restorer (João o Restaurador) was a sort of romantic underdog figure: the monarch of a plucky little country giving the finger to the massive Spanish/Habsburg empire. Des Boys decided to offer his services to this new Portuguese king.

He slipped out of La Flèche and travelled to La Rochelle, on France's Atlantic coast, where he hoped to get passage aboard a ship bound for Portugal. In La Rochelle, he took up with a group of other disaffected young aristocrats like himself—three Frenchmen, two Germans, and a Swede—who also intended to offer their services to King John (these are the men whose names he mentions in his narrative). Because of his family connections, des Boys was also able to acquire a commission from the Commandeur de la Porte (Commander of the Port, the titular head of the La Rochelle city government) to carry some important papers to the French ambassador in Lisbon.

So all looked well. The seven young adventurers were off to perform great deeds and make a name for themselves, and des Boys had a secret mission of some importance to fulfil. Together, they boarded a ship and set sail for Lisbon.

All their plans came to nothing. As they drew near to Cabo da Roca, off the Portuguese coast near Lisbon, their ship was attacked by Algerine corsairs and everybody aboard taken captive. Des Boys subsequently spent two years as a slave in Algiers. There, he found himself in a particularly uncomfortable position. He came from an aristocratic family, and if this fact became known in Algiers, he would have been bought by somebody hoping to demand a huge ransom for him. Because of his estrangement from his family, however, there was no chance of such a ransom ever being paid (he had burned that particular bridge when he fled La Flèche). So if he were to stand any chance of being liberated at a reasonable cost, he had to disguise his origins—a task that was not so easy.

Years later, back in Europe and in his mid-forties, des Boys published an account of his experiences titled *L'Odyssée ou diversité d'aventures, rencontres et voyages en Europe, Asie et Afrique, divisée en quatre parties* (*The Odyssey, or a Diversity of Adventures, Meetings and Travels in Europe, Asia, and Africa, Divided into Four Parts*). Only two of the four parts promised in the title were ever published: the first part, which recounts the details of des Boys' life as a student, and the second part, which describes his experiences in Algiers—the part translated here.

The original French text of *L'Odyssée* is quite eccentric, and des Boys can be painfully long winded at times. So my translation is not an actual word-for-word rendering: I have abridged the original and trimmed things down in order to achieve the most straightforward narrative I could.

As far as I know, *L'Odyssée* has never been systematically translated into English before, so the text below is the first ever English rendering of des Boys' story.

This is one of the longer and more complete narratives in this book. It contains a comprehensive account of des Boys' experiences, from the original attack of the ship he and his companions were travelling on, to his experiences as a slave in Algiers, to his eventual ransom and departure from that city.

Here, then, is Part Two of René du Chastelet des Boys' *L'Odyssée*. We begin once again *in medias res*, as the ship the young adventurers are travelling on approaches Cabo da Roca.

The wind grew more and more favourable and soon carried our ship to within sight of Cape de la Roque [Cabo da Roca]. At this point, one of the sailors on lookout announced that a ship was approaching us, propelled by both sails and oars. We at first mistook it for a Biscayne frigate, but when we saw its flag, which bore crescents, suns, and stars, we knew it for a Barbary corsair.

Previous meetings and false alarms had hardened us and considerably decreased our fear of these pirates, and so the resolution was taken to run out the cannons, distribute muskets to the passengers and daggers and pocket pistols to the sailors, and to unfurl the sails to catch as much wind as possible.

Some of those aboard advised that we gain the coast as quickly as we could. Others, young and impatient, argued that we should stay and defend ourselves, for the corsair ship was no larger than ours, and it could not have carried more than six cannons. It was finally agreed that we would make as much sail as possible and flee into the night in hopes of escaping our enemy. And so we sailed on through the darkness until daybreak. In the light of day, however, we saw the same corsair ship still in pursuit.

Then six large vessels suddenly appeared, Dutch flags raised on their masts. The corsair ship that had been pursuing us backed away, and we began to think ourselves saved. But when the newly appeared ships came close enough to be within a musket shot's distance, they abruptly lowered their Dutch flags and raised new ones: multicoloured, enriched and embroidered with stars, crescents, suns, crossed swords, and unknown scriptures.

This unhappy revelation, taking us completely by surprise as it did, caused panic and horror. People ran everywhere, up into the rigging, down among the cannon, into the bottom of the hold.

The lead ship of this corsair armada fired at us and smashed our bowsprit with a broom [an iron bar linked to two balls fired out of a cannon]. We were so close that they could shoot at us with their muskets, and they wounded one of our sailors and killed one of the passengers. All hope of organized resistance died. The ship's crew, terrified, lowered the sails and waved handkerchiefs as a sign of surrender. The corsairs then put their ships' boats into the water and rushed to board our sorry vessel.

Onboard our ship, the passengers attempted to hide what riches they possessed. Some hid bracelets up their shirt sleeves. Some stuffed jewellery into their socks. Others tucked their valuables inside their belts or under their hair. The Sieur de Cahaignes d'Escures hid some gold coins in the back of an old book, which he resolved to keep carefully in his hands, or at least to give into the hands of some French renegade or Christian slave among those who first came aboard from whom he could later arrange to get it back.

People tossed into the sea most of their money, their flashy clothes, golden swords, embroidered harnesses, boots, precious letters, and other signs of wealth and quality, for spite—so that the corsairs could not have any of it—and to disguise their position in hopes of avoiding having to pay a large ransom. I myself threw away the best part of my clothing and all my letters.

The corsairs clambered up our hull without encountering any resistance, poured over the gunwale, and immediately began searching the ship for valuables, shouting excitedly, poking into every corner and smashing apart chests with their axes.

Amid their dreadful, exalted cries, we kept a dreadful silence.

As the corsairs approached us, we were overcome by a melancholic lethargy. There were some known sea adventurers among us, and some experienced sailors, but we were too overwrought to be able to give or receive advice. Our imaginations froze us with fear, persuading us that these brutally martial corsairs, now that they had come aboard, would sacrifice each and every of us to their scimitars.

In the grip of such fear, several of those on deck fled below, thinking to hide themselves down there and so stay alive. As I stood, uncertain what to do, a large Moor came towards me, his sleeves rolled up to the elbow, brandishing a sabre in one broad hand. I stayed frozen where I was, without speaking. The ugliness of his animated, charcoal face, his sharp yellow teeth, his two eyes like medallions of ivory flickering hideously, and the wide, shining steel blade terrorized me more than the flaming sword of the guardian of the Earthly Paradise had the first humans.

However, I was able to somewhat soften his fury by handing over a little blue leather purse that I had bought before my departure from La Rochelle, into which I had put what small change I had, having sunk, in imitation of the others, most of my ready money along with my good clothes when I tossed everything overboard. The Moor then signalled me to stand aside, and he continued on in his quest to discover any riches hidden by my companions.

I saw a young janissary, armed with a hatchet, force the Sieur de Molinville, my friend and confidant, to give up some monies he had been concealing upon his person. The Sieur de Cahaignes d'Escures was searched and robbed by a *renegado* named Abdallah Maillorquin, who took the old book in the back of which he had, as I remarked above, hidden several gold coins. Sieur l'Anier was no happier, having fallen into the hands of a young Kouloughli named Kara Mourad who, having knocked him over, threatened him so direly that he fairly spewed coins at him.

While the nobility were being stripped of their wealth, the ship's officers and crew were also searched in their turn, and, like the passengers, gave up everything, including the keys to the storage chests, which delighted the more libertine and less miserly of these barbarians, for it gave them access to tobacco and liquor.

As for me, I lost everything. Some little time before, I had hastily concealed what small treasure I possessed belowdecks. But the corsair Admiral, Braham-Effendi, seeing that the captives had all been searched, now ordered that we be dispersed to the seven vessels that attended our capture. Thus I had no time to collect any of my treasure or even hide it better.

The corsairs who had been first to board our ship, having now smashed in all the storage lockers, searched every nook and cranny, and gorged themselves with loot, were ordered by the Admiral to stay on board and to remove the ship's anchors, sails, and ropes, and then to await further orders.

After all this upheaval, we were rowed across to the Admiral's ship. The captain and the sailors appeared most distraught at having been forced to forsake their ship. The uselessness of our resistance produced in all of our minds a kind of helpless passivity, and our misery was so extreme that when the wind picked up and threatened to capsize the boat we were in, we almost welcomed it.

Admiral Braham-Effendi, before whom we were presented, wished to know all he could regarding our faculties, ages, professions, and status. Jacques Denyan, the ship's captain, was brought before the corsair captain and thrown to the deck. He was then cruelly beaten on the soles of his feet to force him to reveal every detail about the ship's cargo. The captain handled himself well, declaring that there is nothing aboard the ship except wheat, and that he could prove that by showing the ship's cargo manifest. Two French *renegados*, one from Marseille, the other from Calais, jointly examined the manifest and agreed that it made mention of nothing but wheat.

Nevertheless, the Admiral commanded that the captain be beaten again. The captain cursed and loudly protested that he knew of no other cargo. They pressed him hard then concerning the faculties and professions of those aboard his ship. He declared abundantly that he only had sailors and passengers on board, and that he knew neither the destiny nor the professions of his passengers, nor their degree of wealth, having learned nothing about them except that they were going to serve the new king of Portugal, and that they had simply paid him for their passage and their food.

The constancy of our captain saved him from further maltreatment. His first mate, however, acquitted himself less well. This poor man trembled at the first hint of brutality and, without further pressing, confessed that, in addition to the wheat listed in the ship's cargo manifest, there were four small bundles of fine hardware hidden in the hold, as well as three bags containing a thousand pieces-of-eight each, hidden at the bottom of the hold near one of the bilge pumps. Regarding the passengers, he confessed that he had no knowledge of them, but that he had seen one—and here he glanced at Lord Arthur Penns—dressed in embroidered silk and scarlet brocade while on shore.

The first mate's perfidious confession gave birth in a single instant to a thousand suspicions, and as many hopes of rich booty, in the minds of the pirates. They dragged the unfortunate Arthur Penns forward and pressed their interrogations by threatening to lash the soles of his feet with a length of well tarred rope, an instrument which they habitually use when questioning new captives. The poor man, terrified by such treatment, fully confessed to everything he could possibly think of, declaring, sometimes in Italian, sometimes in German, all his plans concerning his departure and return. He also said that one of the corsairs had, upon boarding, stolen what little money remained to him, though he could not identify which one. The fear tightening his heart also induced him to confess that he had borrowed some money from one of his French comrades. When pressed to tell who it was, he finally pointed at me.

This confession made me extremely nervous, since I feared that the corsairs would think me to be a wealthy man. The corsair captain commanded me to approach and considered me, and then ordered that I be questioned. I claimed that I was a simple adventurer seeking employment in the king of Portugal's new wars, and that what small amount of money I had was taken from me by a great black corsair, whom I pointed out—the animated, ebony colossus with the yellow teeth and ivory eyes, whom I have already mentioned.

The corsair captain wanted to know more, and he was suspicious that the negro had taken from me a notable sum, so he had the man questioned very roughly about the quantity of money he had taken from me. The Moor insisted he had taken nothing. As a result, he was caned severely, a punishment he endured stoically without further confession.

Once all this had transpired, our unfortunate ship was stripped of its sails, anchors, and guns, and everything else that the corsairs needed and wanted, and it was then set adrift at the mercy of the winds, taking with it my little fortune of coins, which the corsairs had failed to discover. It was, it seemed, my destiny to have everything taken from me.

After this, the corsairs raised sail and set off, with a good wind at their backs.

Of the thirty-two of us aboard our ship, there were only five sent to the Vice Admiral's ship, all sailors except for me. The others were distributed among the other corsair vessels. We stayed there the rest of that day, throughout the night, and for much of the next day. Then, in the evening, the corsair ships weighed anchor. The Vice-Admiral's ship, on which I was held, crossed the sea along with the rest for two days, using the mainsail alone, avoiding the land.

On the third day, as they were drawing near the coast of Spain, the ships raised Spanish flags. They did this to disguise their true identity, both in order to be able to surprise any Spanish ships returning from the New World that they might encounter and capture, and to escape the Spanish ships that cruise incessantly in the Strait of Gibraltar. This sort of disguise, using all sorts of different flags—those of Hamburg and Denmark as well as Spain—is the general custom among corsairs.

The younger corsairs, ashamed to have got such a puny amount of booty so far, which was not worth sharing out among seven ships, were of the opinion that their small fleet should reprovision and then continue hunting, in hopes of better success. A council of war was held. The older corsairs wanted the return to Algiers, the younger to continue on.

Before they could resolve the issue, a thunderstorm arose. They recited repeated prayers, lit magically arranged candles, poured oil into the water, and sacrificed four sheep, carving them into quarters and offered them to the sea, but none of this prevented the storm from driving them into the bay of Calis, on the Spanish coast. The pilot, however, was able to come about and cross the Strait of Gibraltar. After that, the corsair ships continued on eastwards in the direction of Algiers—the storm having made their decision for them.

Eventually, as we approached Algiers, we caught sight of its mosques, and we began to be curious in spite of ourselves, for it is one of the great sights on the coast of Mediterranean Africa. From a distance, it looks somewhat like a ship's sail. As one draws nearer, it resembles the gallery of a theatre. Outlying forts defend the city and make the approach to it dangerous and deadly for strangers, for these forts bristle with cannon.

We arrived at midday. The Admiral, Braham-Effendi, being impatient to be seen and recognized by the inhabitants of the town, fired off all his cannons. The other six vessels followed suit. The Vice Admiral's ship, on which I was, discharged most of its guns, so that we became dazed by the sound of the artillery, choked by gunsmoke, and poisoned with the smell of sulphur. Following this, we passed the end of the Mole, a long breakwater with a pentagonal fort set at the end of it, studded with cannons, and approached the quay.

A board causeway was put into place, and our miserable troop marched down it onto dry land. From there, we were taken to the Pasha's palace, accompanied all the way by crowds and the sounds of trumpets and drums. This barbaric ovation just increased our grief.

At the palace, we each underwent multiple interrogations, sometimes by the Moorish inhabitants of that country, sometimes by long-time slaves, or *renegados*, or by the Turks, all with the design of determining our countries and our professions. Eventually, weak from thirst and bathed in sweat, we were taken to a second courtyard of the palace, where an old slave of the Pasha's presented himself. After receiving a command from the man in charge of us, this slave led us into a room with reeds strewn across the floor, in which the furniture consisted merely of rush carpets suitable only for a small person to lie on.

The old slave spoke Lingua Franca, which he had learned in the Levant when he was there with his master, Issouf Pasha, who had brought him, along with many others, when he came to Algiers to take up the position of Pasha [Ottoman Governor of the city]. Lingua Franca is a sort of gibberish composed of the Spanish, Italian, and French languages. It came into being because a means of communication between so many nations was necessary. It is used throughout the Levant, especially onboard galleys and sailing ships.

The Pasha's slave consoled us the best he could, and brought us water, oranges, and lemons. Everyone among us was eager to confer with Estevan (for such was the slave's name) and learn from him what our fate might be. But this charitable slave could not provide answers to the questions he was bombarded with. The only clear conclusion was that the next day we would be presented to Issouf Pasha who would claim one fifth of us at his due.

At this point, two young men, dressed in the Turkish style, appeared and greeted us civilly in Lingua Franca. The youngest asked me the place of my embarkation and of my birth. I replied that La Rochelle was the one, and Anjou the other. To this, he replied that negotiating my freedom would be difficult, because there was little commerce between those cities and Algiers. He advised me to avoid being chosen by the Pasha if I could, since it would be almost impossible for me to recover my freedom after that, for the Pasha took all his retinue with him when his term as Governor was expired and he returned to the Levant, where he would sell his slaves in Alexandria, or Istanbul, or Cairo, or in other places in that part of the world, and afterwards nobody would ever know where I was.

I thanked him for his advice and urged him to teach me how to avoid such dangerous patronage. To this, he replied that the most assured expedient was to hide any education or skills that I possessed, and that when I was questioned by the Jews who serve as experts to the Pasha on such matters, I must say that I was devoid of any education, ignorant of any trade, and merely a simple soldier of fortune.

As we were finishing this conversation, a *Biclas*—a royal kitchen officer— with a huge moustache brought two rolls to each of us. After that, it being already quite late, we succumbed to our weariness and, despite our grief, fell eventually into sleep, trying not to dwell upon what the results might be of our meeting with the Pasha on the morrow.

❦

At sunrise, having slept uneasily, we prepared ourselves as best we could for our encounter with the Pasha. Out of fear of being chosen by him as part of the one fifth that was his due, none of us washed ourselves or combed our hair, for we all wanted to avoid looking like we might be wealthy, well positioned, or clever.

We waited, not knowing what to expect.

Estevan, the Pasha's old slave, appeared, relieving our impatient curiosity. He had not yet finished cleaning the entrance and the stable of the royal palace (this being an ordinary task of his), but he came to us, panting and out of breath, to let us know that he had learned from those who had to attend the Divan that we would not this day be exposed in the eyes of Pasha, nor led to the Souk known as the Badestan, to be auctioned off there to the highest bidder.

After this, we relaxed a little. A short while later, however, the moustachioed *Biclas*, the royal kitchen officer from the day before, came to find us and advise us be patient, for it was Ramadan, and since Muslims abstaining from eating or drinking throughout the day at this time until the appearance of the first star, we slaves would get nothing to eat until then.

Once the *Biclas* had finished his admonition of us, Estevan asked him if we could, without fear of mistreatment, leave our room and walk through the courtyards and offices of the palace, for perhaps, in doing so, we might be able to render some small service to the Turks and guard officers who had no private slaves. The *Biclas* replied that as long as we did not go anywhere near the door leading out into the courtyard—for if we did, those on guard there would think we were trying to escape—we could go where we wanted without fear of criticism.

After this, there was nobody among us, except for three who were very sick, who did not take advantage of this opportunity to escape the confines of the room we were in.

I ventured out, still wearing the scruffy sailor's clothes that I had donned to disguise my true station. The first person I met was the *renegado* named Osman, the man with whom I had conversed the previous evening. After greetings on both sides, he returned to our earlier conversation and offered to be of what service he could to me, and he promised to find me a good master. I thanked him politely, but I refrained from telling him anything about myself, for I had received warnings that one should not trust men like Osman, who feigned concern and loyalty, but whose real interest was to discover if I was a man of consequence, and thus somebody for whom a large ransom could be expected—a ransom from which Osman himself would receive a share as an informant.

I met with a number of other Turks as I wandered the palace halls. One of them gave me some *aspers* [small copper coins used in Algiers] wrapped in a little cone of paper. Others wished upon me a good master, and freedom even. All this made me realize that these Turkish infidels are more charitable than is commonly conceded.

I spent the rest of the time that needed to be passed until the apparition of the first star in contemplating the palace, where I walked with complete freedom and without any untoward encounters except for some kitchen officers who shouted at me in their incomprehensible language and from whom I quickly retreated.

At this point, the reader might be interested in a description of the Pasha's palace itself.

To tell the truth—and this may seem a little surprising—after seeing most of it, I concluded that the palace was not so beautiful as I had imagined it might be. It is located in the middle of the city, but there is nothing illustrious or remarkable about it. Outside, there is a large, fairly messy courtyard, and the only thing to attract the eyes of viewers is a double gallery of mediocre size, supported by a double row of porphyry columns enriched with marquetry and mosaic antiques. The rest of the palace is vast and confused and not worth the trouble to describe. As I walked around, I saw the kitchens where there was an abundance of dishes being prepared for the end of the day, all of rice or couscous (which is a composition of flour formed into very small, round shapes), along with forcefully boiled chickens, all intended for the table of the Pasha or his officers. There was ample enough food there to drive away hunger, I suppose, but I saw nothing even close to the delicacies that may commonly be found on the tables of Europe.

Eventually, after wandering throughout the palace unhindered, I returned to the room where we were being kept and found my fellow captives all already there.

As I sat with my comrades, we experienced an unexpected moment of panicky terror, for all the rooftops round about the palace were suddenly covered with a thousand kinds of people, all shouting 'Aalla, illa, alla!' They were rubbing their faces with their hands looking up at the sky, all turning in the direction of the sea. The continuation of this cry, without any forthcoming disorder or threat, persuaded me to go upstairs, where I stood gazing at the rest of the city. The houses there are raised in terraces and by degrees, because the city is built on the slope of a steep mountain, so that the whole place is like an amphitheatre which conveniently provides for the inhabitants a view of the vast expanse of the sea and the coastline, with its points, capes, and extraordinary eminences.

From my vantage point, I could see that every single rooftop was crowded with men, women, and small children, all contributing to the hubbub. My imagination, still tinged with a suspicion of panic, convinced me that these shouts from so many different people of all genders and ages must have been caused by some sort of signal by a sentinel more clear-sighted than I, who by some means had discovered enemy vessels at sea, or saw a terrible meteor in the sky.

An old slave, however, informed me of the secret of the ceremony: they were shouts of joy rather than howls of outrage or fear. That evening, because of the serenity of the sky, the moment of the appearance of the first star (which marked the ending of their day's Ramadan fast) was especially easy to discern, thus rendering the populace more excited than usual.

After this, we were given food and then went to bed, but with uneasy hearts, for the next day we were to be taken before the Pasha.

The following morning in the courtyard, we saw some of the officers of the militia diligently lining up before the Divan [the ruling council of Algiers]. I noticed both Jews and Mores confusedly entering into the anteroom of the palace, but nevertheless with restraint, to ask for justice—and coming out happy with each other, without quarrelling. Small disputes are resolved by lower officers, before whom individuals meet. Matters of importance, however, are decided by the Divan, which is the least corrupt jurisdiction among these barbarians, since it is composed of too many judges to be swayed by the solicitations of the great, the commiseration of the small, or by bribes.

In the courtyard, there was a large gathering of janissaries, Turks, Jews, *renegados* and slaves. From among this throng came two men, dressed differently, one with a turban and red jacket, the other with a cape and a black cap. They came up to us and faced Estevan, grand master of our unhappy proceedings, and began to question him persistently about our professions, our goods, our destination when we were taken captive, and the like. They also asked clarification from the two *renegados*, whom I mentioned above, who had already tormented us with their false solicitude.

One of the two men before us was Turkish, the other Jewish. They were not fully satisfied with Estevan's responses, and so they spoke directly to me, demanding to know if there were any gardeners, whom the Turks call *bostanjis*, among us, or any ship's caulkers, or gunners, and I do not know how many other different vocations. I answered them by saying that all those of our group were either ordinary sailors or private soldier-adventurers. They frowned at this and then said they had heard there were *papasses* (their name for Catholic priests) among us, for, they insisted, it was seldom that a ship captured at sea contained so many images, candles, and talismans as ours had, and they were looking for a *papasss* among us. Their purpose, they said, was not to profit from his ransom but, rather, to convert him.

At that moment, a young Turk with a gilded copper belt pulled the Jew by the sleeve advised him to go find the Pasha, which he did immediately.

Soon afterwards, I and the other slaves were herded together to see the Pasha. We found him seated, legs crossed tailor fashion, in the middle of a rather large but poorly lit room, on an elevated platform covered with Persian rugs. Any defects the room might have had were hidden by a large brocade cloth that hung on the wall, displaying a great array of different colours, well matched and nuanced. The Pasha reclined upon several silk cushions. The cushion on the right, which he leaned upon, was larger and more variegated, shining, and adorned with four long tassels of gold and silver mixed with some intertwined jewels. On this, he supported a copy of the Koran, covered with gold and ornamented with precious stones.

We were presented before him, our heads and feet bare (having, before entering the room, left our shoes at the door). The Pasha held long conferences with several Turks and Jews, who discussed us very carefully, one after the other seeming to give him advice. Eventually, we were ordered to depart, all but ten, whom the Pasha had chosen as his due, and who remained in the palace. The rest of us, fifty in number, were taken to the Badestan, the market where slaves were sold.

After we had all been well walked around there to show us off, our sellers began encouraging auction bids on each of us. As an old Flemish slave later explained to me, the man selling us auctioned off eight of the youngest and most vigorous among us to Ali Pegelin, General of the galleys. As for me, I was bought by a man named Oge Ali, whose name meant Ali the Scribe. Ali was the official scribe for the Divan, as I learned later. As Oge, he had the right to a small tax on each slave sold at the market. I had to stay in the market with him while he waited to receive the tax due him from the slaves sold that day.

After that, Oge Ali led me to his home, constantly questioning me about my age and country, and, with great eagerness, about my trade or profession. Once we arrived, he made me wait a good quarter of an hour in the entrance hall of the house. Then, warning me to take off my shoes, he ordered me to cross the courtyard. I entered into a fairly clean room, where he introduced me to his wife, who sat in the same posture as I had seen the Pasha sit. As she was young and quite beautiful, I did not feel in myself a great reluctance to start slave duty. I kissed the back of her hand when she presented it to me to show her approval of the purchase made by her husband.

Oge Ali made part of his living from the tax he was due from every slave sold in the Badestan, but he also made a profit from trafficking in slaves. There was no trick that he did not practise in order to find out if the investment he had made in me was good, and if he might profit from it. Along with many other questions, he pressed me hard on the subject of my trade and profession, hoping to discover if I was a man of wealth and position. I insisted to him that I was just an ordinary soldier of fortune who had been travelling from France to Portugal to enlist in the armies of the Portuguese Crown.

To my surprise, upon hearing this, Oge Ali fetched an enormous arquebus [a kind of musket], so heavy that I could not hold it up to my cheek without support. Having loaded it himself, he presented it to me with a smile and a command to fire it. Since I had no idea how to use such a heavy weapon, I found myself unable to do anything but lay it down in an admission of defeat. When, with a mocking smile, he asked if there were many soldiers like me intending to serve the Crown of Portugal, I hardly knew what to reply.

Still smiling, he then told me that I was from now on going to carry water from the public fountains into the city and sell enough so that I brought back twenty *aspers* every evening. If I failed to do this, he said, I would receive a hundred strokes with a stick each time.

The next morning, I was provided with two large jugs of brass, which I could hardly carry empty Fear, however, gives strength, so I shouted through the streets just as other slave water sellers did, calling out 'Ab el ma!' (that is, 'My water is good!').

At day's end, I had only managed to sell twelve *aspers* worth of water, which I brought with me to my owner's house. Finding that I was eight *aspers* short of the twenty he had demanded from me for each day, he prepared to execute his threats and commanded two of his English slaves to turn me upside down and attach my feet to a contraption of rope and wood which they lifted up, holding me immobile with my feet in the air. He then began striking me on the soles of my feet with a rope.

In that most uncomfortable position, having already received five to six painful clouts of the rope on the soles of my feet, I saw my owner's wife appear, returning from a trip in the city. Luckily for me, she softened her husband's temper, reminding him that I was a new slave who did not know the streets of the city, and that my small profit was excusable. In future, she insisted, I would surely be able to earn the twenty *aspers* a day just as well as the old slaves who had their regular routes and knew the streets well.

They finally untied me then, and, after I had rendered proper reverence to my owner and master, Oge Ali, I was sent to join the other slaves, who were in a small gallery in the vestibule of the house. When I got there, limping, the other slaves who sold water laughed at me instead of consoling me, for they had learned that I had only been able to make twelve *aspers*, while they were obliged to pay each evening twenty-four, which they did easily.

Our meal that evening was hard bread and a few spoonfuls of a soup made from boiled camel meat. I had just started to close my eyes, when I received a message from the oldest of the slaves that Oge Ali was going to order me to go out the next day with some others of his slaves and wield a *chappe* (a type of hoe) and work the soil at his *macerie*, or farming estate, outside the city, and that if I was not more successful in tending his garden than I had been in selling water, I would be sent to the galleys.

These new orders made it difficult for me to sleep, for I was very anxious about what might happen to me.

Early the next morning, I and three others each took up a *chappe*, along with the bread intended for our food for that day, and walked out through the city gate called *Bab-el-Oued* at the north end of the city, from which a road led out into the countryside. Oge Ali's *macerie* was a quarter of a league from his house, near the sea. It consisted of a small country cottage, fairly well built, located in the middle of a garden dotted with fountains. The best comparison for it I can think of is a country house outside Marseilles.

We set to work immediately upon arriving, but no matter how I tried, my job was neither well done nor progressed like that of my fellow workers. As the sun was starting to go down, Oge Ali arrived, either on purpose to surprise us, or simply because he came out on a walk, for the countryside around there was, I must admit, amongst the most beautiful I have ever seen, with an endless vista of the sea and long lines of lemon trees and charming orange trees exuding their pleasant odour.

Oge Ali noted well the trouble I was having and my obvious inexperience in this manual trade. I concentrated as hard as I could on the handling of my *chappe*, since I was afraid that he would suspect something of my birth because of my ineptitude.

A short time after his arrival, the sunset giving us the freedom to retire, Oge Ali led the four of us back to town, questioning us one after the other and pointing to the ships that were anchored in the bay. On entering the city, we were carefully observed by the soldiers in the *Bab-el-Oued* guardhouse.

I endured the fatigue of cultivating the earth for another five or six days, until I found myself so exhausted that I could hardly put one foot in front of the other. Besides, the terrible heat of the place had caused a rash all over my body, which made me incapable of doing anything except very slowly. Added to this was the vexation of my fellow workers, who, because of my inability with the *chappe*, did not want me working in the same place as they.

Informed of my incompetence, Oge Ali appeared and recommenced his threats and reproaches and reiterated his expectation of getting a good ransom for me. He said disgustedly that unless I was of noble birth or had some sort of skilled profession, it would have been impossible for me to have remained alive and in good health until the time I was captured. I continued to insist that his claims about me were groundless. More importantly, I practised restraint and concealment with the other slaves when we were together for fear that guesswork based on their report and observation might give me away.

After a time, I adjusted to the work and no longer suffered from sorrow and fatigue quite so much, having reached a point where my body and mind no longer felt tormented. I also began to be less worried about Oge Ali's interrogations, which seemed to be lessening.

And then one day, to my surprise, a negress (she was a slave from Angola or Guinea) brought me refreshments from Oge Ali consisting of local delicacies, including honey, *manteca* [fritters fried in butter], and a cake composed of lupines, almonds, honey, and milk. She gave me all this and instructed me to take it to the *macerie* cottage and sleep there until further notice.

This sudden change of employment relieved me, but it also puzzled me greatly, since I did not understand Oge Ali's intentions. I waited for the negress to leave and then conferred with one of the other slaves, a Portuguese man whom I trusted more than the others, who were English, Flemish, Sicilian, Mallorquin, and Spanish. I learned from this slave that Oge Ali was to place me in charge of some negresses, fifteen or sixteen of whom he kept out at the *macerie*. The Portuguese slave further informed me that Oge Ali kept them in order to produce *mulattos*, that is, children of mixed race, white and black. From time to time, he chose from among his slaves the whiter and more vigorous ones to impregnate the negresses. He carried on this business through correspondents in Alexandria and Istanbul, where he sold these *mulatto* children. From this, he made a large part of his main income.

Such was to be my new occupation.

Night passed, and the next morning, a large black eunuch came to fetch me at the *macerie* cottage where I had been sleeping. He carried with him some provisions, and a long drum on which he beat loudly—this being apparently his idea of a pleasant way to awaken me. I got up and dressed myself and went out, escorted by Mustapha (for such was this ugly black eunuch's name). He continued pounding on his drum throughout our journey until we reached another house nearby. Barely had the door to this dwelling opened when I found myself surrounded by a whole troop of dark bodies.

I tried to turn and slip away, but the eunuch pushed me forward, redoubled his drumming, and cried out in a loud voice: 'Barca, Maria, Fatima, Israëlita…' the names of the black angels who appeared at the door of Oge Ali's earthly paradise.

After saying a quick word or two to them, Mustapha closed the door behind me, having left the supplies he had brought, along with a bottle of date brandy. The next day, and the next, and other days thereafter, he brought more supplies, and, morning and evening, never failed to give us loud serenades on his drum. After six days, the door was opened, and, after he had private conference with each of the negresses to ascertain that they were satisfied, he returned me to the city and to my master, Oge Ali.

Fatima and Barca each gave me a tobacco snuffbox, which I carried back with me.

Having been returned to Oge Ali's household in the city, I now found myself left entirely alone, with no set tasks to accomplish and nobody to talk with. I grew progressively unhappy with my lot, and eventually began searching for expedients by which I might free myself from my onerous master. Eventually, I settled upon the idea that if I were to counterfeit being an epileptic, Oge Ali would decide to put me up for sale.

Accordingly, I procured a small vial in which I mixed blood from my nose with liquid soap scum and charcoal and then waited for my master as he was returning from prayers. When I saw him coming from the mosque, I covered my stomach with the bloodied foam and lay down at the entrance to the hallway of the house just a few moments before Oge Ali entered through the doorway. I executed my little charade with such great skill that my master was shocked and dared not enter. He waited for a slave to rouse me and demand what had happened to me. I pretended to come back groggily, as from a slumber. After all of them questioned me persistently, I pretended to be ashamed to admit to them that my illness was very extraordinary, and that sometimes for as much as three months I would not experience an attack, but that at other times I was tormented four or five times a moon (for so they counted their months).

My ruse worked even better than I had hoped. The very next morning, I was led to the public baths, and was there well washed and shaved. I was then led to a Jewish second-hand shop where I was bought the sort of clothing a Flemish sailor would wear. The next day, at the slave market, after some bidding, a local Arab bought me and put me in the hands of his sister, Fatima, the widow of a Flemish *renegado*, for whom he had purchased me.

I then entered Fatima's service—after first kissing the back of her right hand, according to the required ceremony. She made me responsible for the chores needed to keep her household going. She had no slave other than a negress, for she was not very wealthy, being just the widow of a Flemish *renegado* who had been a ship's carpenter. She was also neither so young, nor so well made as the wife of Oge Ali, whose house I had just left.

The tasks she assigned me were neither very rigorous nor very difficult, and the negress did her fair share, so that we lived together in reasonable harmony. My ordinary task was to fetch water from the nearby fountain to be used in the house, and, for the rest of the day, to carry around in my arms a small child of two to three years of age. In the afternoons, I followed my mistress to the door of the public baths, where, once she had received linens, depilatories, and other necessary things from me, she kept me waiting at the entrance until she was done, after which I accompanied her back to the house.

Such public baths are very common and convenient in Algiers. They are necessary both because of the great heat of the country and the scarcity of decent clothing. Men go to these baths in the morning; women go in the afternoon. For the women, these necessary and pleasant places were a retreat where they could indulge in libertinage, for in the baths they were not watched over, as they always were elsewhere, and they could spend time there both with their friends and with certain other friends in disguise.

Men are forbidden, under penalty of death, to enter these public baths in the afternoon, when the women are there. Therefore, the men cannot surprise them, nor come upon them—unless the women concur in it. I followed Fatima to the baths, carrying the linen, ointments, and other necessities, and, as I said, waited at the door for her. On one occasion, she called me inside to render her some service. The other women with her questioned her loudly about my trade and profession, asking her how much she had paid for me. Once she told them the price, they smiled and said she had made a good bargain.

When we were back in her house again, Fatima asked me if I were to have a change of owners, which one of the women who had inquired about me I would like the most as a new mistress. To this, I responded that if there were any pleasure in slavery, it was in having a reasonable owner like her. To this, she said that when she looked at me, she could not help but recall memories of her late husband.

I remained in the house of Fatima, my patroness, for another four to five days. Then, upon the advice of her brother, who counselled her to sell me, for he considered me to be a useless slave (and far too familiar with her), I was led to the slave market for the third time. And so I ended up in the hands of my third owner, an Ouda Bachi—a company commander in the janissaries. I passed out of service of the house of Fatima for sixty pieces of eight. She received the money from my auction through the hands of her brother. I took my leave of her with some regret.

The Ouda Bachi who purchased me was called Beiram (family names being unknown among the Turks). He had a nickname: Topeclaure, meaning 'big leg'. I thus became known as the slave of the Ouda Bachi Topeclaure.

The price for which I was sold was quite low. I had made the walk through the slave market several times already, remember, and the Jews and other kinds of experts found my body weak, and found me stronger in the teeth than anywhere else. One said he had seen me with Oge Ali's negresses at the *macerie* outside the city. Another had seen me attempting to sell water with little success. A third remembered that Oge Ali had sold me in the Badestan at a loss, that a *renegado* woman had bought me, and that it was now she who was selling me.

Despite my poor reputation, my new owner bought me and brought me to the janissary barracks in which he lived. There, he put me in charge of the cooking, which was done in the evening in common among the soldiers. The janissaries were divided up into brigades and housed close to each other in dormitories, like the cells of our religious houses. In the middle of the building in which they lived was a large courtyard, resembling the cloister of an abbey.

I was soon able to set myself up successfully as a cook in the Beiram brigade, having learned in a few days how to season white cabbage with chili and orange, how to prepare rice and couscous with chicken, and how to lay out honey and oil with hot bread. Cooking fish was just as easy, for frying and poaching were the only methods employed—the Turks being neither so greedy for, nor so fond of food as we are in Europe.

Beiram was satisfied enough with my service that soon he commanded me to organize supplies needed for him to join a corsair expedition aboard one of the more important corsair vessels, named *The Small Moor*. Onto this vessel, I carried, in a single case, his basic necessities, which included a bunch of onions, a stick of tobacco, and a small barrel of brandy. As well as these, I brought along the staples that all Turkish soldiers going to sea carry with them: oil, olives, vinegar, and hardtack biscuits—since onboard provisions do not consist of very much and are distributed among them only twice a day.

There were fifteen other slaves on board this corsair ship, mostly Flemish and English, with me being the lone Frenchman. There were also fifty Turks on board, plus ten or twelve Kouloughlis, who were the sons of those among the Turkish janissaries who had married local women. Kouloughlis were not included among the ranks of Algiers' state militia [the janissaries]. The garrison payroll is intended solely for the Turks whom the Pashas bring in from the Levant, or for the *renegados* among their ranks. Any children got with native women are usually excluded.

A dozen years ago, these Kouloughlis—the term means 'mixed-race' in their language—launched a rebellion and, in an attempt to take control of the city and the state, captured the Alcassave [*al-Qasaba*, the fortress at the top of the city of Algiers]. They were besieged by both Turks and *renegados*, many of them fathers of the rebels. The Kouloughlis' resistance was so stubborn that they blew up the Alcassave. Those who survived lost their heads. In my own time, some of these severed heads still decorated the walls around the *Bab el-Oued* gate—a pitiful relic of paternal revenge, for most of the besieged and the besiegers were fathers and sons, uncles and nephews, or at least first cousins. Since that time, the Kouloughlis have had no voice in the government of Algiers, do not receive any public pay, and are permitted to join corsair expeditions only on the condition that they receive no wages or salaries but just a simple share in the common profits.

Notwithstanding all this, the captain of *The Small Moor* was, in fact, a Kouloughli, a man named Joseph Reis, who was the son of a young janissary from the Levant who had married a Morisco woman. Although my master, the Ouda Bachi, did not consider Joseph Reis to be a man of any importance ashore, he nevertheless yielded to his authority aboard ship because the ship owner so wished. This man, who had armed and equipped the ship himself, had given command of it to Joseph Reis because of his leadership skills, loyalty, and experience.

The day of our departure dawned, and a brisk wind from the land moved us quickly away from the port. The coast of Barbary dwindled behind us. Algiers diminished visibly… and finally disappeared. And so we began our expedition, on a sea that seemed like a giant, unpolished emerald, still turmoiled by a recent storm.

Joseph Reis was superstitious, and in order to make preparation for a successful hunt, he called into his cabin the ship's cleric and all the other notables on board, including my master the Ouda Bachi. I, however, was banished, along with the other slaves, to the depths of the ship's hold. I only learned the next day, from a Sicilian *renegado*, the secret and the mystery of the ceremony they performed, which is a kind of enchantment used among them, and which is practised in the following way.

They take two arrows or two knives, one of which designates the Turkish ship, the other any possible Christian ship they will encounter. After some conjurations and words from the Koran, the arrows (or knives) are placed between the right hand and the left of one of them, or put in the hands of two of them. These men then fling them down and allow them to land as they may on a table or some other appropriate surface. If the one that designates the Turkish ship ends up on top of the one that designates the Christian ship, then the corsairs will be so reassured that they will act bravely to the point of recklessness, and, however weak they might be, they will persevere in the hunt and will not be turned back, even by armed Christian ships of war.

Much of that first day at sea was spent with this superstitious ceremony. In the evening, with the sun already beginning to sink toward the horizon, the slaves were ordered to go aloft and work to unfurl the sails. I did the best I could with this seaman's duty, but I was clumsy and kept getting tangled up in the ropes, and I did not know how to clamber up past the top [the platform on the mast]. I hid my absolute inexperience as best I could.

We sailed on throughout the night. When the sun appeared the next morning, it ushered in a day as bright as the one before, lighting our way into the Strait of Gibraltar. We passed through this dangerous area without encountering any of the ships of Charles V, the Spanish king, and so passed the Pillars of Hercules without incident.

As we rounded Cape Spartel, we poor Christian slaves could gaze first upon Tangier and then Larache, both Christian strongholds. Then, after some time, we passed by Azamor and Safi, Muslim towns on the Moroccan coast. After passing Cape Cantin only with the greatest of difficulty, because of contrary winds, we sailed for two days out into the open Atlantic until we encountered a large English ship.

As soon as the news reached Joseph Reis and the principals of the ship's council of war, the order was given to open the gun ports, prepare the cannons, and hoist the sails to catch every bit of wind possible. Everyone on board prepared: the *renegado*s got ready to seize the booty; the janissaries equipped themselves for combat, and the Moors, of whom there were many on the ship, took to tobacco and brandy. The slaves, meanwhile, were tormented by the half-hope of possible liberation.

Broadsides were fired by both ships, and this cooled the Turks' ardour for boarding the English ship. The two vessels drew close but did not grapple. Then the English ship sped away northwards. We gave up the chase and cruised in the general direction of the Canary Islands.

Several days passed after this without adventure, stars and fish being the only objects we saw. Then the great peak of Tenerife, called by the Spaniards *Pica de Terraria*, came into view—still at least some forty leagues distant, according to the more experienced seamen aboard the ship. It is well known that this upthrusting of the Earth can be seen from as far as sixty leagues away. Its top, incessantly covered in snow, persuades people to see it as connecting Earth and Heaven. The islands of El Hierro, La Palma, Gomer, Tenerife, Gran Canaria, Fuerteventura, and Lanzarote then all came into view.

Soon we spied a fishing boat passing from Tenerife to Fuerteventura, which we took easily, surprising them before they were able to think of fleeing from us. We learned from the fishermen on board this boat that two brigantines [small, two-masted sailing ships] from Gran Canaria had set sail a couple of days previous in search of some Dutch ships returning from Fernambouk [in Brazil]. In hopes of encountering these ships first, and with the desire to gain booty without too much risk, Joseph Reis decided to cruise around the Canary Islands, for he felt his ship was equipped to deal with the two brigantines, which, if they encountered us, would find themselves involved in a more dangerous business than they imagined.

So we sailed between the islands, which appeared on all sides, and cruised in a triangle between Cape Bojador, Gran Canaria, Tenerife, and Fuerteventura. In the meantime, the Ganches—for so the inhabitants of the Canary Islands are called—who were as dismayed as the fish they caught, the hooks they used not being all that different from the shackles they were confined by, informed us of the wonders of their country. There were five of them, three from the city of Las Palmas, capital of the island of Gran Canaria, and the other two from the isle of Fuerteventura. They tried to convince us that their islands had a climate so perfect that the terrestrial Paradise had had none better.

While the Ganches were thus enchanting our ears, a confused noise arose from the ship's stern. Above in the rigging, some of the sailors cried that they saw a large vessel which looked to be Dutch—because of the lines of the ship, which were that of what is called a fluyt, with no castle on either stern or bow. Such ships are merchant vessels, and they handle better in rough seas than other sorts of ships do. They are, however, poorly armed and lack sufficient cannon to properly defend themselves with a broadside. The Moors call them *pinques*.

More sailors clambered up into the rigging, the gunners ran to their cannons, the soldiers looked to their muskets, and the slaves, of whom I was one, went to stand diligently beside their masters. I took my place near Ouda Bachi Topeclaure, who commanded me to stay alert and to keep the wick for his arquebus lit.

We began to give chase.

Joseph Reis, our Captain, called upon Dominque, the oldest of the captives we had taken near the Canary Islands, to know his thoughts on the discovery of this Dutch ship we had spotted. He learned nothing much other than the fact that Dominque had a general distrust of vessels from the Netherlands and that he could not tell if this ship was one of the ones the Canary Islands brigantines were hunting. This doubtful information left Joseph Reis unsure for a considerable time, for he did not know if the fluyt we were chasing might be filled with men and artillery and might already have defended herself well against the two brigantines. If that were the case, there was little to expect now but an exchange of unwelcome and destructive cannon fire.

His irresolution diminished, though, when the corsairs saw the fluyt raise its sails and change course to flee. Never did a hunting dog leap more quickly after a hare than Joseph Reis's ship did after that fugitive fluyt. After a chase, the Dutch ship was forced to either surrender or to fight. Those aboard chose the latter, but it was not a very spirited defence. There were, apparently, few among them who were willing to risk their lives, for they eschewed the liquid tomb that desperate maritime defence provides and chose instead to accept bondage in return for staying alive.

After three volleys of cannon fire, to which they replied with but a single shot, they raised a white flag... and the dropping of the sails and the movement of handkerchiefs denoted the surrender of the miserable flute. They then put their ship's boat in the water and rowed over to receive the orders of Joseph Reis, who, at the same time, dispatched fifteen of his men to board the fluyt. The Ouda Bachi, my master, was the leader of this group, and I went along with him and his soldiers. We all clambered aboard pell-mell.

The fluyt was carrying a cargo of woad [a plant used to make blue dye] and cedar wood. It was in the employ of merchants from Antwerp who had armed and equipped the ship in Lubeck [in northern Germany]. From there, it had sailed to Terceira [in the Azores], and was on the return leg when it had the unhappy luck to meet with Joseph Reis and his corsairs.

Since slaves share the same common miseries, whether old slaves like me or new ones like those taken from the fluyt, the Ouda Bachi, my master, ordered me to find out everything I could about these new captives of Joseph Reis. I did what I could to fulfil my slave duty, but yet tried to do so without prejudicing Christian charity, and also without prejudicing the interests of the new captives. Accordingly, I assured the Ouda Bachi that the fluyt's crew all had no expectation of ever being ransomed and had no other home than their floating wooden house, out of which they had now been driven in perpetuity. The Ouda Bachi put faith in my report and so left the captives alone during the rest of our journey.

Joseph Reis, happy with the booty he had taken, gave orders to return to Algiers. We had good following winds and soon entered the Strait of Gibraltar, through which we passed without any encounters other than with several small fishing boats which immediately fled back to their ports upon seeing us. The favourable wind continued, and although this channel that separates Europe from Africa is usually infested with galleys and warships, we sailed through it without misadventure. At one point, we gave chase to two brigantines from Malaga that we spotted, but they retreated from us in good order and without fear.

When we reached Algiers, Joseph Reis omitted nothing that could contribute to his triumphant entry: the waving flags of the captured fluyt, the banners, the strident music of trumpets, the firing of the artillery on board... all announced to his friends, and any others waiting interestedly on the shore, the importance of his catch—which consisted of woad, cedar, sugar, and Spanish *reales* [pieces of eight].

After the ordinary ceremonies, the booty was brought and deposited in some stores near the harbour, except for the Spanish *reales*, which were loaded upon the shoulders of a few Moors and carried in a procession along with Joseph Reis and the new captives. I followed this procession to the courtyard of the Pasha's palace, where we were commanded to remain until his return.

The Pasha, alerted by the noise and commotion, soon appeared. The Ouda Bachi went in to see the Pasha, along with Joseph Reis but ordered me to stay behind and determine the faculties, countries, and ages of the captives they were bringing to the Pasha. Once the meeting with the Pasha was over, they all came back, apparently fully satisfied. Joseph Reis returned to his home, and the Ouda Bachi returned to the janissary barracks, followed by me.

Throughout my various trips over sea and land, I never stopped thinking about possible ways of recovering my freedom—the charms of which tasted sweeter after their loss. Eventually, I decided to attempt asking my fellow slaves if they had any notions about how to go about obtaining freedom from our wretched situation in Algiers.

A few days afterward, on a Friday—which is a holiday for the Turks, like Saturday is among Jews and Sunday among Christians—I met by chance in the *bagnio* [the slave pen] of Ali Pegelin, the General of the Algiers galley fleet, the Sieur Anier Levallois, one of those who had been captured with me. He had a small concession stand by the main door of the *bagnio* where he sold tobacco and brandy.

After the usual welcome and courtesies, I learned from him that the Sieur de Cahaignes d'Escures, who had also been captured with me, had reached an agreement with his owner, Car-Ibrahim, to be ransomed for the sum of twelve hundred ecus. Having negotiated this agreement, the Sieur de Cahaignes was now looking for some fellow countryman whom he could trust so he could send him to Provence to see the Archbishop of Aix, his relative, friend, and protector, in order to acquire the needed ransom funds as soon as possible.

I then talked with the Sieur de Cahaignes himself, who assured me that he could bear the loss of twelve hundred ecus without much resentment or notable alteration in his fortune, and that the only difficulty he foresaw was that there were no trade relations of any sort—and so no means of communication—between the city of Rouen, the place of his birth, and North Africa. He had faith, though in the Archbishop of Aix, who he said could make the necessary arrangements for his parents, from whom he expected the required funds.

The Sieur de Cahaignes was in truth more impatient than worried, having no doubt that his father and mother would do their best to free him from the hands of the infidels. He had, accordingly, convinced his owner to purchase a French slave, for whom he could pay a low ransom, whom he could then send to France to solicit the funds to buy them both free.

I offered myself to the Sieur de Cahaignes, my colleague in misfortune, with such sincerity and repeated oaths that he said he was disposed to accept me. He needed to be certain of the lowness of my ransom, though. I assured him that my master, Beiram Ouda Bachi, was quite satisfied with my duties to him as a slave, and that he had once said that, if he sold me, he would ask no other price for me than what he paid at the Badestan. He was a soldier, and a brave man, and little interested in making a profit from his slave.

Sieur de Cahaignes and I decided that we must convince Beiram Ouda Bachi to sell me to Car-Ibrahim. Our deliberations complete, I returned to my owner.

Beiram Ouda Bachi asked my where I had been. I told him about how the Sieur de Cahaignes wished to send me to his country to ask his wealthy and accommodating parents to pay his ransom. Car-Ibrahim was somebody Beiram Ouda Bachi knew very well, having drunk sorbet with him many times in the Souk, and Beiram seemed open to the idea.

When I went to bed that night, an army of a thousand thoughts bristling with a million difficulties besieged me, ruining my peace of mind. When the dawn removed the darkness, I had hardly slept at all. I rose early and kept close to my master in order to be able to present my proposal to him yet again.

First, though, it was necessary to know how much I had cost him. Fortunately, I was informed (without him knowing it) by a Portuguese *renegado* who was present at my auction, that the price Beiram Ouda Bachi paid to buy me from Fatima, my previous owner, had been sixty pieces of eight. It was true, however, that by now I was worth something more, being healthier and better equipped than when I left the said Fatima.

I still was not certain that Beiram Ouda Bachi actually would part with me for what he paid for me. But one has to beat the iron while it is hot. So I asked him if he would agree to accept ransom money for me from Car-Ibrahim and then pressed him further to know what he had paid for me, in case Car-Ibrahim, at the urging of the Sieur de Cahaignes, did indeed offer to buy me from him. Beiram told me, with a frown, that if he was going to sell me, he would rather accept payment to set me free than to sell me as a slave into the hands of another owner. I convinced him, however, that selling me to Car-Ibrahim was in fact my best chance of returning to my own country a free man, since I was not able to arrange anything for myself, for I was only a simple soldier of fortune, as he knew.

He accepted all this and agreed to sell me for the sixty pieces of eight I had originally cost him, plus four more for the clothes he had provided me with, and two more for the port tax that would be incurred by my sale—which amounted to a total of sixty-six pieces of eight.

We met with Car-Ibrahim the next day in one of the booths in the Badestan where he and Car-Ibrahim used to meet to drink sorbet and take tobacco together. We waited there for two endless hours before Car-Ibrahim and his slave finally appeared. After a fairly short conference, they agreed on my price—seventy pieces of eight. Car-Ibrahim then went off and returned in a little while with the money wrapped carefully in a handkerchief and handed it over to Beiram Ouda Bachi.

Beiram gave me a parting gift of thirty *aspers*, which equalled half a piece of eight. I thanked him sincerely for his kindness and generosity and then walked away with my new owner.

On the evening that I entered Car-Ibrahim's household, the taste of half-liberty granted to me by my change of owner was quite pleasant, and I spent that first night in tranquillity. This did not last, however, for I grew apprehensive about the Sieur de Cahaignes' plan to send me off to a Christian land. Also, I realized that my new owner's main trade consisted in the purchase and sale of slaves—that is, he was a professional slave dealer—and that his only concern was profit. While I was there, he had fourteen or fifteen slaves of different ages, sexes and nations, for which he hoped to recoup large ransoms.

Car-Ibrahim had sufficient wealth to maintain three spacious *maceries* near the sea. He financed these primarily by his trade in slaves, purchasing these slaves cheaply and reselling them at a high price. He prospered also, with the help of the Jewish merchants of Livorno, by providing supplies for the city militia and the corsairs, especially grain, sails, and rigging.

The day after I entered his household, Car-Ibrahim granted the Sieur de Cahaignes and me the freedom to go about the city—so long as the plan to send me to collect the Sieur's ransom remained in place. This gave me hope. But I still worried that something could go wrong. For though the Sieur de Cahaignes seemed completely sure of the assistance he would get from his family, I was not so confident. So I waited anxiously and impatiently for the arrival of some Christian ship that could provide me passage out of Algiers.

Finally, such a ship did arrive.

As was the custom, the ship's sails were brought ashore and stored in a shed set aside for such things. I learned that it was a ship from Livorno, in Italy, belonging to some of that city's Jewish merchants, who traffic in the stolen goods which, thanks to the corsairs, can be found inexpensively in the cities of Barbary. I went to Car-Ibrahim, to whom I gave news of the ship's arrival and explained to him that this ship proved a convenient way for me to get to Italy, and that from there I could easily travel to France, where I could set in motion arrangements for the ransom of the Sieur de Cahaignes and myself.

Car-Ibrahim seemed quite willing to go along with this, not asking me for any assurance other than the particular promise to complete the ransom arrangements. He even offered to provide me with a document to serve as a safe-conduct and offered to let me go whenever I and the Sieur wished—for he considered the risk of loss in this venture small, and the potential profit great.

I then took leave of Car-Ibrahim and went in search of the Sieur de Cahaignes. I heard that he was at the residence of the consul of France, and it was there that I found him. He had just finished talking with the newly arrived merchants from Livorno. From them, he had learned that his friends and family had already made arrangements for his ransom. This news was carried in a letter stating that some Trinitarians, carrying funds derived both from public alms and private donors, were in the harbour at Marseilles waiting for a good wind in order to make the passage to the Barbary coast. In keeping with their pious mission, they intended to ransom as many of the unfortunate slaves in Algiers as they could, some with money derived from public charity, others with funds provided by relatives and friends for the special assistance of certain individuals—among whom, the Sieur de Cahaignes believed, was himself.

Upon learning this, and considering his chains broken and his slavery ended, the Sieur dismissed my upcoming expedition, considering it now a useless and ineffective intrigue.

I tried to accept this setback with patience, but I could not help but complain to Car-Ibrahim about the wrong the Sieur de Cahaignes, his slave, had done me, having forced me away from my previous owner, Beiram Ouda Bachi, by whom I might have been given my freedom eventually, and how I now found myself abandoned, for there was nobody putting up special funds to ransom me. Car-Ibrahim reassured me that he would not allow me—or him—to be taken advantage of.

A few days later, Car-Ibrahim called me and the Sieur de Cahaignes into his presence and declared that he had come to a decision about our ransom. He insisted that we stick to the original plan, that one of us would go away to Christian lands to solicit the ransom for both, while the other would stay with him. It was, he said, his choice as to which of us would go. And since the loss of my ransom would not be as great as the loss of the Sieur's, he had decided that I would be the one to go.

The Sieur de Cahaignes seemingly acquiesced to this, but I could tell that he secretly refused to accept it because of the hope that had been given to him by the letter received from the Livorno merchants. I, however, began to feel despondent about my chances of ever being freed, and for two or three days I entered into a kind of retreat, trying to console myself and escape the grip of anger and resentment.

One day, I was walking along the breakwater of the Mole when a Turk, descending from a frigate mounted with four iron cannons, approached me. After greeting me in good French, he pulled me aside and asked me which canton of France I was from and offered to render me what assistance he could to alleviate the sufferings of my slavery. I replied, not without some unease, that I was a native of Anjou, without designating any city in the province, and was a soldier by profession, without specifying anything else.

After this, the man pointed to the frigate which lay at anchor and told me that in five or six days it would sail, and that if I wished I could go along with him to Salé, where I would stay. Or I could go to Marrakesh, which is not far away, to look for an opportunity for a ship to La Rochelle, for traffic from La Rochelle to Safi, Azemmour, Salé, Marrakesh, and other cities in this empire provided abundant opportunities for travel. This Turk was, by his own confession, originally from La Rochelle. He seemed about aged forty years, quite dignified and polite. He was a creature of Ali Calcris, one of the captains and governors of the city and castle of Salé, held on behalf of Muley Musmagnan Abdelmelek, Emperor of Morocco and King of Fez.

This offer by Ali Alcaide, *renegado* from La Rochelle, sorely tempted me to abandon my design, which was now nothing less than to wait for the arrival of the Trinitarians in hopes that I could somehow manage to get myself ransomed by them. I thanked Ali Alcaide, without either accepting or rejecting his offer, for I was not sure what I might now do.

As fate would have it, the Trinitarian expedition, which was led by Fathers Lucien Hérault and Boniface Duboys, arrived before the ship of Ali Alcaide, the *renegado* from La Rochelle, had left the harbour. I therefore declined Ali Alcaide's offer and watched his ship set out to sea without too much regret, though still far from certain I had made the right choice.

When the Trinitarian friars came ashore, they were mobbed by a large crowd of slaves of all nations. The French especially were there in greater numbers. The friars hurried through this crowd and made their way to the house of the Sieur Picquet, Consul of France. Up until this point, the Consul had been more concerned with the affairs of the Marseilles merchants—especially those who trafficked in coral at Bastion de France, near Tabarka—than in the negotiations to free French slaves, groaning under the weight of their chains. (Special interests, although baptized with different names, always produce the same effect.)

The said Sieur Picquet was associated with the Sieurs Constant and Hauterive, in whose house the leaders of the Trinitarian mission took up residence. After getting settled, they began to inquire about the quantity and quality of the French slaves and the intentions of the Pasha and the Divan. As preparation for their mission, they first presented the Pasha with a letter from his very Christian Majesty Louis XIV and distributed gifts to the said Pasha, to Ali Pegelin, the General of the Galleys, and to others of the highest rank in the Divan.

I went to see Fathers Lucien and Boniface, leaders of the Trinitarian mission, as confessors rather than as redeemers. Father Lucien heard my confession, and I told him about the continuation of my persecution and the fecklessness of the Sieur de Cahaignes, who no longer wanted me to leave Algiers to arrange his and my freedom. Father Lucien gave me his absolution, which reassured me and gave me hope that if I just resigned myself to the actions of divine Providence, a way to break the chains of my slavery would appear.

However, the Sieur de Cahaignes, having been assured by Messrs. Mailland and Riboüillet (who commanded the ship on which the Trinitarians travelled) that his family were fully prepared to provide money sufficient to pay his ransom, pressed his freedom with Car-Ibrahim, offering him with authority to pay not only his own ransom but also all the cost of the various taxes and duties added on that were required before a ransomed slave could leave the city.

Car-Ibrahim was fairly well-intentioned, and he assured me that if I could guarantee that he could get back what I had cost him plus a modest profit, he was willing to ransom me. His good disposition prompted me to ask the Trinitarian Fathers to advance me my ransom money from the public alms in their treasury. I explained to them that I was beginning to despair of the continuation of good intentions on the part of my enslaved comrade, whose freedom was nonetheless being advanced by them. Fathers Lucien and Boniface, besides the goodly sum deposited into their hands, had ample authority jointly with Commanders Mailland and Riboüillet to provide funds and make advances as they deemed appropriate. So they went to find Car-Ibrahim.

They had no difficulty at first with the ransom price for the Sieur de Cahaignes, it having been previously settled. But during the discussion, Car-Ibrahim smiled and asked Father Lucien about me. He said that I and the Sieur de Cahaignes were jointly liable, and he did not think that one could go be freed without the other. This surprised the Fathers, and they were afraid that Car-Ibrahim was trying to sabotage the discussion as a ploy in order to raise the price. They paused uncertainly, unsure what Car-Ibrahim's intentions were.

Car-Ibrahim took the Sieur de Cahaignes and me aside and told us that he expected a ransom of 900 ecus for our liberties, 800 for the Sieur de Cahaignes, and 100 for me, and he vowed that he would either ransom us together or not at all.

Car-Ibrahim's resolution greatly disturbed the Sieur de Cahaignes, who did not know which way to turn. He tried pleading and lamenting his sad fate, but these had no effect on Car-Ibrahim. I stood silently while the Sieur implored Car-Ibrahim to reconsider. Finally, having no other option, he offered to pay for my ransom with money loaned to him by the commanders of the Marseille ship.

Without further delay, we went to find the Trinitarians, Commanders Mailland and Riboüillet, and the Sieur Picquet at the house of the Sieurs Constant and Hauterive. There, we completed the necessary formalities. Fathers Lucien and Boniface officially ransomed the Sieur de Cahaignes for 800 ecu, a price that did not include the taxes and duties added on that were required, which amounted to an extra 150 crowns. I did not cost nearly that much. Commanders Mailland and Riboüillet gave as payment for my freedom 100 crowns worth of opium, coral, and woollen cloth instead of cash money.

The recovery of my freedom initially gave me such an excess of joy that I was unable to sleep. So impatient was I to get to a Christian country that I remained violently agitated. However, Fathers Lucien and Boniface encountered so many obstacles that we languished among the infidels for six whole weeks, trying to be as patient as we could while waiting for the occasion of our departure.

Finally, as the Ottoman Easter holidays [Ramadan] commenced, we were informed that the process of departure was about to begin. Fathers Lucien and Boniface ordered the redeemed slaves to gather with the Sieur Picquet and to be ready in three days for departure.

The day of our impatiently awaited embarkation being finally come, each of the redeemed slaves joined the crowd surrounding the Trinitarian Fathers. Baby chicks that take shelter under the shadow of the wings of the hen hurry no more than we did. The tears, wails and cries of rage on the part of the many remaining unransomed slaves were moderated somewhat by Father Lucien's promise to return promptly with more funds collected through public alms.

The sails and the rudder having been returned to the ship, we went aboard with Commanders Mailland and Riboüillet. The Fathers stayed a little longer, to deal with any last-minute problems or confusion that might arise, and also to try to console their unfortunate and desperate compatriots who were left behind.

Finally, the Fathers were rowed out to our ship and climbed aboard. After the Algiers port guards had completed one final inspection of the ship and had departed, the Commander gave the order to raise the sails.

And so I left Algiers, a free man, finally... after more than two years of miserable servitude.[1]

---

1. My translation is based on the French text contained in René du Chastelet des Boys, *L'Odyssée ou diversité d'aventures, rencontres et voyages en Europe, Asie et Afrique, divisée en quatre parties*, which was serialized in *Revue Africaine*, 1866-1870.

# Francis Brooks: Barbarian Cruelty

In early August, 1681, Francis Brooks, from Bristol, had the misfortune to be aboard a merchant ship that was captured by Algerine corsairs. At the time, Algiers had entered into a treaty with England, and so Algerine corsairs were legally obligated to leave English shipping alone. Some Algerine corsair captains simply ignored such treaties, however, for there was a simple way around them: capture the ship, take all the booty aboard it, sink it, and then transport the captives to a corsair port that did not have any treaty with England, and therefore would accept such captives without hesitation—like Salé.

This is what happened to Francis Brooks. The ship he was on did not flee the Algerine corsair ship when it approached because those onboard thought the treaty would protect them. By the time they realized their mistake, it was too late.

It was severely unfortunate timing for Brooks and those captured with him. Being a slave anywhere in North Africa in the seventeenth (or any other) century was a bad experience. Being a slave in Morocco in the last couple of decades of the seventeenth century was about as bad as it could get.

There was a new dynasty in power in Morocco at the time—the Alaouite dynasty (the same dynasty that rules Morocco today). In 1672, the second Alaouite Sultan, Moulay Ismail Ibn Sharif, came to power. Moulay Ismail had enormous ambitions, and he proved enormously effective at achieving those ambitions. He was also one of history's most brutal tyrants.

This sounds like a trite cliché, but in Moulay Ismail's case, there simply seems no other way to put it.

One of his grand ambitions was to build a palace in Meknes (located about 50 kilometres/30 miles southwest of Fez, in northern Morocco) that would dwarf Versailles (he had heard all about Versailles). He set about doing this by purchasing thousands of slaves and putting them to work constructing his dream palace. He was so committed to this dream that he regularly rode through the sprawling construction site personally overseeing things and—by all accounts—terrorizing everybody in sight.

After surviving a decade of miserable servitude, Brooks managed to escape Morocco and return to England, where he wrote a book, which he titled *Barbarian Cruelty: Being a True History of the Distressed Condition of the Christian Captives under the Tyranny of Mully Ishmael Emperor of Morocco.*

Brooks had such a bad time as a slave that he included the following in his preface to the reader:

The chiefest design of my publishing this book is to caution all seafaring men, whose particular voyages carry them into the Strait of Gibraltar, that they take all possible care not to be trapped by the subtle pirates who infest those coasts, where we unfortunately fell into their hands. Considering the barbarities those whom the pirates capture must expect to suffer from such merciless enemies, it will be in their surest interest to defend themselves to the utmost of their power, even to the last extremity, for death itself is to be preferred before that, or any other slavery.[1]

Here, then, is Francis Brooks' description of what it was like to be a slave under Moulay Ismail Ibn Sharif, whom he refers to simply as the Emperor or the Tyrant.

The poor Christian captives that are taken by any of those hellish pirates belonging to the Emperor of Morocco are brought up to Meknes, where they are kept at hard work from daylight in the morning till night carrying earth on their heads in great baskets, driven to and fro by barbarous negroes at the Emperor's order. When they are led by the negroes at night to their lodging, which is on the cold ground, in a vault or hollow place in the earth, laid over with great beams a-thwart, and iron bars over them, they are herded in there like sheep, and out again in the morning.

The slaves' food is bread made of old rotten barley, and their drink only water—when they can get it. Many times after they have been hurried to their work in the morning (not knowing whether they shall be able to bear their afflictions till night) and have survived and been driven back to their lodging, expecting rest, the Tyrant sends some of his negroes to hurry them out again to work, either to haul down walls, brace the gates, or the like, keeping them working both night and day many times without either bread or water—which is all their sustenance. Even after they have done all that, the negroes dare not to drive them home again before the Emperor gives the order, lest they be killed

---

1. Francis Brooks, *Barbarian Cruelty*, pp. xviii-xix.

for so doing. When they finally receive his order, they drive the slaves home and lock them up until daylight.

One day, coming to inspect matters (as he used constantly to do), although it was raining very hard, as the Emperor was going into one of the buildings, he saw the Master Workman and his assistants hoisting up a piece of timber. The rope that held it broke, and the timber fell, forcing the Emperor to suddenly retreat. He then sent for the Master Workman in a great passion, threatening him for taking no better care. The Master Workman returned he was as careful as he could be, saying it was a mischance he could not prevent. Nevertheless, the Emperor took a gun from out of the hands of one of his guards and shot the Master Workman to death.

He then went among the Christians, raving and threatening as if he would have killed them all, setting his negroes and guard to beat both the Moors and the Christians that were at work, which they did with such violence that many of them had their heads and arms miserably broken, making his building more like a slaughterhouse than a place of work. At the same time, he ran two of his Moors through with his lance. He made no more out of killing a man at his pleasure than out of killing a dog.

Every one of his black guards has a gun, and he has three or four lances which he carries with him, and several guns always ready charged, to kill with at his pleasure either the Christians or his own natives. When he falls out with his guard, he strips them, puts them in irons, and sets them to work.

He seldom returns home after his going out in a morning without killing some one or other, by running of them through with his lance, shooting them, or dragging them across the ground tied to a mule's tail, both men and women, seldom repenting for what he has done. The Emperor believes that if he kills anyone, he merits Heaven by so doing; but if any person should kill him, that person cannot avoid going to Hell. He has short sticks carried around for him daily, so that he can beat the poor slaves at his pleasure, which is hourly, to vex and punish them, delighting in nothing more.

Coming a certain time to view his work one day, this Tyrant demanded to know why it was progressing so slow. He was answered that several of the Christian slaves were fallen sick. Hearing this, he went to the place where they lay, which was underground, and ordered his negroes drag them out of that place. When the poor slaves, in such weak and feeble condition that they could barely stand on their legs, when hauled before him, he instantly killed seven of them, making of their resting-place a slaughterhouse. The very Moors themselves were terrified to see so inhuman and bloody an action.

The proverb says: 'The more rain, the more rest.' But God knows it was most commonly our lot to be driven and kept closest at our work when it rained. Yea, when it rained most hard, our work was nothing lessened, but the more increased. Besides the Christians, the Emperor set thousands of his own natives to work with great shovels and to carry earth on their heads in baskets from one place to another. And though it rain ever so fast, (there are heavy rains in the winter season) he will stay by them, setting his negroes to drive them with whips of small cords and with sticks from morning till night; and if he is of a mind to eat, he often sends home to his castle, and hath his victuals brought to him, lest the slaves should neglect his work.

In the Year 1688, the Tyrant, coming out one time to see his works, as constantly he did, examined the stuff they used instead of mortar: earth, lime, and sand mixed together, which they use to build their walls with. Taking up a handful thereof, he did not like it. Upon this, he sent his negroes to fetch the Master Workman to him, who, being hailed by the neck before him, he asked why more lime was not mixt with the earth. The Master Workman answered that he lacked lime, and that was the reason the stuff was no better. The Emperor then sent for the man responsible for the lime and demanded of him what the problem was. This man replied that he lacked mules to bring the lime. The Emperor then sent for the mules to see how many there were. One was missing, which a negro said he had at his house because it was lame. The Tyrant ordered several of his negro boys to hold this man fast, while he sent some of the rest to see if what the man said was true. When they found no mule, the Tyrant ordered the man to be immediately stripped unto his drawers and fastened to a mule's tail, which was done, and he was dragged for the space of half a mile to prison, there to remain. He had the Master Workman stretched out by four negroes, two at his hands and two at his feet, and beat him till he could not turn himself, bidding him take better care of his mules, saying that if, when he came again, he found such bad stuff for his work, he would cut off his head.

Immediately after this, the Emperor sent his negro boys to fetch the seventy Christians that were at hard labour making a wall. He asked for one of them who could speak his language. When a man volunteered, he examined him in like manner about the mortar. The man answered that he durst not reply for fear of acquainting him with the badness of it. So the Tyrant took one of the sticks he used to carry with him and, calling the slave a dog, bid him hold his head fare to strike at. Having struck that man down, he knocked down all the rest with his own hands and broke their heads so miserably that the place was all bloody like a butcher's stall. None of them durst make any resistance, for if they had, he would presently have killed them. He then bid them rise, saying that if they used any more such bad mortar in his work, he would kill them all.[2]

---

2. Francis Brooks, *Barbarian Cruelty,* pp. 39-62. I have modernized the vocabulary and spelling and mildly edited the original of this and the other excerpts from Brook's text that appear in this chapter.

*Barbarian Cruelty* mostly focuses on Brooks' experiences as a slave, but it also includes the stories of a number of other people, including a young woman. Narratives about female captives are uncommon. Brooks' offers a rare glimpse into the sort of thing that happened to women who were captured by Barbary corsairs.

❀

In the Year 1685, a ship was bound from London to Barbados, in which were four women, two of them being mother and daughter. One of those heathenish pirates meeting this ship, gave chase, and coming up to it, demanded to know from whence they came, and whither bound. They told the pirate they were from London, bound for Barbados. The pirate was Captain Venetia the younger, who had 300 men and 18 Guns. When the captain of the English ship inquired the same of the pirates, they told him that they came from Algiers. They then demanded that he show his Pass, and said he must hoist out his boat, for they saw that he was not provided with any guns with which to defend himself, and so could make no resistance.

When the English captain and some of his men came aboard, the pirate captain took them into his cabin and showed himself to be kind to them, giving them dates. In the meanwhile, his lieutenant and Moors girded their pistols and cutlasses on their waists, and in the Englishmen's boat rowed to the English ship and captured all who were aboard, including the four women.

The pirate captain asked who the young woman was, and whether she was married. Account being given him concerning her, he ordered her to be put in his cabin, lest any of his own barbarous crew should offer to lie with her, and after that he sailed away for Salé.

Being come there, the pirate captain arranged for all the men from the ship and the four women to be brought up to Meknes. The women were brought before the Emperor's Eunuchs, and an account given to the chief of them by the pirate captain that one of them was a virgin, and she was immediately sent to the Emperor's women. The Eunuch went to the Vice-Roy, acquainting him with how he had disposed of the virgin. The Vice-Roy ordered the other women to be brought to his house and ordered the negroes to drive the poor Christians to hard labour.

At night, they were locked up amongst the other Christian captives, having no sustenance allowed them for that day, and what their poor brethren offered them they could not eat, it being bread so bad that the beasts in that place refused to eat it. Between their diet and lodging on the cold ground, together with the negroes' hard usage, many of them fell sick. And to add to their extremity, were threatened and abused by the negroes to turn Moors [i.e., convert to Islam]. They daily prayed to God to strengthen them in their afflictions and that in his great mercy he might work some way for their deliverance out of this dreadful bondage.

Afterwards, the chief eunuch sent word to the Emperor that he had a Christian virgin amongst the rest of his women. The Emperor ordered him to send her up to the camp where he was staying, with a parcel of his eunuchs to guard her thither. When she came to the camp, the Emperor urged her, tempting her with promises of great rewards if she would turn Moor and lie with him [sex with non-Muslim women was prohibited, even for the Sultan]. She earnestly desired of the Lord to preserve and strengthen her to resist his persuasions and proposals, which he offered in order to have his desires fulfilled.

When he could not prevail upon her, he fell to threatening her, and put her amongst his negro women, and he threatened to kill them if they offered to show her any kindness. These women kept her, beating and abusing her for several days. She prayed still to the Lord to strengthen her and maintained her resolution to withstand him.

The Emperor again sought to prevail with her, tempting her and promising her great things if she would turn, which she still refused. So he caused her to be stripped and whipped by his eunuchs with small cords, for so long till she lay for dead. He then caused her to be carried away out of his presence and charged his women that none of them should help her till he sent for her, which was not till two days after. In the meantime, she had no sustenance but that black rotten bread.

At length, the Emperor sought again to prevail with promises and threats, which she still withstood, praying to the Lord that she might be preserved from him, and be delivered from his cruel hands. Then he pricked her with such things as commonly his women use instead of pins, being just as sharp. Thus this beastly and inhuman Tyrant, by all ways he could invent, sought to force her to yield, which she resisted so long, till tortures and the hazards of her life eventually forced her to yield and resign her body to him, though her heart was otherwise inclined.

So he had her washed and clothed in their fashion of apparel, and he lay with her.

Having his desire fulfilled, he inhumanly, and in great haste, forced her away out of his presence. She being with child, he sent her by his eunuchs to Meknes, where they presented her to the chief Eunuch. After that, she was delivered of two children.[3]

3. Francis Brooks, *Barbarian Cruelty*, pp. 27-34.

That is the whole of the story Brooks relates about the young 'virgin'.

It is telling that he does not reveal to us anything about the other women, and that he does not continue the 'virgin's' story much past her deflowering and pregnancy. In fact, he does not really seem all that interested in the women themselves. He never provides their names or says anything at all about their characters. The only information about them that matters is that one of them is a virgin.

What Brooks seems to really be doing here is recounting a melodramatic morality tale: one in which a pure Christian heroine is besmirched by a wicked Muslim villain. Despite that, however, the general outlines of this story are probably pretty accurate. The Moroccan Sultan, Moulay Ismail Ibn Sharif, was renowned for several things: his grand architectural ambitions, his cruelty, and his enormous harem. By all accounts, he treated his women no better than he treated anybody else, and the poor 'virgin's' treatment was probably pretty common—including her abrupt dismissal once Moulay Ismail had had his way with her.

The general outlines of this story are accurate in another, more general, sense as well: in North Africa, young and attractive female captives—anywhere from as young as eleven or twelve to thirty or so—were much sought after as sex toys. Young boys were as well. Both fetched high prices in the slave markets, and both were offered as presents to curry favour with important men—in this case, no lesser a personage than the Sultan himself.

Such were the times.

# Elizabeth Marsh:
# The Female Captive

There are few captivity narratives about women, and even fewer written by the women themselves. Accounts like that in Francis Brooks' *Barbarian Cruelty* about the unhappy young 'virgin' are rare. The unfortunate fact of the matter is that throughout the time of the Barbary corsairs' ascendency—roughly from the early 1500s to the early 1800s—European captivity narratives tended to be written by men, about men, for men.

There are a few exceptions, though.

One is a first-person narrative written by Elizabeth Marsh, a young English woman who was captured by Barbary corsairs in 1756 and, eventually, wrote a book, titled *The Female Captive: A Narrative of Facts Which Happened in Barbary in the Year 1756, Written by Herself*, in which she described her experience.

Marsh's family were not wealthy, but they aspired to be 'respectable people', and she received what could be termed a genteel education. Her fate was to marry a man and tie her (and her family's) fortunes to him. Before that happened, though, when she was only twenty-one and engaged but not yet married, she had the bad luck to be aboard a ship captured by corsairs from Salé.

Marsh's experience as a captive was similar—though not identical—to that of the 'virgin' in Brooks' story. As a young, attractive European woman, Marsh would have been a highly prized (and highly expensive) commodity in any North African slave market—and exactly the kind of woman the Moroccan Sultan would be very, very interested in acquiring for his harem.

Marsh's narrative—the longest one in this book—provides a woman's perspective on what it was like to be in such a situation.

I have added a fairly extensive series of explanatory footnotes laying out the historical background to the events she describes. You can make sense of the story without consulting these notes, but they provide details about the Mediterranean and Morocco that help make both the events themselves and the motivations of the various characters clearer and more meaningful. As with other extracts in this book, I have abridged the original somewhat to streamline the story and have modernized the spelling and language to make it clearer for modern readers.

Here, then, is Elizabeth Marsh's narrative.

I was the daughter of a gentleman whose principles and abilities procured him a very respectable employment under the government, on the island of Minorca. We resided in this place until a war commenced between Great Britain and France, which occasioned our removal, for our safety, to the Garrison of Gibraltar.[1] We had been happily situated in Minorca, and this change would have been very disagreeable to me if I had not been engaged to a gentleman who was stationed in Gibraltar,[2] and the pleasing hopes of meeting him made my departure less irksome for me than it otherwise might have been.

I was, therefore, greatly disappointed on my arrival to find him gone. However, his servant, whom he had left behind, delivered me a letter in which he informed me of his having been obliged to sail to England, and he earnestly requested that I follow him as soon as I conveniently could.

At that time, an opportunity presented itself in the form of a merchant ship which, along with many others, was to be convoyed as far as Lisbon. The fact that a friend of my family, a Mr. Crisp,[3] was going as a passenger convinced me to solicit my family's permission for me to return to England. At first, they were unwilling to grant this, but knowing Mr. Crisp was to go on the same ship, to whose care they thought I could be entrusted, they eventually consented, and my father acquainted that gentleman with his intention. He, with great pleasure, accepted the charge, and he assured my father that nothing which he could prevent should happen to me while I was under his protection.

The time of our departure arrived, and I parted with my family and embarked on board the ship.[4] We were supposed to be part of the convoy protected by a naval warship, but we were unhappily deserted by that ship soon after we lost sight of the Garrison at Gibraltar. When our captain perceived the warship's

---

1. The war that 'commenced between Great Britain and France' was the Seven Years' War (1756-1763), known in North America as the French Indian War. The removal of the Marsh family and other British subjects from Minorca, which was then a British possession, turned out to be a sensible precaution, for the French captured the island a couple of months after they left it.

2. Marsh's fiancé was a Captain Henry Towry, of the Royal Navy.

3. James Crisp came from a successful merchant family. Though Marsh makes no mention of it in her narrative, Crisp had apparently proposed to her while she was living in Minorca, and she had turned him down in favour of Captain Towry. Crisp was in fact the captain of the ship—a smallish merchant ship named the *Ann*—that took Marsh away from Gibraltar rather than a mere passenger. Marsh published *The Female Captive* anonymously, and she purposefully omitted or obscured personal biographical details.

4. The *Ann* left Gibraltar on July 27.

intention of leaving us, he put on all the sail he could in an unsuccessful attempt to keep up with it, so much so that our lives were endangered, for there was six feet of water in the hold before anyone knew of it, which obliged the sailors to be at the pumps, and only with much difficulty did they save the ship from sinking.

I was entirely ignorant of the danger we had been in until it was over, when my friend [Mr. Crisp] told me of the alarm that we had met with and that it proceeded from the ship having crowded on too much sail.

From this fateful accident, I date the whole of my misfortunes, for very soon after that, our ship was chased by a vessel which our captain at first imagined to be a French privateer, but on further inspection found it to be a Sally rover [a corsair ship from Salé].[5] This vessel soon caught up to us, and it was thought more prudent to wait for them than, by trying to escape, run a risk of being put to death if they should attack us, for their ship was well armed and the men aboard very numerous.[6]

The Moorish commander instantly came on board our ship and inquired into the number of passengers. Our captain thought it proper to bring him into the cabin where we were waiting, and, after asking a number of unnecessary questions, the Moorish commander told the gentleman (there being two others besides my friend)[7] that they were to accompany him to his ship. He promised only to detain them for half an hour, upon which they attended him.

I made myself tolerably easy until night drew on, when fear seized my spirit at their not returning at the time appointed. I continued in that state until morning, which brought on new afflictions, for instead of seeing the gentlemen returning, I saw boats crowded with Moors rowing towards our ship. They came aboard, and the sailors from our ship were sent on board theirs.

In this miserable situation, I remained for three days, until I had the pleasure to finally see my friend return. He told me that he had, with much difficulty, obtained leave from the Admiral of the corsair cruiser to visit me, telling him that I was his sister. But his permission was under restrictions. My friend stayed and dined with me, but then he unwillingly took his leave, the time being elapsed which had been granted him. I was in great distress at this second separation through dread of being exposed to those merciless Moors who would certainly have behaved very insolently had it not been for our ship's steward, who was a good man and prevented them from tormenting me with their impertinent discourses.

As soon as the next day dawned, the Admiral and officers of the corsair cruiser came on board and brought an interpreter with them who, in bad

---

5. Marsh's fateful encounter with the Salé corsairs happened on August 8.

6. The Salé ship was armed with twenty cannons and had a crew of over 100. The *Ann* was a smallish merchant ship, unarmed, with a crew of only about a dozen. There was no practical way for them to resist the corsairs.

7. The other two passengers aboard the *Ann* were an Irishman named Joseph Popham and his son William.

English, told me I must go with them. This alarmed me exceedingly. I desired to know what they intended to do with us and reminded them that a truce had lately been concluded between the courts of Great Britain and Morocco.[8] The corsair Admiral replied that no harm would be done me, but that they simply wanted our assistance in navigating their ship, for they had missed their coast. I did not know whether to believe this or not, but, having little in the way of choice, I acceded to his command.

In the ship's boat, I was greatly terrified by the sea, for we were some considerable distance from the wretched abode of my unhappy countrymen, and the waves looked like veritable mountains, often hindering my seeing the vessel we were going to. When I came on board, my disconsolate friend received me, his countenance sufficiently denoting the anguish of his mind. I had summoned up all my fortitude on so shocking an occasion, but the sight of our sailors tied together drew tears from me, notwithstanding my resolution to the contrary, and my appearance had the same effect on them.

My friend led me to the cabin allotted to us, which was so small it did not allow us even to stand upright. In this miserable place, four people were to live. Provisions were likewise extremely bad, being a kind of paste resembling Sago and dressed something like a *pilaw*. The Moors called it *cuscusu* [couscous]. It was mixed with bad butter and served in a wooden dish for our lunch, and it was then again repeated for supper. My appetite, however, was not keen enough to partake of this sort of diet, for I felt very ill and fatigued from seasickness and want of rest.

My friend did all in his power to render my situation tolerable. I wish I could say as much in praise of another of my fellow captives, but he seemed to delight in terrifying me with stories of the cruelties of the Moors and the dangers my sex was exposed to in Barbary.

I passed many days in a very uncomfortable manner, having vile accommodations and no provision which I could eat—save for almonds and raisins, which were my only support. On the fourteenth, we saw land, and soon after we were off the town called Marmora. The corsairs fired two guns and hoisted their colours. At nine o'clock in the evening, their ship anchored in the Salé road.[9]

---

8. Marsh is likely referring here to the treaty concluded in 1750 between Great Britain and Morocco and to the Additional Articles of Peace and Commerce agreed to in 1751 by the English King George II and the Moroccan Sultan Moulay Abdallah (the father of Prince Sidi Mohammed, who plays a prominent role later in Marsh's narrative). Sultan Moulay Abdallah and Prince Sidi Mohammed were members of the Alaouite dynasty, a dynasty that still rules Morocco today.

9. Marmora is modern-day Mehdya, located on the Atlantic coast of Morocco about 210 kilometres/130 miles south of the Strait of Gibraltar. Salé is modern Rabat-Salé, located about 32 kilometres/ twenty miles further south of Marmora/Mehdya. The 'road' was the stretch of water outside a harbour where ships could anchor.

Boats immediately came out from land, beating drums and sounding a sort of music which pleased those infidels but struck me with the greatest terror imaginable. I learned that this rejoicing proceeded from our being brought in, as it is customary with them to make proclamations of joy upon such occasions.

My spirits were violently agitated. Perceiving this, the Moorish Admiral told me in his uncouth way to be of good cheer, for all would be well by and by.

We remained on board that night. The next morning, we were ordered to our own ship to take what necessaries we thought proper, which I was thankful for, as I wanted a change of clothing. I stayed in the ship's boat that brought us across while my friend endeavoured to get what was needed. He found it impossible, however, and therefore only procured a small quantity for present use, as well as our bedding, but he was not permitted to take any provisions or liquor.

We then left our ship, and they ordered us ashore. But the tide would not permit our passing the bar, and therefore we were obliged to anchor and remain there for three hours exposed to the scorching sun—with no fresh water, and my thirst intolerable. I implored Heaven for relief or for assistance to support my misfortunes with patience, which the Almighty requires of us whenever He thinks it proper to afflict us. We were tossed about for a considerable time and then, with difficulty, passed the bar, it being very dangerous. They landed us on a sandy beach which I believe might extend half a mile, and which was covered with some thousands of Moors shouting and hallooing like so many infernals. [10]

My friend did all he could to keep my spirits up and displayed the courage and resignation which proved him to be what I had ever found him: a man of honour and a Christian. When we landed, I was almost smothered with dust, and I was put upon a mule without a saddle. My friend was placed upon another, and he kept as near to me as he could. A man rode on each side of me to guard me from falling. In this manner, we travelled two miles over heavy sand. A band of

---

10. Salé was located on the south bank of the Bou Regreg River, which flows northwestwards into the Atlantic Ocean from its headwaters in the Middle Atlas Mountains. The river carried considerable quantities of silt. This created a shifting sand bar across the river mouth that ships had to cross over in order to get to the docks, which were some little ways upriver. Calm seas and a high tide were needed to cross the bar safely; otherwise, it could present a dangerous obstacle. Events as described by Marsh are not very clear, but it seems that she and her friend were conveyed from the Salé corsair ship in which they were being held to their own ship in a 'jolly boat'—a ship's boat about 5.5 metres (eighteen feet) long, propelled by oars. They were then stranded in the jolly boat, waiting for the tide to turn so that there would be sufficient depth of water over the bar for them to cross it safely. Typically, captives brought into Salé were taken directly to the docks upriver. Marsh and those with her seem to have been landed on the beach in the jolly boat because their captors wanted to get them ashore as quickly as possible and decided not to wait until the tide was high enough to float the corsair ship across the bar.

their musicians went before us, playing music more dismal, in my opinion, than a funeral march. The insults of the populace were intolerable. The other passengers were on foot, and our sailors were dragged along and used with severity.

We proceeded to the Pashaw's [the Governor of Salé's] residence, who received us with seeming concern. After going through the customary ceremonies, he ordered his guards to conduct us to a place about half a mile off. All the way, we were entertained with a confused noise of women's voices from the tops of the houses, which surprised me very much until I was informed it was a testimony of joy upon the arrival of a female captive.

When we got to the habitation destined for us, the door was open, and a long dark passage presented itself to our view, at the end of which was a square ground floor with two rooms opposite each other and a gallery at the top. No words, however, can properly express the wretchedness of the place. The best of the rooms was allotted to me and the other passengers, and the rest for our servants and the ship's crew. A strong guard stood at the door and examined everyone who came in. Soon after, a slave brought some grapes, bread, and a picture of water, all of which he placed before us and then retired.

I endeavoured to reconcile myself to this most severe turn of fortune as well as my age and the circumstances of my case would admit by trying to submit to my unhappy fate. But my heart was faint within me.

In the evening, to our great surprise, we received a very genteel letter from Mr. Mountney in Old Salé, along with a present of provisions and wine, refreshments which were very agreeable, as I have not tasted much of anything solid since the day we were taken.[11]

At the same time, I had a visit from the Admiral, the hated monster who had brought me to this country, attended by most of the principal Moors of the place. He assured me we should have our liberty as soon as the Prince's answer was returned to a letter which they had sent to Morocco concerning our being

---

11. In the eighteenth century, the situation in Morocco was complicated. Moroccan corsairs regularly attacked European ships, especially the corsairs operating out of Salé—known to the English as the Sally rovers. At the same time, however, Morocco had not only negotiated treaties with various European powers but was also involved in numerous legitimate commercial enterprises with European merchants and traders. In order to conduct such business, European companies needed to have commercial representatives *in situ* in Morocco. Mr. Mountney was one of these commercial representatives. He lived in Old Salé, a city located on the north shore of the Bou Regreg River, across from Salé (which was referred to as New Salé). Such commercial representatives not only oversaw business operations but also sometimes acted as unofficial consuls and facilitators. Mountney was not in a position to push for the release of Marsh and her companions, but he was able to offer them aid. Marsh received help from a number of such European commercial representatives during her time in Morocco. She refers to them simply as 'merchants'.

brought in.[12] They then took their leave, and I had some little time to myself, which I employed in preparing my things in the most comfortable manner the place could afford. I endeavoured to rest, but the fatigues of the preceding day had made me ill and deprived me of that happiness.

On the next day, we had the pleasure to see Mr. Mountney and Monsieur Ray, merchants of Old Salé.[13] The former was an English gentleman and therefore much concerned about our situation. The latter was of the French nation and behaved with the politeness peculiar to it. The other unfortunate captives, as well as myself, experienced many proofs of their generous friendship. They passed the day with me and my friend, and they gave us hope that his Imperial Highness's answer to the Salé Admiral's letter would be favourable, and that he would undoubtedly order us our liberty. This news induced me to be a little cheerful.

But this interval of tranquillity did not last, for when the gentleman left us, my apartment was crowded with men women and children, nor could I prevail (even by bribery) on those villains our guards to prevent it.

Among the number of my tormentors was a nephew of the Moorish Admiral, a man devoid of any sentiment of honour or honesty. He brought others of his own disposition to assist in separating us from our baggage, in order no doubt to plunder it. But my friend insisted that they should not take possession of it unless they had the Admiral's or the Governor's order in writing. This baffled his expectations, and he left us, much offended.

Our friends, the two merchants, advised us to write to the Garrison at Gibraltar and said that they would provide a courier who should safely convey our letters there. But they cautioned us to be very silent, lest our guards should suspect what we were doing. We accordingly passed the night in writing to my family, to my Lord Tyrawley, Governor of Gibraltar, and to Admiral Hawke, in command of his Britannic Majesty's fleet in the Mediterranean. By night's end, we had our packets finished and ready to deliver.[14]

---

12. The 'Prince' was Sidi Mohammed ben Abdallah, son of the Moroccan Sultan Moulay Abdallah (who had signed the treaties with England in the early 1750s). In the summer/ autumn of 1756, when Marsh was in Morocco, Sultan Moulay Abdallah resided in Fez, in northern Morocco. Sidi Mohammed was Governor of Marrakesh, in central Morocco. Sultan Moulay Abdallah was aging—he died in his sixties in 1757—and Sidi Mohammed was already beginning to unofficially assume the role of Sultan. So it was to him that the Salé corsair 'Admiral' (i.e., captain of the corsair ship) communicated the capture of Marsh and her companions. In Marsh's time, the city of Marrakesh was known as Morocco, so when she refers to 'Morocco,' she is referring to Marrakesh.

13. Monsieur Ray was another commercial representative.

14. Whatever letter(s) Elizabeth Marsh wrote disappeared long ago, but those written by Joseph Popham (the Irishman who, along with his son, was captured with Marsh) and James Crisp (Marsh's 'friend') have (amazingly enough) survived. They can be found in the National Archives at Kew, in London: SP 71/20, Part 1, fols. 65, 67, 69, and FB fol. 21.

Mr. Ray was with us early the next morning, attended by three Danish gentlemen. He brought provisions of wine and fruit. They favoured us with their company until lunch and added to the repast by their agreeable conversation. We passed the day tolerably easy, and I flatter myself after they left us that I should soon get some rest. But that satisfaction was prevented by the lower sort of people being very intruding and extremely troublesome. My friend often attempted to prevent their admittance, but he was always ill treated and never able to succeed.

We had an invitation from the Captain of the Port, for he desired to see us. We therefore waited on him the next day and found him sitting on a carpet. He immediately rose upon our entrance and guided me to a cushion. He conversed a little time with my friend in Spanish[15] and then, conducting me to the apartment of his ladies, introduced me to them and retired.

One of these ladies drew my attention as much as I seemed to do hers. She was surprisingly tall and stout, with a broad flat face, very dark complexion, and long dark hair. She wore a dress resembling a clergyman's gown, made of muslin, and buttoned at the neck, like the collar of a shirt, which reached to her feet. She had bracelets on her arms and legs and was extremely inquisitive and serious in examining my dress and person and seemed highly entertained by my appearance.

When she had finished, I was permitted to leave and was again shown to the room where the Moor and my friend were sitting. I found preparations had been made for supper, which was a collation after the Moorish taste and consisted of a dish of *cuscusu* and fowls mixed with butter and sugar. The other dishes were of different sorts of fruit and some sweetmeats. I ate a little to complement him, having heard that they esteem it a favour for Christians to partake of their repasts when invited.

This honest Moor, for such I thought him, often expressed infinite concern regarding my misfortune and would readily have rendered me a service, but though he was a man of high station and Captain of the Port, he did not dare openly to pity our distress on account of the dread these people live with in regard to each other. This is the reason that the good men in the country (who I believe are but few) show not the least signs of humanity for Christians, for they fear to suffer ill-treatment from those, who are very numerous, who set less value on Christians than they do on dogs.

---

15. In the early 1600s, close to 15,000 Spanish speaking Moriscos, exiled from Spain, had settled in Salé, and Spanish was still the common language in Salé at this time. There is some indication that James Crisp might have been born in Spain. Whatever the reason, he was apparently fluent in both Castilian and Catalan. So it is no coincidence that the slaves he later ends up communicating with—and on whose aid and advice the captives rely—are of Spanish origin.

When we parted from the Captain of the Port, I underwent a second mortifying examination, at another house, from their indelicate women. My friend, on our coming ashore, had taken on himself the character of my brother in order to be of some little protection to me. He was therefore always permitted to wait without until they thought it proper to release me, and I accordingly found him there, where he had been waiting with the utmost impatience for my dismissal, ready to attend me.

We hastened to our place of confinement, where I passed the night with many afflicting thoughts and confused ideas of what another day might produce. Indeed, my anxieties were not groundless, for before I had breakfasted, the Moorish Admiral's nephew, with a great number of others, made us a visit. He insisted on placing us in another apartment and leaving our baggage under guard in the room we were then in. This behaviour raised various conjectures of what they intended by acting in such a matter. My friend endeavoured, by many just arguments, to prevent their designs. But this only served to heighten their malice, and they redoubled their insults. This obliged us to acquiesce, and as every other means but patience was wrested from us, we had no other recourse save that sovereign remedy for all the calamities of life.

The room appointed to us, as I have already observed, was much the best in the prison in which they chose to keep us. It had, however, one end of the ceiling open, occasioned by an earthquake. I found this a great inconvenience from the dew and caught a violent cold.

The Moorish Admiral gave positive orders that none of our friends should be admitted. This they strictly observed, and when some gentleman came to visit us, they were treated with great indignity and obliged to return without being permitted even to leave a message. The Moors carried their cruelty to such lengths as to hinder our servants from going out to procure us the necessities of life. At the same time, however, they did not prevent the rabble from entering my apartment at any hour.

My friend had recourse to bribery and paid our guards very handsomely,[16] but this notwithstanding, they were base enough to admit a great number of people and continue to deny us the pleasure of seeing our friends, which was a distressing circumstance and threw me into a dejected state. My cold daily worsened, and I could get no assistance for it.

Being deprived of the satisfaction of the company of the gentlemen who had shown as so many civilities grieved me much, so I tried what a further gratuity

---

16. At this point, the status of Marsh and her companions has yet to be officially determined. They are being detained, but they are not treated as outright prisoners and have not been robbed of their possessions or their money—so Crisp has ready cash on hand to use for bribes.

might do. This fortunately had the desired effect, and we were so happy as to see Mr. Mountney and Monsieur Ray again that same evening. They gave their opinion that the Admiral of the corsair ship had no authority for taking us and advised that we should be as cheerful as possible, for they were certain our detention would be of short duration. We therefore flattered ourselves that it would prove so, and I tried to keep my spirits up.

The next morning, a Spanish *renegado* came in great haste to tell my friend that he had heard there was an hourly expectation of a person of consequence from Morocco [Marrakesh] who was to conduct us safely onboard our ship and protect us from the mob. This intelligence in no way elevated my spirit, as I was possessed of the notion that the news wanted further confirmation to be believed. Soon after this, my friend received a letter from Mr. Ray informing him of a messenger who had arrived from Morocco whose mission was to convey us there.

We had just got this information when his approach was announced to us. Entering with the Governor of the place and many others, he told us that we must prepare in five days for a journey to Morocco and that he was one of those delegated to escort us on our journey. His orders, which were from his Imperial Highness, were to travel gently on my account, resting in the day and proceeding during the night, so that I might not be too fatigued.

This was some little comfort for my afflicted heart, but I was terrified beyond expression. The messenger, perceiving this, flattered me with hopes that as soon as the Moorish Sovereign had seen me, which I was made to believe was all that he wanted, I should be sent back immediately to Salé with liberty to leave Barbary.

They then left us, and the Almighty ordained that I should receive consolation from the lies told us by this barbarian. For such is the composition of the human mind that where there is the least glimmer of hope, we love to cherish it, and it is happy that we do so, for otherwise souls endowed with a superior share of sensibility instead of surmounting difficulties or bearing distress with fortitude would be plunged into despair in the hours of affliction—a calamity which those of less elevated sentiments would be exempt from.

We were now favoured with the company of Don Pedro, a slave from Minorca, who was at Salé trading on behalf of his Imperial Highness. This man was uncommonly affected by my unhappy situation and was of infinite service to us, both as an interpreter and a friend. He prevented our baggage from being plundered and saved us from receiving many insults which undoubtedly would have been offered us but for his protection.

Don Pedro told my friend that I should be in less danger of injury in Morocco if he said he was my husband rather than my brother. My friend replied that he imagined I should be entirely safe by his appearing in the character he did now, and that as he had been examined by the principal people at Salé concerning the truth of it, it was too late now to alter that scheme.

The conversation then lagged, and Don Pedro left us. But his advice, and the manner in which he had given it, greatly alarmed me, and I earnestly wished to be removed from a world where I have no reason to expect any felicity.

Tears gave me some relief, but I remained in a very melancholy condition till the dawning of the day and a severe shock of the earth gave a turn to my thoughts and roused me from the state of despondence I had indulged in the preceding night and occasioned some religious reflections which in great measure resigned me to my state.

We received a very kind invitation from Mr. Mountney and Monsieur Ray to visit them before our departure, and we solicited the Moorish Admiral for permission, which he agreed to. We then asked if he would allow us to take our baggage, to which he likewise consented. However, when we applied to his nephew, offering him a handsome present, he refused to deliver.

Monsieur Ray came to convey me and my friend to their house, but I first was made to attend the Moorish Admiral and submit to another inspection by Moorish women. Monsieur Ray accompanied me there, and I made this mortifying visit as short as possible.

We had then a burning sand to walk over, and I was almost scorched to death with the sun before we reached the beach. Unfortunately, the boat we were to take was aground when we arrived, which obliged us to sit there nearly an hour till the tide changed. After that, though, we soon landed on the opposite shore, where I was received with the greatest respect by a number of merchants of all nations.[17] I thought myself happy, not only on being delivered from my detested prison but also by the satisfaction of being with Christians.

Many gentlemen of the place were invited to supper with Mr. Mountney and Monsieur Ray, and we were entertained with as much elegance as such a place could allow. After this, I retired.

We had many invitations from the gentleman of that place to dine with them before we left the town, and I was sorry I could not have that pleasure, but my time was very short, and a great deal of preparation had to be made for the long journey ahead.

The Governor of Salé, a good old gentleman, waited on us with a letter that he had received from Morocco ordering that the greatest care to be taken of

---

17. New Salé was located on the south bank of the Bou Regreg River. To reach Old Salé, on the north bank, Marsh and her companions had to take a small ferry boat that had previously been moored near the river shore. The tide had gone out, stranding it, and Marsh and company were forced to wait until the tide had risen enough to float the boat free. Mr. Mountney and Monsieur Ray were part of the community of European commercial representatives who lived in Old Salé—hence the 'number of merchants of all nations' who received them.

the captives, and especially of me. He was a very solicitous companion and stayed and drank coffee and assured us he would do everything in his power to contribute to our peace.

We were told that the ship we had been captured on was brought over the bar and was plundered of every valuable thing on board. A large quantity of excellent wines of different sorts the Moors had sold by the dozen to some Dutch ships that lay in the harbour, but we could not prevail on them to let us have any part of it.

Monsieur Ray passed much time in contriving to have a man's saddle altered into a woman's, after the Spanish fashion, for me to ride on. We found great difficulty in getting our baggage from the Admiral's nephew and, as no arguments had the least weight with him, my friend made him a considerable gratuity, money being the one thing that motivated him in all his actions.

On the 30th of that month [August], we left the town of Salé.

I was deeply affected by our parting from our hospitable friends. They had been so solicitous as to provide plentiful provisions for the journey we were about to undertake, and they also made us a present of a tent along with all the necessities belonging thereunto.

These gentlemen, attended by the Governor, walked with us as we left the town in order to keep the crowd, which was prodigiously great, in some sort of order. When we were a quarter of a mile from the place, we parted and mounted the mules provided for us. My friend, the other passengers, and the ship's company rode on pack saddles, I on the saddle that Mr. Ray had contrived for me—though we had not proceeded many miles before I discovered that it was most uncomfortable. But I thought it useless to complain, as there appeared no remedy.

We stopped at seven o'clock in the evening on a large plain, where we decided to pitch our tent. The road had been tolerably good, but we had travelled at the tedious rate of four miles an hour.

Our trusted friend Don Pedro, the slave of the Prince, had accompanied us thus far, and I believe he would gladly have remained with us, since he well knew the many inconveniences we should be exposed to without his assistance. He seemed remarkably pensive and very observant of me, which I was at first displeased with and thought his behaviour ungenteel—until I overhead what he said in conversation with my friend, which was much to the following effect:

'Sir, I must beg you excuse the liberty I am about to take and to be attentive to some advice I must offer you concerning this young lady. As a Christian, I cannot but be deeply affected by your misfortunes, but the danger to which your fair companion is exposed gives me inexpressible concern. I therefore hope you will be persuaded to comply with my instructions.

'The anxiety I am under on her account induced me to accompany you as far as this day's journey, and I wish from my soul it was in my power to continue it with you, but as that cannot be, I have determined once more to represent to you how very necessary it is for her safety that you should pass for her husband.

'I have been a slave to Sidi Mohammed since the year 1750, and you must conclude that I cannot be unacquainted with his temper and his inclinations. Such, I can assure you, is his despotic power that if she is at all to be preserved from being detained in the Seraglio, it must be by the means above proposed.'[18]

My friend argued the impossibility of his acting the part of my husband, as he had hitherto publicly assumed the character of my brother.

That difficulty was obviated, however, by Don Pedro assuring him that he would undertake to settle the matter: namely, by writing a letter to Juan Arvona, a fellow slave in Morocco, and giving it in confidence to a Moor who was in the caravan, advising this Moor to be as expeditious as possible in delivering this letter in order that he might be there a day or two before us.

In this letter to the said slave, Don Pedro would desire him to acquaint the Prince with the fact that my friend and I had been misrepresented and that we were married and had been going to settle in England when we were captured. Don Pedro would give the Moor at the same time instructions to spread this report in the palace and throughout the city of Morocco.

My friend, seeing me affected by this conversation, addressed himself to me in a very earnest manner, begging me to be assured of his honour and that no conduct of his would give me the least cause for offense. He only wished to preserve and deliver me safe into the arms of my afflicted parents. He also said that if I approved of what the slave Don Pedro advised, the other passengers, the master, and the seamen would all be acquainted with this deception so that, in case of an examination, everyone might be in on the same story.

This sudden change in my situation shocked me beyond expression, and I could only answer with my tears. My heart was too deeply oppressed for me to

---

18. Prince Sidi Mohammed was powerful enough and wealthy enough to possess a large harem (the 'Seraglio'). Don Pedro knows the Prince wants to add Marsh to that harem. Sidi Mohammed could not just arbitrarily force Marsh to become one of his women, however. There were Quranic rules regarding such matters. Verse 4:24, for example, states the following: 'Also forbidden to you are women already married, except those whom your right hands possess.' The phrase 'those whom your right hands possess' is a standard way in the Quran of referring to slaves. At this point, Elizabeth Marsh is not a slave. So if she and her friend, Mr. Crisp, can maintain the fiction that they are married, Prince Sidi Mohammed cannot take her for his harem—for to do so would contravene the Quranic injunction.

be able to give an opinion for or against the idea of it. Indeed, I was unable to determine whether I was for or against it.

Upon reflection, however, the arguments of Don Pedro appeared very reasonable, and I thought it most prudent to submit to his judgment and accede to what he thought to be the most expedient pretext, given the extremity of our situation.

After that, we sat up the remainder of the night settling this affair with Don Pedro.

Very early the next morning, he took a friendly leave of us, recommending me to the protection of Divine Providence and the care of my friend. After that, we mounted our mules and took the road to Morocco.

Some little time afterwards, I had the misfortune to be thrown from my mule, by which accident I was on the point of being killed. My friend instantly jumped off his mount to assist me. He entreated our guides to stop for me to recover myself, but this they would not agree to. Instead, they told us that we would pitch the tent early in the evening. (My fall was occasioned by the fellow who led my mule, for he held a grudge against me for complaining of him back at Salé, while he was one of our guards.)

I therefore was again re-seated upon my mount, but in great pain. My friend continued his importunities for a short respite, telling our guides I should certainly die if they did not stop soon. I was incapable of speaking, and my tears never ceased for some hours, on account of the ill treatment I had received. They merely continued assuring us with promises that we should soon stop.

Instead, we travelled for many hours over dangerous deserts, and the roarings of the different kinds of wild beasts in the mountains filled me with terror.

After all that had happened to me, and was likely to happen, I earnestly invoked Heaven to put an end to my days, which promised me such a dismal prospect of nothing but misery, and though I was so far preserved, yet it was only for still greater sorrows to come.

Our guards eventually permitted us to dismount, and I, being extremely ill, desired my friend to entreat them to stop so that my tent might be pitched, but they told him it could not be done, as they should only rest an hour at that place and then set off again. Our conductors, however, assured us, that they would stop for the night at a castle five miles farther. By this ill-natured artifice, they persuaded us to proceed, though no castle was seen, or so much as a house, or even a track where any human foot had ever been. The howlings in the mountains and dread of the wild Arabs greatly afflicted us, and I often melted into tears at my sufferings. Whenever my friend observed this, he endeavoured to relieve me by many kind words, soliciting me to be as composed as possible, and to rely on Providence to extricate us from our afflictions.

We travelled all that night until ten o'clock the next day. When they lifted me off my mule, I could not stand on account of the violence of the pain in the side on which I fell.

The Moorish Admiral (he who had originally captured us), observing that I was very ill, ordered a tent to be pitched, and allowed me two hours for my repose. But I could not rest, the uncertainty of my fate continually employing my thoughts and keeping me awake. When my time was expired, a messenger came to tell me I must proceed.

I told him they acted contrary to the Prince's orders, and probably would kill me before they reached Morocco. At this, he seemed to be shocked and was rather inclined to be compassionate. However, the great number who were for proceeding overpowered him, and he hurried from me.

My friend asked the interpreter what their reason was for going at the rate they did. He answered that the feast of the Ramadan was to begin in a few days, which occasioned their haste. It being a high festival at Morocco, everyone was desirous of being present for it.

Our caravan pressed on and passed over very high mountains and bad roads, until we came to a *duar*, or town of tents, where they told me they would procure me a machine such as the Moorish women make use of, instead of a saddle, on the road.

This machine was placed across my mule, over a pack, and held a small mattress. The Moorish women lie in it, as it may be covered by cloth. I sat with my feet on one side of the mule's neck, and I found it very proper to screen me from the Arabs, who would not now offer to come near me, imagining I was one of their own countrywomen going to Morocco. Had it not been for such a convenience, I could not have continued a journey of 300 miles in that rough part of the world.

At twelve o'clock that night, we stopped on account of my being fatigued, and, indeed, unable to proceed farther. I suffered more than can be expressed for the want of good water, for that they had with them was extremely nauseating from its being put into the hides of hogs, tarred on the inside, and slung across the mules. Bad as it was, I often accepted of it to moisten my mouth.

My friend had the tent pitched, and I should have been happy to get some rest, but the tiresome noises which the camels made (by reason of the heavy burdens those poor creatures are constrained to carry, who often lie down with their baggage on their backs for the night) prevented me from sleeping.

At break of day, the caravan began to stir, and, consequently, my tent was to be removed; and, as breakfast was a meal we were entirely unaccustomed to, we had little to do before we set out.

The heat of the sun, as the day advanced, was extremely great, which obliged our guards to stop at a large town of tents, where I purchased some watermelons and distributed part of them among the sailors, which was a great refreshment to them. But the crowd which surrounded us shortened our stay, what with everyone striving to get a sight of me. I at every moment expected they would force me from the caravan, even though our people kept near me.

The day had been most disagreeably hot and fatiguing, but we were not permitted to stop until eleven o'clock at night. This, however, was an early hour for us and gave me an opportunity for having some rest, after a slight repast of eggs and milk, which was our chief diet. For want of anything better, the poor sailors had to eat of the Moors' provisions.

At three o'clock in the morning, we received orders to get ready. We set out at four. At one point, as I was very faint, the guards permitted the tents to be pitched, being under a necessity of indulging me with an hour's rest for fear of any bad consequences from their unjustifiable proceedings. They no doubt trusted to my youth and constitution, or they never would have run the risks they did in travelling night and day.

We set off soon after, and never stopped until twelve that night. Notwithstanding the fatigues I had suffered, and the dew which fell very heavily, our tent was not allowed to be pitched.

My friend, who was greatly affected by the brutality of the Moors, wrapped me in his cloak and stayed beside me. His uncommon concern and assiduity might have induced me to entertain a suspicion that he had a stronger attachment to me than mere friendship—but that he knew of my engagement to another gentleman. Besides, his words and actions were always so extremely circumspect and even delicate that they dispelled any apprehensions to his disadvantage.

When our company awaked, they were resolved to travel as fast as possible,

The heat was intolerable, and steep rocks, which we were obliged to pass over, continually presented themselves everywhere we looked. There was no appearance of a house, or a tree, only a large tract of country abounding with high mountains, affording little worthy of notice. At twelve o'clock that night, our guards informed us that we would make no long stay, and therefore would not pitch the tents, as they intended to be at Morocco the following day.

We proceeded over very rugged, narrow roads and between mountains which reached above the clouds, and sometimes we went down steep precipices, and then up again. In this manner we travelled till eight in the morning. When we arrived at the river of Morocco, we stopped there for an hour, and then advanced nearer the capital. But we had a severe trial of our fortitude before we reached it, for when we were within eight miles of the city, my tent was ordered to be pitched, and I received a message from the Moorish Admiral to change my dress.

The meaning of this, according to the interpreter's explanation, was that I should 'make fine clothes.' I did not readily understand this, but my friend, with concern, explained it thus: that they would have me dressed in such a way as to make a fine figure upon entering Morocco.

I entreated them to excuse me from so disagreeable a task, acquainting them with how very inconvenient it would be to unpack my baggage and dress in such a place. My entreaties had no effect, and I found it was their habit to carry in, adorned in this manner, all captives who, by appearance, seemed above the vulgar.

As I found it in vain to contend, I had a chest opened, and they fixed upon the clothes I was to put on, which were rich and new. I wrapped up my head in a night-cap, which almost covered my face, as I was told they did not intend to let me wear my hat.

When I was ornamented to their satisfaction, instead of being placed, as before, on my own mule, I was seated in front of my friend on his. At the same time, one of the guards pulled off my friend's hat and carried it away—which treatment amazed us extremely. To our further astonishment, our fellow-sufferers were made to dismount, and walk, two and two, bare-headed, though the sun was much hotter than I had ever felt it, and the road so dusty that the mules were almost knee-deep in it.

We had not proceeded far before we were met by Juan Arvona, a Minorquin slave, who was the Prince's treasurer and great confidant.[19] He intended to accompany us into Morocco and had brought with him a horse for my friend to ride on. However, the Admiral would not permit him to leave the mule he was on. Upon this, the slave returned to the city. His departure was of bad consequence to us, as his presence might have been a check to their arbitrary proceedings.

As we approached Morocco—a walled city with great towers of mosques and mountains behind—a multitude confronted us that could not have been less than about twenty thousand, horse and foot, most of whom were well armed, and attended us with shouts and hallooings. Parties of them continually galloped backwards and forwards, loading and firing their muskets in our faces.

I was almost dead with grief and fatigue, and my friend expected at every moment that we should be thrown from the mule. His legs were scratched in a terrible manner from the horsemen riding by us with great fury. But he did not seem to regard this, as his attention was intensely fixed on my preservation from those accidents that fell in my way. The almighty, however, whose

---

19. Juan Arvona was the man to whom Don Pedro, the helpful Spanish slave, had sent a letter in order to spread the story of the husband/wife relationship between Elizabeth Marsh and her friend, Mr. Crisp. Juan Arvona was originally from the island of Minorca; hence he was a 'Minorquin slave'. The fact that both Marsh and Crisp had recently lived on Minorca would have given them something in common with Juan Arvona.

watchful providence had defended me from innumerable dangers, continued his goodness, and supported me through the distresses of that dismal day.

About noon, we arrived at Morocco. My friend and I were taken to an old castle dropping to pieces with age. There, we were led up a number of stairs to a dismal room and left to our own reflections. We were seated on the floor, lamenting our miserable fate, when a French slave entered with some water, a loaf of bread, and some melons. The latter was very agreeable, and all the refreshment we had had for many hours.

We remained in that place till four o'clock in the afternoon, when the rest of the captives and their guards assembled to take us from that horrible abode. I was so ill with fatigue that they were obliged to carry me down the stairs. They placed me on the mule, as before, and we passed through the city, amidst a great loud concourse of people, to the palace, which was three miles beyond the castle we had just left.

When we came to the palace gates, we halted. After we had been waiting near two hours, his Imperial Highness came out and received us in a public manner. He was mounted on a beautiful horse, with slaves on each side fanning off the flies, and guarded by a squadron of his Black Regiment.[20]

The Moorish Admiral and his crew presented themselves to him, falling on their knees and kissing the ground. As they arose, they did the same to his feet. Then they retired. The Prince addressed himself to us by means of his interpreter and informed us that the reason of our being taken was on account of Captain Hyde Parker's insolent behaviour—as he was pleased to term it—for

---

20. During the seventeenth and eighteenth centuries, Morocco underwent a long series of bloody internecine conflicts, during which different tribes—Moroccan society was tribal—contested with each other for primacy (think modern-day Afghanistan or Iraq). The Sa'adian dynasty, which preceded the Alaouites, had collapsed in bloody chaos so devastating that one chronicler of Moroccan history described it as dreadful enough to make the hair of a suckling infant turn white. In such an environment, ruling was fiendishly complicated and required pitting one tribe against another in a Machiavellian game of divide and conquer. To avoid relying on untrustworthy tribal allies, Prince Sidi Mohammed's grandfather, Sultan Moulay Ismail, created an army composed entirely of black African slaves—known as the *Abīd al-Bukhārī*—loyal only to him. The *Abīd* became a formidable, well trained fighting force numbering perhaps as many as 150,000, and they enabled Moulay Ismail to consolidate his position as Sultan. After his death, however, the *Abīd* rebelled and became king makers in their own right, backing various candidates for Sultan over the years. By Prince Sidi Mohammed's time, the *Abīd* had been brought to heel sufficiently to serve dutifully as the Prince's 'Black Regiment.'

having treated him in a very disrespectful and rude manner when Ambassador from the court of Great Britain.[21]

The Prince assured us, however, that we were not slaves, but that he should detain us until the arrival of a new Consul.[22] He then dismissed us. Upon this, we returned through the gates.

We were thereupon conducted by a Jew to a house which had been provided for us in the Jewish district of the city,[23] which afforded us a most dismal prospect. It was a square ground floor, much like our place of confinement at Salé, only with this addition: the walls were covered with bugs, and as black as soot.

As soon as I perceived this, I desired that my tent might be pitched in the courtyard, thinking I should thereby escape being tormented by those vermin. It was, accordingly, done, and I intended to go early to rest. However, an order came from the court for me to attend on his Imperial Highness there.

I would gladly have been excused, but, as a slave was sent to wait on me, I was constrained to comply.

My friend, being extremely uneasy, was unwilling I should go with the man, and intended to see me there himself, but the slave told him his orders were that none of the captives should accompany me.

We then set out, the slave and I, and I was conveyed into the palace at the garden-door. We walked through a part of the garden which contained a great

---

21. 'Captain Hyde Parker' was Sir Hyde Parker, the fifth Baronet Parker of Melford Hall, in Suffolk, England. He is described as being a stern yet brave naval officer, but also vain, pompous, ignorant, fussy, lacking in imagination, and disdainful of ornamentation. In his later years, he was nicknamed Old Vinegar because of his acerbic temper. He eventually rose to the rank of Vice-Admiral. Some little time before Marsh and her companions arrived in Morocco, when Parker was just a captain, he was sent on a mission to Morocco to negotiate the release of English captives/slaves. Parker apparently had no idea what the appropriate protocol was when dealing with a Moroccan Sultan, for he mortally offended Sidi Mohammed. According to one story, Parker arrived for his introductory meeting with the Prince in scruffy travel clothing and wearing dirty boots. This incensed Sidi Mohammed, who interpreted Parker's appearance as a personal slight upon his dignity as Alaouite royalty.

22. Sidi Mohammed seems to have been conducting a sort of 'gunboat diplomacy' with the British. By having one of his corsair ships capture Marsh and the rest and then holding them hostage in Morocco until he got what he wanted, he was sending a message to the British government that he was not to be trifled with. His ultimate goal here was to drive the hardest bargain he could in terms of the commercial relations between the two countries. Marsh and company were just pawns in the game—though Marsh turned out to be a particularly attractive pawn for Sidi Mohammed.

23. Non-Muslims were prohibited from living with Muslims, and so they were traditionally housed in the Jewish quarter.

number of fine statues. But as the slave seemed to be in haste, I could not make out the persons represented by them or for whom they were designed. The next place we came to was a noble gate of curious workmanship. Two soldiers stood before it. They stopped me as I was going in and directed the slave to tell me I could not pass without first pulling off my shoes.

For a long time, I refused to comply. However, finding there could otherwise be no admittance, I threw my shoes from me. The slave informed me that the Prince was considered a saint, and therefore no Christian, unless barefoot, could be admitted into his palace.[24]

We were obliged to pass many more guards, but eventually we came to the apartment wherein his Imperial Highness was waiting for me. I felt most disagreeably faint and distraught but stepped forward, having little option.

To my great surprise, when I entered into the apartment where I was to meet the Prince, I was received by him with great respect. Four ladies were with him, who seemed as well pleased at seeing me as he was himself—not that my appearance could prejudice them much in my favour, for I had put on my riding-dress, and my face had suffered extremely from the scorching violence of the sun. The Prince took notice of this and turned to the slave who attended me, saying that I had not been taken care of the way he had commanded, and he seemed highly offended.

I should have been happy, could I have spoken Morisco, in acquainting him with the ill treatment I had experienced on the road. I entreated the slave to represent it to the Prince, but he begged me not to force him to do me this service, for if he should do it, he claimed, the Moors would never be satisfied until they had his life. And so those wretches escaped the punishment they deserved, and I was prevented from receiving any satisfaction for what I had endured.

The ladies made many remarks on my dress, greatly recommended their own, and importuned me to put on some clothing they had brought with them. But as I would by no means oblige them in their request, they eventually desisted from any further solicitations.

One of the most agreeable of them, and one who showed me the greatest civility, was the daughter of an Englishman who had become a *renegado* and

---

24. The Alaouite dynasty claimed to be *sayyids*, that is, direct descendants of the prophet Mohammed. The term was used as an honorific, and the 'Sidi' in 'Sidi Mohammed' was a contraction of the Arabic *sayyidī*. 'Sidi' served essentially the same function as the title 'Lord,' though with the explicitly religious denotation. Marsh had to remove her shoes as part of formal protocol because she was approaching a member of the highest nobility in Morocco, a man who was venerated—at least in theory—as a member of a dynasty that accrued saintly status from its connection with the prophet Mohammed. Captain Hyde Parker's offense—if the story about him is true—had been not only to wear muddy boots in the presence of Sidi Mohammed, but to wear boots at all.

married a Moorish woman. She took the bracelets off her arms and put them on mine, desiring that I should wear them for her sake.

The slave told me that I might now take my leave whenever I pleased, which I did immediately, being very glad to retire. But my conductor, instead of taking me to my lodgings, introduced me into another apartment, where I was soon followed by the Prince. Seating himself on a cushion, he enquired concerning the reality of my marriage with my friend. This inquiry was entirely unexpected, and though I positively affirmed that I really was married, I could perceive he much doubted it from his persistent interrogation of me.

At one point, he observed that it was customary for English wives to wear a wedding ring. I answered that mine was packed up, as I did not choose to travel with it.

Finding that I persisted firmly in my story, the Prince, questioned me no farther, and instead gave me assurances of his esteem and protection. He said that he would take pleasure in helping me and, ordering the slave to take particular care of me, he gave me leave to depart.

The slave and I went, with all possible speed, to the garden gate, where I found my faithful friend, who had waited impatiently for my dismissal. He received me from the slave, and we soon arrived at our dismal habitation.

Amends, however, were speedily made for the inconveniencies of the place by the agreeable company of two gentlemen merchants who resided in that country, and who had been so kind as to leave their places of abode in order to meet with us in Morocco. They invited us to sup at their lodgings, but I was too much fatigued to accept their friendly invitation and instead retired to my tent in hopes of rest.

But I had not lain an hour before I was constrained to get up again, the bugs having found me out and joined with my other tormentors in preventing my repose. As it was in vain to complain, I tried to content myself with the hopes of changing my situation.

The following day, Mr. Court, one of the two gentleman merchants, provided company for me at breakfast. Perceiving me ill from want of rest, he went in quest of another lodging for me—though he was not so fortunate as to succeed.

Juan Arvona, the slave, soon after waited on me with a small basket of fruit from his Imperial Highness, who had ordered him to inquire particularly concerning my health. I desired the slave to return my thanks to the Prince for the regard he was pleased to show me. As this slave was leaving me, my friend stopped him and asked, as a favour, that he would endeavour to procure me a more comfortable apartment. This he readily complied with and arranged for part of a new house which belonged to some Jews.

My friend and I accompanied Mr. Court to his house, where we dined and were treated with the greatest kindness imaginable. I had to leave them sooner than I wished, however, as I had things to settle for my new lodgings—not that

I was encumbered with furniture, for a chest served me as a table, another for a chair, and a third to lay my mattress upon. The mosquitos were extremely troublesome, notwithstanding a net which Monsieur Ray had given me as a present whilst I was still at Salé.

Mr. Court was constantly with us and proved not only a valuable acquaintance but also an agreeable, sensible companion: Whenever he perceived that I was distressed by the recollection of my unhappy change of fortune, he endeavoured by a thousand ingenious contrivances to substitute a train of cheerful thoughts instead of those I had entertained.

The other gentleman merchant, Mr. Andrews, visited me and would gladly have had my company to dine with him, but he did not wish me to be exposed to the view of the populace, assuring me that the Prince had many spies to observe my actions, and, if he should by an unguarded event, discover the deceit I had made use of, I undoubtedly would be confined to Seraglio and so lost to my family forever.

I therefore flatter myself that great allowances will be made for my situation, which, though nothing more than a necessary fiction, gave me the greatest uneasiness, as it rendered me apprehensive that the ill-disposed part of the world would unmercifully, though unjustly, censure my conduct. But I had no reason to be under any apprehension regarding the man whom Providence had allotted to be my protector, for his behaviour would always bear the most careful inspection, and the attention he paid me was as to a sister and friend, as he ever studied to reconcile me to my fate by his tenderness and care.

We seldom had the pleasure to see our fellow captives during this period, as they found much more amusement in the company of the ship's crew than with my friend and myself, whose conversation could not be entertaining to them, it being generally about our misfortunes. The sailors lived well by reason of my friend's generosity, for he allowed each man sixpence per day while in that country in order to prevent them becoming Moors, which they must otherwise have done or else starved. For as they were not slaves, the Prince would have nothing to do with their subsistence.

A very agreeable day was passed by us with Mr. Court, and, after his departure, I desired the steward (who had been so careful of me on board our ship and attended me as my servant while we were in Barbary), not to admit any Moors into my apartments. He was a faithful man on whom I could always depend, and whose behaviour merited my everlasting gratitude.

I was disturbed early the next morning by Arvona, the slave, who brought me another basket of fruit, dressed with a variety of flowers, from his Imperial Highness, who request to see me and had ordered Arvona to bring me to the palace. Accordingly I dressed myself in a suit of clothes and did my hair up in the Spanish fashion.

Just as I had made myself ready, Mr. Court visited me as usual, but he seemed to be surprised at my appearance and walked very pensively about the room without speaking a word—behaviour I could not then account for.

I parted with him and my friend, and, attended by the slave, I walked to the palace. At the first gate, as before, I was obliged to leave my shoes under the care of the soldiers. We then hastened through the different apartments, and I was once again brought into the presence of the Prince.

When I arrived at the Prince's apartments, the slave who had conducted me there was dismissed. Then a French lad, who could be admitted into the women's apartments, was sent for to interpret between us, for the same ladies whom I had seen before were at the other end of the room. The Prince demanded that a cushion be placed near him, and I was ordered to be seated thereon.

The Prince was tall, finely shaped, of a good complexion, and he appeared to be about five and twenty.[25] He was dressed in a loose robe of fine muslin, with a train of at least two yards on the floor. Under that was a pink satin vest, buttoned with diamonds: He had a small cap of the same satin as his vest, with a diamond button. He wore bracelets on his legs and slippers wrought with gold. Taken all together, his figure was rather agreeable and his address polite and easy.

A low table, covered with a piece of muslin edged with silver, was placed before him, and on that was an elegant serving tray containing a small tea kettle and lamp and two cups and saucers that were as light as tin and curiously japanned with green and gold. These, I was told, were presents from the Dutch. The tea was made in the kettle, and he presented me a cup of it, which, as it came from his hand, I ventured to drink, though I should have refused it from the ladies, for very substantial reasons. When the table was removed, I was introduced to a young Prince and Princess and had the honour to kiss their tawny hands, after which they retired.

A slave then brought a great collection of rarities, which were the produce of different nations, and showed them to me. I greatly admired everything I saw, which pleased the Prince exceedingly, and he told me, by means of the interpreter, that he did not doubt of my preferring, in time, his palace to the confined way of life I was then in. He also assured me that I might always depend on his favour and protection, and that the curiosities I had seen should be my own property. I thanked him for the honour he did me, but I explained that, as I was very happy with a husband who was my equal in rank and fortune,

---

25. Sidi Mohammed was born sometime between 1710 and 1720 (sources differ), which would put him in his mid-thirties to mid-forties rather than his mid-twenties when Marsh met him. It is not clear why she perceived—or possibly misrepresented—him as being so young.

I did not wish to change my situation in that respect and, whenever it was agreeable to him, I would take my leave.

He looked very stern at my answer and made no response. Instead, he conversed in Morisco a little while with those in the room. Eventually, one of the ladies guided me to the other end of the room and seated me before them.

One of them in particular observed me very closely and seemed to be out of temper. She was a large woman but low in stature, of a sallow complexion, thick lipped, with a broad, flat face and black eyes, the lashes whereof were painted a deep red. Her hair was black, combed back from her forehead, and hung down a great length in various ringlets. She wore a large piece of muslin, edged with silver, round her head, raised high at the top. Her earrings were extremely large, and the part that went through the ears was made hollow for lightness. She wore a loose dress much like that of the wife of the Captain of the Port back at Salé, only with the difference of a diamond button at the collar and its being made of the finest muslin. Her slippers were of blue satin worked with silver, and she had bracelets on her arms and legs.

The lady whose father, as I have already remarked, was an Englishman talked to me in Morisco and was seemingly fond of me. By her gestures, I imagined she was urging me to learn their language.

I asked the French boy what she was saying. He answered, 'Rien de conséquence' ['Nothing of consequence']. I, therefore, concluding that what she said related to nothing more than common conversation, and being desirous to oblige her in trifles, I imprudently repeated some words she had said.

Too late, I discovered that I had renounced (completely innocently) the Christian religion by saying in Morisco: 'There is no God but Allah, and Mohammed is His prophet.'[26]

---

26. This is the *Shahadah*, the Muslim profession of faith: *Lā 'ilāha 'illā Allāh wa-Muḥammad rasūl Allāh*. By Islamic tradition, all a person needs to do to become a Muslim is recite the *Shahadah* in Arabic. Apparently, Marsh was deliberately tricked into reciting the *Shahadah*. As a result, she technically converted to Islam on the spot. What seems to have happened here was that the Prince involved his wives and the young French translator in a scheme to trick Marsh into technically converting to Islam (or perhaps the wives took it upon themselves to do so). If Marsh had in fact become a Muslim, the Prince could have licitly added her to his harem. Sidi Mohammed was prohibited by the Quran from acquiring her if she was legally married and not a slave (see footnote 18 above). However, verse 60:10 of the Quran states the following: 'O ye who believe! When there come to you believing women refugees, examine them...If ye ascertain that they are Believers, then send them not back to the Unbelievers. They are not lawful wives for the Unbelievers, nor are the Unbelievers lawful husbands for them.' So if the Prince could declare that Marsh had converted to Islam and was a 'Believer,' he could claim the Quranic-sanctioned legal right to pry her away from her husband and add her to his harem.

The palace was immediately plunged into the utmost confusion, and there was joy on every face.

I was surprised and frightened, for I knew not the cause of the commotion. Perceiving this, the Prince ordered the noise to cease and, at the same time, spoke to the ladies, who instantly left the room, taking me with them to an apartment remote from that wherein we had been, adjoining to the garden. It was a large room, much longer than broad, and crowded with women, most of them black. One of them spoke French and inquired very civilly after my health. I asked her if the palace we were in was the Seraglio. She said it was a small part of it and offered to show me around. I, however, would not venture myself out of sight of the door through which I had entered.

The ladies who had conducted me thither left me as soon as the black women were in conversation with me, and I saw them no more.

An old slave brought me a cup of chocolate, but its appearance did not please me, and I declined taking it. Indeed, I had been cautioned by my friends against drinking anything that might be offered to me. After some time, I began to be impatient and extremely uneasy at my being detained in that place, and I entreated them to permit my departure. Instead of granting my request, they endeavoured to assuage my anxiety by assuring me that I should not remain there much longer.

I nevertheless continued my entreaties.

Eventually, a young lad came in. He was one of those who attended the women. I immediately addressed him in French, which, fortunately for me, he understood. I asked him to convey my respects to His Imperial Highness and inform him that I besought him, as I was very ill, to give me leave to depart.

The boy cheerfully complied, and in less than a quarter of an hour, I had an answer from an English *renegado*: that I must attend the Prince in a private apartment. I was shocked at the oddity of this message, but, as it appeared to be my fate to be reduced to passive obedience and non-resistance, I had little choice but to follow the man.

The English *renegado* led the way through a series of noble squares, some of which were of white Marble, with the pillars of mosaic work. There was a variety of delightful fountains, the water of which fell into large basins, along with lattices above to keep out the sun. But such was my distressed condition that it was beyond my power to make any material remarks on the magnificent objects presented to my view.

When we entered the salon where the Prince was waiting to receive me, I was amazed at the elegant figure he made. He was seated under a canopy of crimson velvet, richly embellished with gold. The room was large, finely decorated, and supported by pillars of mosaic work. At the far end of the room, lay a range of cushions with gold tassels. A Persian carpet covered the floor.[27]

The Prince commanded me and the English *renegado* to draw near his person. He conversed for some time with the latter in Morisco. After that, the *renegado* informed me that his Imperial Highness wished to know if I would become a Moor [i.e., convert to Islam] and remain in his palace, desiring me to be convinced of his esteem for me and hoping that I would properly consider the advantages resulting from doing as he desired and promising me every indulgence he could possibly favour me with.

Though I was alarmed and even greatly terrified by these interrogations, I had the resolution to reply that it was impossible for me to change my sentiments in religious matters, and that consideration was entirely unnecessary for me, for I was peremptorily determined to remain a Christian. I assured him, however, that I would forever retain the highest sense of the honour he had done me, and that I hoped for the continuance of his Highness's protection.

I could easily perceive that he was disgusted with my answer from his remaining silent for some minutes. Then, throwing off the mask he had hitherto worn, he cruelly informed me that I had that very morning renounced the Christian faith and turned Mohometan [i.e., Muslim], and that a capital punishment—namely burning at the stake—was, by their laws, inflicted upon all who recanted from or disclaimed their religion.

---

27. The Moroccan Sultans of the eighteenth century were certainly cruel tyrants by today's standards, but they were apparently neither unsophisticated nor crassly brutal (except when it suited their purposes). Prince Sidi Mohammed's father, Moulay Abdallah, took into his harem a young Scottish woman named Bet Whitson, who, like Marsh, had been captured by Salé corsairs. Here is a description of Bet Whitson's first night with Moulay Abdallah (referred to as 'the Emperor'): 'She was conducted to the Emperor's bed. Bet had seen many large and splendid apartments in the palace, but the magnificence of this bedchamber exceeded all conception. She trembled when the Emperor entered, but the kindness of his manner soon quieted her apprehensions. She said his features were regular and manly, and his air indicated majesty blended with condescension. The fire in his eye was softened by feelings of love and tenderness. Above his underdress, which was extremely rich, he wore a beautiful velvet robe, lined with ermine, and embroidered with gold. His turban was tastefully disposed, and in the front was a star of diamonds. His whole conduct to the young woman was characterized by feeling and delicacy. Next day, Bet received the formal congratulations of the ladies of the seraglio, though some of them could ill conceal their chagrin at her good fortune' (James Thompson, *A New, Improved, and Authentic Life of James Allan, the Celebrated Northumberland Piper*, p. 388). The Sultan's 'feeling and delicacy,' the overwhelming opulence of Bet's surroundings, and the privileges that accrued to her as one of the Sultan's favourites did not alter the brute fact that her union with the Sultan had been forced upon her against her will, and Bet escaped after some years and made her way back to Scotland.

The shock of this pronouncement was so severe that it was with difficulty that I prevented myself from falling, and I invoked Heaven for assistance in my distress. As soon as I was capable of making a reply, I assured the Prince that, if I was an apostate, it entirely proceeded from my being tricked, and not from my own inclination. I further assured him that if my death would give him any satisfaction, I no longer desired to avoid that last and final remedy to all my misfortunes, for to go on living under the terms he proposed would only add to my misery, and I therefore was resolved that the preservation of my life no longer deserved my care and attention.

The Prince seemed greatly perplexed by my resolute declaration, and, though he continued his importunities, yet it was more with the air of a supplicant than that of a sovereign—though he was still inflexible to everything I urged against what he proposed.[28]

I, therefore, on my knees, implored his compassion and besought him, as a proof of that esteem he had given me reason to expect, to permit me to leave him forever. My tears, which flowed incessantly, extremely affected him.

---

28. Sidi Mohammed seems to have been attracted to European women. Of his dozen or so official wives, two were European. The second woman that he married, sometime in the late 1740s, was an Irish girl referred to in the records as Lalla (Lady) Sargetta. In Elizabeth Marsh, he clearly saw another European woman he wanted to add to his collection—so to speak. Marsh seems entirely unaware that he already had a European wife. Lalla Sargetta bore Sidi Mohammed two sons. The eldest, Moulay al-Yazid, was born around 1750, so he might conceivably have been the 'young Prince' introduced to Marsh along with his sister earlier in the story, whose 'tawny hands' Marsh had 'the honour to kiss.' In his day, Moulay al-Yazid seems to have been fairly well known among the English. Here is a contemporary description of him: 'The Emperor of Morocco's Eldest son is half an Irishman, his mother, who is alive, being from that country. The young prince is remarkably fond of the British nation. He speaks English tolerably, and has been taught the military discipline, and even the small sword, at which he is very expert, by masters from Gibraltar. The father and the son hate each other mortally. They seek each other's death with great avidity. The son is beloved by the whole empire, except, indeed, the Negro slaves [i.e., the *Abīd*; see footnote 20 above] who are as faithful to the Emperor as the Swiss Guards are to Louis. They are supposed to be 50,000 strong. When the son comes to the throne, he means to abolish all slavery of the English, and invite them, by particular exemptions, to settle in his dominions' (Johann Wilhelm von. Archenholz, *The British Mercury, or Annals of History, Politics, Manners, Literature, Arts etc. of the British Empire*, Volume 7, pp. 267-268). Much of the above seems to be pure wishful thinking. Moulay al-Yazid was certainly not 'beloved by the whole empire,' and the notion that he would 'abolish all slavery of the English' is risible. He did, however, have a fractious relationship with his father: he rebelled unsuccessfully against him three times (and was pardoned each time) before finally becoming Sultan. Lalla Sargetta clearly had some hold over Sidi Mohammed, for she prevailed on him to have her mother brought out from Dublin to keep her company (*The British Mercury*, p. 268).

Raising me up, and putting his hands before his face, he ordered that I should be instantly taken away.

The English *renegado* held me by the hand and hurried off as fast as possible to the gates. We found it no easy matter to pass these, however, for a great crowd had assembled there.

My worthy friend was on the other side, with his hair all loose and with a distracted countenance, demanding me as his wife. The inhuman guards had beat him down for striving to get in. The black women took hold of me, hallooing out, 'No Christian, but a Moor!' and tore all the plaits out of my clothes. My hair hung down about my ears.

After a number of intense arguments, my friend prevailed and, having torn me from the grip of the women, took me in his arms and, with all possible expedition, got me out of their sight.

Back at my lodgings, I was kindly received by Mr. Court, who displayed a silent satisfaction at my deliverance, for, as there were spies about us, it was dangerous for my friends at that time to say anything concerning what had passed relating to me.

My friend sent for a French surgeon, a slave to his Imperial Highness, to bleed me. This news was carried to the palace, and the Prince, as we afterwards heard, was extremely concerned. Bleeding in that country is looked upon as very extraordinary and is never practised but in cases of extremity. This was, therefore, a fortunate circumstance, as his Highness imagined it was occasioned by his behaviour.

Three people, that day, ran the greatest risks to their lives on my account. One of them risked himself by acquainting my friend with what they were doing with me at the palace. Another, we were informed, was sent for by the Prince just after he had dismissed me, who ordered him, if I was not yet out of the gates, to bring me back to him, to which that good man answered with the untruth that he had met me, with my husband, near our lodgings. I am under the greatest obligation to this worthy slave. He knew all too well the fatal consequences of my returning to the Prince, and he risked his very life by deceiving his Imperial Highness in order to preserve my safety. My Friend, also, had been in imminent danger, for he had attempted to force his way through the guards in order to rescue me.

I was advised to keep myself very retired for the remainder of the day, and I soon went to my bed. It was impossible, however, for me to sleep. I had too much of a dread on my spirits, for I knew that I was not yet safe.

On the next morning, I got up very early to see our friends, the merchants, who heartily congratulated me on my safe return, though they advised me to keep myself still, in appearance ill, and to admit no one to visit me but themselves.

A visitor, however, presented himself, to whom it would have been very ungenteel to have denied admittance. His name was Moulay Dris, and he was a Prince of the Blood. He was tall, of a sallow complexion, and had fine black eyes. He was also very polite, and a great friend to the English. He conversed with my friend in Spanish, and when he went away, he wished us well and desired that I should keep my spirits up, for he did not doubt that all would end well.

I was in continual dread, however, and could get no rest, night or day, so that my life was wretched beyond imagination.

Mister Court was extremely obliging and devoted most of his time to our service. I was much entertained with his agreeable company, his conversation being always new and improving. Providence was particularly kind in providing me, in that country, with so agreeable a companion.

This gentleman and my friend were breakfasting with me one morning, when the latter received a message from the palace commanding the presence of himself, the other two passengers, as well as the ship's master and crew. The two merchants were also to come along.

They all accordingly waited upon his Imperial Highness, the Prince. This worthy told them that the reason for his sending for them was to grant them liberty to proceed on their voyage, and that he would issue proper orders for their journey to Salé. He explained that he did this despite the indignities he had suffered at the hands of the Ambassador from the court of Great Britain and the further ill treatment he had met with from the British, who had furnished his rebellious subjects with arms and ammunition.[29] He added that he would set an example of moderation, as well as justice, by permitting us to quit his domains.

The gentlemen no sooner returned than they told me what had passed. I was very happy and flattered myself with hopes that I might, once more, see my dear, disconsolate parents.

---

29. Sidi Mohammed is referring here once again to Captain Hyde Parker (he of the dirty boots). The furnishing of arms and ammunition to 'rebellious subjects' is likely an incident that happened in 1755, when some English naval vessels traded guns for provisions with some of the tribal leaders on Morocco's Mediterranean coast. At this time, Morocco was wracked by internecine strife, with different tribal groups vying with each other for supremacy. The situation was so volatile that Sidi Mohammed's father, Moulay Abdallah, was removed from the throne and replaced no fewer than six times by various tribal factions and the *Abīd*. Given such rampant instability, Sidi Mohammed had to quash any flare-ups of rebellion quickly and forcefully. Among other actions, he imprisoned all the European merchants in the area and was especially brutal to the English. According to one story, he had a captive Englishmen tortured so severely, and so traumatized the man, that he committed suicide. The English (along with the Dutch) had been supplying arms to Morocco since the end of the sixteenth century, and it is quite possible that the English naval captains who initiated the trade thought they were simply conducting business as usual and had no idea of the consequences that would follow.

We supped that night with Mr. Court and Mr. Andrews at their lodgings, and it was the general opinion that we could not set out without proper guards to protect us and letters to the Governor of Salé to ensure he received us as free people.

The next morning, a slave brought us information that the Prince had altered his intentions, and that he was now determined that we should first go to Safi, and from thence to Salé. This greatly stupefied us, and we feared he had not been sincere in his first proposal. This was a double mortification, since he had obliged the gentlemen and the ship's crew to sign a letter to the Governor of Gibraltar, wherein he promised to release us, and this was immediately sent by express. We now feared that he had only done this to deceive our countrymen and so deter them from demanding our liberty.

We nonetheless made preparations for the journey, though we received no dispatches from the palace.

Mr. Court passed the day with me, and in the evening, we had a very disagreeable visitor: the messenger who had travelled to Morocco with us. He behaved in a very insolent manner, telling me I was a Moor, and that he hoped his Imperial Highness would oblige me to remain in his domain. He demanded fifty pounds for the care he had taken of us on the road. My friend would have treated him as he deserved, but he was a dangerous man to have any dispute with. Therefore, on my account, he gave the man twelve ducats, which seemed to tolerably satisfy him. After he left us, I was in great distress at what he had said, fearing he might use every artifice he could against me with his Highness.

This prevented me from getting any rest that night.

The next day, however, the wished-for dispatches were brought to us, along with proper guards to attend us to Safi. We immediately acquainted the gentleman merchants, who were to accompany us. They were at the abode of Mr. Andrews, who very kindly invited us to make use of his house during our stay in the part of the country to which we were travelling. We were entirely indebted to those gentlemen for providing necessaries for the journey, it being out of our power to make such a provision.

Our baggage was ready by eight o'clock in the evening, and we walked out of town. We met with no interruption, since the Moors were obliged to retire into the city after sunset, and the Jews were easily kept at a distance from us by our guards. We mounted our mules and soon crossed the river of Morocco and rested there for the night. Mr. Court had dispatched some of our attendants in advance to prepare the tents and have our supper ready, which was a most comfortable change from that we had experienced on the road from Salé.

We set out early next morning after breakfasting on milk. The roads were very good, and the prospect of the country extremely delightful. Mount Atlas, at the back of Morocco, with a chain of mountains about thirty miles before us, presented to our view the most agreeable of objects. We rode close to the

Enchanted Mountain, so called from it appearing to travellers to be very near when in fact it was many miles distant. It was dramatically deceiving and drew my attention more than anything I had seen before.

We stopped about noon, for the sun was very hot and made travelling most fatiguing. We dined and then set off again in the evening and passed over a high mountain, the top of which commanded a most heavenly view of the Atlas, the city of Morocco, and its extensive plains.

We then turned our backs on the place, in fervent hope that we had seen the last of it.

After resting for the night, we set out again at daybreak and travelled all day, pitching our tents in the evening near a salt lake three miles long and two broad, which from November through April is a river and, at other times, quite dry and hard. It is esteemed a great curiosity, being fifty miles from the sea.

We rode over part of it but only proceeded a few miles further before the tents were again fixed for the night, this time on a large plain (called Roseline) that was very fine but entirely uncultivated. We passed the night at this charming spot and then prepared to continue our journey. It was the Jewish Sabbath, however, and our servants who were of that religion refused to attend us on that day. Our guards, by very severe usage, forced them to comply. It was shocking to see the subjugation these poor creatures are forced to endure under the Moors, for the greatest miscreant amongst them, or even a boy, may buffet and abuse the Jews without their having the least redress. But if a Jew should lift his hand against a Moor, he would be instantly put to death.

We were happy in the company of Mr. Court, who was always cheerful and entertaining. Mister Andrews was likewise very kind to us, all of which contributed to render short and pleasing an otherwise tiresome journey.

When we reached Safi, we stopped about three miles distant from the town, where all the Christian merchants had assembled to meet us, bringing refreshments with them. A little time was here spent in ceremony, and then we proceeded to the gates of Safi itself. There we were forced to dismount on account of a great crowd, drawn by curiosity, that gathered about us and obstructed our passage, which gave us much uneasiness.

Having at length entered into the town and the house of Mr. Andrews, we were kindly received by his partner, Mr. Conneller, and welcomed in a particularly hospitable manner to their habitation. We were entertained with a genteel supper, and I was afterwards conducted to the room allotted to me.

My first thoughts were to return thanks to Providence for the happiness I then enjoyed in being under the roof of those who professed the same faith as I. I slept tolerably well, considering the fatigues of the journey, and, in the morning, I met the gentlemen for breakfast.

In the meanwhile, the Governor of the place made us a visit. He told us that he had received orders from the Prince that our stay was to be fifteen days, during which we were to be treated as free people. In the interim, he was waiting to receive further instructions in relation to us.

This communication was in no way agreeable to me, for I feared the Prince might be reconsidering his decision to grant us liberty.

Whilst we were at dinner, a number of Moors surrounded the table. I found that it was customary for them to enter the houses of Christians whenever they might want, and the owners could not prevent it, though they were sensible how disagreeable it was to me.

When I retired to my chamber, I employed myself in putting up all such letters as would have revealed me to be a single woman and delivered them into the care of Mr. Andrews. My friend also procured me a plain gold ring from a Swedish captain. I locked this in a chest, fully expecting a search to be made of my effects in order to know whether I was really married or only made a pretence thereof. Such precautions were necessary in order to guard against the danger to which I was still exposed.

I desired my friend to write to Arvona, the slave who had aided us and who remained in Morocco, to learn what had passed at the palace after my departure, for I was ever in dread that his Imperial Highness would again send for me, for I had heard from undoubted authority that I was of great interest to him, and though he had shown a benign condescension in permitting me to leave him when it was in his power to detain me, yet I knew him to be an absolute monarch, and therefore I had reason to be extremely uneasy.

I had entertained great hopes, now that we were in Safi, of receiving letters from my family and friends. The disappointment of not receiving any made me very unhappy. This and many other reasons kept me in perpetual misery, and I often wished to be taken from this world, for it afforded me no consolation.

I was in one of my desponding reveries when Mr. Court entered the room. Seeing me extremely dejected, he attempted to dispel my fears. Any satisfaction I may have derived from this was but of short duration, for he informed me that he had had just received an express from his partner in business desiring his return, as his partner stood in need of his assistance.

This unwelcome news so greatly afflicted me that I bade adieu to cheerfulness.

He left us early in the evening to prepare for his journey, and I was entirely miserable when I reflected on the loss of our best adviser and protector, and I could not help but fear what the future might hold in store for me, trapped as I was in this place and still at the mercy of the Prince should he choose to exercise his power with regards to me.

When Mr. Court came to take his leave of us, he assured me that he had been some time with Mr. Andrews and had recommended me to his care and protection in order to prevent, if possible, by their united endeavours, my return to Morocco.

Upon this, he embraced my friend and me, sending up to Heaven a heartfelt wish for our speedy deliverance out of captivity. And then he departed from us with all expedition. Though I was exceedingly distressed by such a cruel separation, I still relied upon Divine Providence for support in all my afflictions.

We now received an unexpected visit from Juan Arvona, the slave, who had been dispatched from Morocco to guard some Spanish bulldogs that the Friars residing in Safi had ordered to be sent from Cadiz as a present to his Imperial Highness. Arvona, in my hearing, told my friend that the Prince was very anxious, on account of my health, that he had called upon Arvona in the middle of the night in order to talk with him concerning me, and that he frequently said that he would have me again in Morocco because Safi did not agree with my constitution.

Arvona added that he much feared his Highness's resolution to permit me to leave Barbary would not continue much longer, despite his assurance on this matter the day I left Morocco. The reason for Arvona's apprehensions was that the Prince, upon being asked if he would not again see the fair Christian before her departure, after a pause, replied, 'No, lest I should be obliged to detain her.'

This honest slave promised to keep us informed regarding what passed at the palace, and then he set out to return to Morocco.

Arvona was no sooner gone than I acquainted my friend with the fact that I had overheard their conversation, and that this gave me the greatest uneasiness. My friend, though equally concerned, entreated me to be as easy as possible, assuring me that he would spare no pains to lighten my afflictions and undergo any torments rather than see me returned to the Prince.

At this time. another post came in, but it brought no letters from my family. This greatly increased my unease, for I feared that my mail was being intercepted, for then my captors would discover my real name and my situation with regards to my friend.

At this juncture, Mr. Andrews introduced to me a Swedish Merchant of Safi who informed me that he could, with certainty, affirm that an English Admiral had arrived at the Garrison of Gibraltar,[30] and that he had ordered that a warship should be dispatched to demand us. This agreeable information, however, gained little credit with me, for I was becoming accustomed to this sort of deception and inured to disappointment.

A little after this, some friars, who had been for a time in Safi for the benefit of the Spanish slaves, desired to be admitted to see me, as they were going to return to the Garrison of Gibraltar. The senior-most among them stayed some time longer than the others, as he had a great deal to say, and he took great pains to encourage us to cheerfully submit to the Divine Will. He likewise assured

---

30. This 'English Admiral' was Admiral Edward Hawke, the first Baron Hawke, who replaced Admiral John Byng as British commander in the Mediterranean in June, 1756.

me that he would see my family as soon as possible after his arrival, and he then parted from us in tears.

I observed that one of his companions delivered a letter to my friend, whose countenance was extremely altered by the reading thereof. When the friars had departed, I desired to know the letter's contents, as I was very certain it came from Morocco.

I found it, however, a difficult matter to persuade my friend to grant my request.

He relented, finally, and told me that the letter came from Arvona, and that it carried news that a Moor of some consequence (and an enemy to the English) would shortly be sent by his Imperial Highness to Safi. It appeared from his manner of writing that Arvona was concerned for my preservation, for he entreated my friend to be particularly attentive to the most effectual means of securing my safety. This advice, however, was unnecessary, for the most affectionate parent could not have been more tenderly careful of me than my friend had ever been on all occasions.

I endeavoured to conceal my apprehensions, but Arvona's letter was never out of my mind and produced many melancholy reflections, which almost deprived me of hope.

A few days after this, a ship arrived from Holland bringing two gentlemen who, as soon as they heard of my distress, paid a visit to me. One of them was a merchant who had formerly resided in Santa Cruz. He was going, with his companion, to Morocco to solicit the favour and protection of the Prince in order to reestablish a house in that city.

This gentleman, had, it was reported, formerly traded with great success in this place, and the prospect of adding yet more to his fortune had so strange an effect upon him that the constant difficulties a Christian was exposed to in that country were treated by him as matters of no importance or consideration.

These gentlemen informed me that they had heard that a messenger had arrived from Morocco whose aversion to the English was implacable. They advised me to keep to my chamber, since it was generally believed that this messenger had been sent by his Royal Highness to look into the conduct of my friend and me. I was greatly obliged to them for this information, but the effect of it was to increase my fears and uncertainty, for if the true nature of the relation between my friend and me was uncovered, I would be lost.

Soon after, as I pensively sat reflecting on the news I had heard, my room door was thrown open with great violence, and a most forbidding object presented itself to my view.

For several minutes, he fixed his eyes upon me without speaking a word. His aspect was as furious as can possibly be imagined. Finally, he narrowly inspected every part of my room, muttering to himself in his own language. Then, giving me another terrifying look, he retired, closing the door after him as violently as he had opened it.

I was struck with great horror at his wild appearance and remained seated as I was for some time, riveted to my chair.

My friend was ignorant of this visit, for he was walking, along with several other gentlemen, at the top of the house. When he returned, I was for some time incapable of acquainting him with what had happened to me. When I finally narrated to him the details of what had transpired, he concluded immediately that this person was the messenger who had been expected. This was soon confirmed by Mr. Andrews, who came to inquire after my health and to introduce the Danish Consul, who was on the point of departing for Salé and had desired to see me before he left.

This gentleman expressed a tender concern for my illness and recommended a person who, in his opinion, had some knowledge of physic. He obligingly sent this man to see me, who advised my being bled. As I was uncertain as to his skill, however, I chose to defer bleeding to another opportunity.

When he visited me again and discovered that my complaint was a dejection of spirits, the intended operation was totally laid aside.

Soon after this, I received a letter from Mr. Ray in Salé that speedily restored me to health, for it had been sent to congratulate us on the arrival of a British warship at that port. The weather being bad, however, they had not reached the shore. I now began to seriously entertain some favourable hopes of once more seeing my dear parents. With these pleasing imaginings, I retired to rest.

My repose, however, was interrupted in the night by two shocks of the earth, which continued a minute and a half. The fright I was in cannot be expressed. Before I was removed from my room, the ceiling was thrown down, and the walls, though of a prodigious thickness, were cracked in many places. The noise of it may be compared with a carriage going speedily over a rough pavement—ending with a tremendous explosion. The sky remained serene, but the sea made a great roaring, and afterwards we heard that shipping had greatly suffered.

When I was taken back to my room and had a little recovered from my shock, I returned grateful thanks to the Almighty for his protection from the dangers of the night.

Mr. Andrews and my friend breakfasted with me the next morning. My friend read to me from a letter, which he had just received from Juan Arvona, in Morocco, which enclosed a copy of that which had been sent from Captain Maplesden, the Captain of the English warship anchored at Salé, to the Prince, which was to the following purpose.

That the Captain was come there, in the name of Admiral Sir Edward Hawke, to know the reason for taking and detaining our ship, passengers, and crew in a time of peace. Further, he related, with great respect how much the

King, his master, would esteem the justice in the Prince setting us at liberty, and that he might depend upon the Treaty that had been concluded between our two nations being inviolably maintained on the part of his Britannic Majesty. [31]

To this letter, his Imperial Highness the Prince answered that, when we were taken, his ship had been out at sea for some considerable time, and the Captain had consequently been unacquainted with any peace having been being made. Further, upon our arrival in Salé, a report prevailed that his Ambassador had failed in his negotiation, which was the reason for his sending us to Morocco. Despite this, however, the Prince declared that, upon our arrival, he (who always kept his word) had declared us free, as well as the ship and cargo, and likewise had ordered the crew back to Salé in order to refit the ship. In the Interim, he declared, I and the other passengers were sent to Safi, to wait there until all was ready for us to proceed on our voyage.

His Imperial Highness further declared that he would, for his part, duly adhere to the treaty. But, he added, if the peace was not soon formally ratified by the Court of England, he would deem this as a declaration of war and order his ships to make reprisals and stop all communication between the Garrison of Gibraltar and his dominions.[32] He ended his reply with complaints against the English for furnishing his rebellious subjects with arms and ammunition.

Juan Arvona further informed my friend in his letter that a Jew would be sent out soon from Morocco to Safi to negotiate on behalf of the Prince with the Captain of the warship.

The Prince also said that we might either embark on board the warship or return to Salé and continue our voyage in the merchantman we had been passengers on. He knew very well, however, that the latter was impossible, as the ship was almost pulled to pieces, and his people were fitting out their pirate cruisers with the materials they had taken from it. Even if the case had been otherwise, though, my strength was too much exhausted by illness and sorrow for me to be in any condition to take so fatiguing a journey.

Several days later, the Jew arrived from Morocco. That very same day, the warship anchored in the Safi road. A boat was immediately sent on shore with

---

31. This English naval captain was Captain Jervis Maplesden, who commanded the *Portland*. Sending Captain Maplesden to Morocco was an act of literal gunboat diplomacy on the British side. The *Portland*, a fourth-rate ship-of-the-line, was 50 metres (165 feet) long and armed with fifty cannons. There was nothing in Morocco at that time that could touch it. The letter Captain Maplesden sent to Prince Sidi Mohammed may have been appropriately courteous and respectful, but it was backed by the brute power the English warship represented.

32. This was the most severe threat Sidi Mohammed could make, for the English garrison at Gibraltar relied heavily on Morocco for supplies of grain and beef. If Sidi Mohammed had cut off such supplies, the garrison would have found itself in serious difficulty.

our letters. Among these was one from my dear father, who encouraged me to keep up my spirits and assured me that nothing should be wanting to procure my release. All these developments filled me with hope. I had had, however, too many distresses and disappointments to be able to fully believe in the promise of these events, and I could not help but anxiously anticipate some last-minute calamity would undo all our plans.

Not long after the British warship had anchored in the Safi road, my friend received a very obliging letter from the ship's Captain, who advised us to be in readiness to depart, though we could not embark until the Jew the Prince had sent as an emissary had gone and returned from Morocco. The Captain entreated us to make ourselves easy, for he would do everything in his power to facilitate our enlargement.

The Jew, who was a principal person at the palace, talked with my friend and asked him what kind of present my friend intended to make him for the trouble he should have on our account. My friend answered that neither the other passengers nor ship's crew could spare him anything, and therefore the whole of his demand must fall on myself and him, who had but little cash left, but he might depend on having as much as we could possibly spare. This pacified him for the present, and he then set out for Morocco.

Five days after this, he returned to Safi with joyful tidings: we were to embark the following day.

However, bad weather prevented any boats from going off, and no gratuity could tempt the Moors into rowing us out while the sea ran so high as it did. Indeed, I cannot say that I really believed that I should ever be permitted to quit the country. Providence, however, was pleased to change the situation in my favour.

The very next morning, I was asked to get myself ready, for the weather would now admit of our going, and the people were ready to take my baggage. The sudden joy of this agreeable news so excited my spirits that it was with difficulty that my friend returned me to a state of tranquillity.

The gentlemen of the house accompanied me to the strand, where I returned them my most grateful acknowledgments for the friendship they had showed me, and I assured them that no opportunity would be neglected wherein I might be capable of making the least return.

After we had taken our leave of these gentlemen, my friend was put into a boat in order to receive me. As soon as the other people had got into it, we set off for the warship. A Moor of consequence accompanied the Jew, who was with us in the boat. This man took great pains to persuade me that I was no Christian. He really seemed mortified at my leaving Barbary. I was in extreme dread until we reached the warship, fearing a signal from shore to order our return.

I was hoisted aboard the warship in a chair and received by the Captain and all the gentlemen aboard the warship with the greatest politeness imaginable and general expressions of joy at seeing me safe from the power of those who wished to detain me. Those who had rowed us out received a handsome present and were discharged in order to return to their own detested shore. After this, the Captain led me to his state room, which he very obligingly resigned to me. I cannot express the enormous comfort I felt at having an apartment allotted to me after the cruel restraints I had been under in Barbary and the uneasiness I had suffered on account of passing for what I really was not.

The agreeable things I was now surrounded by, together with the hopes of my being soon returned to my afflicted family, made me entirely happy. I had, besides, an additional satisfaction: that of having it in my power to acquaint my relations to whom they were indebted (next to Providence) for my preservation—for my friend had, in every respect, fulfilled the promise he had made to my father.

After several days sailing, we arrived at the Garrison of Gibraltar, to the unspeakable joy of my distressed parents. It is easy to imagine how happy I was on such an occasion.

Not long after my return, my friend confessed to me that his affinity for me had proceeded from a stronger attachment than that of mere friendship, and he declared his love for me before myself and my family and the unhappiness he was under at the thought of parting from me. He confessed that he hoped the confidence my parents had already reposed in him by trusting me to his care, along with the esteem I had always possessed for him, would be the means of removing any obstacles which might prevent his future happiness.

I was not much surprised at this declaration, but I had many difficulties to surmount on account of my engagement to Captain Tremont. The Captain's behaviour during my absence, however, had occasioned my father's taking the resolution of never consenting to this alliance.

My friend's good character, the gratitude I owed him, and my father's desire overbalanced every other consideration, and after adjusting some family affairs—which are not necessary to explain in this narrative—my friend and I were married and embarked upon a merchant ship bound for Bristol.

And so my adventure in Barbary finally ended happily.[33]

Elizabeth Marsh published her narrative in 1769—thirteen years after her captivity. She wrote it because she needed the money.

---

33. Elizabeth Marsh's narrative can be found in *The Female Captive: A Narrative of Facts Which Happened in Barbary in the Year 1756, Written by Herself*, Volumes 1 & 2. I have modernized the spelling and vocabulary of the original text and abridged some portions of it to make the story move along a little quicker.

*The Female Captive* is an example of something that happened with commercially published captivity narratives: it was written (and edited) to meet the expectations of the reading public—and to maximize sales. In Marsh's case, this editing is most obvious in the way she comes across in the narrative. The Elizabeth Marsh we meet in *The Female Captive* is (at least on the surface) an earnestly pious, virtuous young lady, prone to tears and bouts of debilitating sickness, needing the protection of men—a classic female stereotype (and a depiction that can become irritating for some twenty-first century readers). It turns out, though, that this picture of Marsh is an exaggeration, apparently done on purpose for the book.

There are two versions of *The Female Captive*: one is the published book, the other a hand-written manuscript. The contrast between the two versions reveals the editing process at work. The book begins with Marsh and her family leaving Minorca for Gibraltar, where her father, a gentleman, had been transferred, and where she is disappointed to learn that her naval captain fiancé has been dispatched to England. She then petitions her father for permission to go after him. The manuscript has a quite different beginning:

I resided with my parents at Minorca, previous to, and at the commencement of, the War with France in the year 1756, which occasioned our removal to the Garrison of Gibraltar, from whence, being desirous of visiting my friends in England, and a favourable opportunity offering a ship in which a friend of my family (James Crisp Esquire) was going as a passenger, I embarked.[34]

The difference between the two versions is clear. In the manuscript, Marsh makes no pretence of her father being a gentleman (he was not; he was a shipwright), makes no mention of her engagement, and makes no claim to have solicited her family for permission to travel.

Here is another example, first from the book, then from the manuscript:

---

34. Elizabeth Marsh, bound manuscript titled *Narrative 1: Narrative of her Captivity in Barbary,* pages 1 & 2 (the manuscript itself has no pagination). There is some debate about whether or not this manuscript was actually written by Marsh herself or copied out by somebody else.

When I came on board [the corsair ship], my disconsolate friend received me, his countenance sufficiently denoting the anguish of his mind. I had summoned up all my fortitude on so shocking an occasion, but the sight of our sailors tied together drew tears from me, notwithstanding my resolution to the contrary, and my appearance had the same effect on them.

When I got on board, I saw our sailors tied together, but my friend and the other passengers were at liberty.[35]

The version of Marsh that comes across in the manuscript is still a pious eighteenth-century young woman, prone to mentions of divine Providence and in need of gentlemen coming to her aid, but she is pluckier and more matter-of-fact than the effete character presented in the book. It is not so surprising that the Elizabeth Marsh of the manuscript has the resilience to endure being captured, the stamina to survive a long, arduous cross-country march in the Moroccan heat, the gumption to maintain the fiction that she is married, and the backbone to stand up to Sidi Mohammed. For that, surely, is the aspect that strikes modern readers most about Marsh: she depicts herself as a frail and sensitive woman, yet she endured and successfully coped with an incredibly stressful situation—and faced down the Sultan when he threatened to have her burned at the stake by daring him to do it.

Marsh's marriage to James Crisp seems to have started out well enough, but Crisp, who was a merchant, went bankrupt and fled to India to try to resuscitate his fortunes. Marsh was left behind with their two young children, with no option left but to live in her parents' house. It was at that point, strapped for money, that she wrote *The Female Captive* in hopes of generating some much-needed cash.

Marsh had her reputation to think of—or what was left of her reputation, rather, since her husband was a notorious bankrupt—and the book was published anonymously. To protect her identity, she left the names of the various characters blank (I have filled them in). More than a few people knew

---

35. Elizabeth Marsh, *Narrative of her Captivity in Barbary*, page 5.

her to be the author, though, an outcome she surely anticipated, and in the interests of her reputation, she presented a whitewashed version of herself. So the Elizabeth Marsh we see in *The Female Captive* is an idealized figure of fragile femininity—an overcharacterization of a woman who was far more than that.

Marsh eventually joined her husband in India. While there, she completed an eighteen-month tour of eastern India on her own—an adventure it is hard to imagine the piously helpless young woman depicted in *The Female Captive* embarking upon. She left a journal chronicling her Indian adventure that was never published and that exists only as a handwritten manuscript (bound together with the manuscript version of *The Female Captive*).

Marsh died in India of breast cancer. She survived a mastectomy without anaesthetic but did not survive the disease. The bound volume containing her two manuscripts ends with the following: 'Mr. and Mrs. Crisp both died in Bengal, leaving a son and a daughter.'

*The Female Captive* is the first full-length captivity narrative written by a woman in English. It was published by subscription. That is, orders (and money) were first solicited, helping to defray the initial costs of printing. The book had some notoriety when it was first published but was never a 'best seller', and only a single copy survives. If that copy had disappeared, it is likely we would never know Marsh's story.

# The View from the Other Shore

This book has focused on the experiences of Europeans captured by Barbary corsairs and their subsequent enslavement in North Africa. The events described in the various narratives really did occur. That is part of the point here. It is a compilation of true stories either based upon the testimony of, or directly narrated by, those to whom the events happened. But the catalogue of atrocities that emerges from these stories makes it seem as if North Africans were inhuman brutes, while Europeans were innocents cruelly wronged.

This is not an accurate portrayal. Terrible, cruel things did indeed happen in corsair ports like Algiers and Salé. That, however, is only one part of the larger story of the age.

Barbary corsairs engaged in a rough business: plundering ships and coastal settlements and trafficking in human beings. But they were not the only ones engaging in such things. As we saw earlier in this book, privateering—the looting of 'enemy' ships for profit—was universally practised by both North Africans and Europeans. Both sides also indulged in human trafficking for profit. There were slave markets in North African cities like Tripoli, Tunis, Algiers, and Salé, but there were also slave markets in European cities like Naples and Livorno, and in Valetta, on the island of Malta. Human trafficking was not limited exclusively to North Africa; it was one of the things that generally characterized the times.

The universalness of these practices is all too easily glossed over or forgotten.

One of the reasons for this one-sided portrayal is that relatively few documents have survived from the North African side, and so, by default, much of what we know about Barbary corsairs, and about the corsair city states, comes from European documents—narratives of escaped or ransomed European slaves or the reports of Europeans who were in the Maghreb in some sort of official capacity, whether as business agents or consuls, or as members of the frequent ransoming expeditions. Such accounts tend to play up the horror of the European captives' situation.

Look at the following extract from Father Pierre Dan's *Histoire de Barbarie*, for instance:

They [captives taken from Baltimore, Ireland] were brought to Algiers, where it was a pitiful thing to see them put up for sale. Women were separated from husbands and children from fathers. Husbands were sold on one side, wives on the other, their daughters snatched from their arms, without hope of any of them ever seeing each other again. I learned all this in Algiers from several slaves from this group who assured me that there was no Christian who did not burst into tears and feel extreme regret at seeing so many honest girls, and so many good women, given over to the brutality of these barbarians.[1]

Here is another description of the sale of human beings:

If you had ever seen them as they were taken, you would have wept blood. Children were separated from their mothers, and husbands from their wives. For the loss of their loved ones, tears streamed down their cheeks. The virgin was paraded in the open, after her *hijab* was torn away from her, and the enemy watched gleefully, as tears choked her moans.[2]

The description above conveys exactly the same sort of heartfelt anguish as Father Dan's, but this author (a sixteenth century Arab poet named Ibn Yajjabsh al-Tazi) is from the other side—the other shore.

Modern readers are appalled by the fact that the Barbary corsairs made a living from violent robbery and human trafficking. But the European states of the time did essentially the same thing, and such practices were woefully common. Like common things everywhere, they were taken for granted. It was a much rougher world than ours, and capturing and selling people for profit constituted a legitimate business enterprise—at least as long as the people being bought and sold belonged to the other side, to the 'enemy'.

---

1. Pierre Dan, *Histoire de Barbarie*, 1649, p. 313.
2. Quoted in Nabil Matar, 'Piracy and Captivity in the Early Modern Mediterranean: The Perspective from Barbary,' in Claire Jowitt, ed., *Pirates? The Politics of Plunder, 1550-1650*, p. 56.

Europeans of the time were outraged and horrified by the treatment of their kin in the North Africa, but they pretty much turned a blind eye to the way North Africans were treated in Europe.

North Africans were outraged and horrified by the treatment of their kin in the various European countries, but they pretty much turned a blind eye to the way Europeans were treated in North Africa.

Human nature, perhaps.

So, yes, during the three hundred years or so of the Barbary corsairs' ascendency—roughly the beginning of the sixteenth to the beginning of the nineteenth centuries—Europeans were in constant danger of capture and enslavement when they sailed the Mediterranean and, later, the Atlantic. But so too were the North Africans.

Below, is an extract from a travel journal written by Abu Hassan 'Al ibn Muhammad ibn 'Ali Muhammad al-Tamjruti. In the late 1580s to very early 1590s, al-Tamjruti travelled from Morocco to Istanbul—where he served as an ambassador for the Moroccan Sultan Ahmad al-Mansour—and back. Here is a series of excerpts from al-Tamjruti's travel journal that reveal how real the risk of attack at sea was for North African travellers.

On August 13, 1589, we left Tetouan by sea. As we sailed, the waves rose against us, the winds blew, and the sea became turbulent, and remained so until the end of the day. After great difficulty, we cast anchor at Tergha, about twenty-four miles from Tetouan. The captain said that we had to reduce the number of passengers lest the ship sink. So he released a group of passengers, including some of our servants. We allowed that for their own safety.

We then sailed to the port of Badis, the ship unstable, rocking left to right. So the captain rearranged the cargo until the ship steadied in the water. At night we sailed past the island of Badis, where there are Christians, may God destroy them. We continued on near Fourk (Cap de Trois Forches), a rectangular mountain protruding into the sea. It is a frightening spot because fishermen from among the Christians and Muslim mariners, who are called in their own language *qarasin* (corsairs), lurk there. They seize whomever they find of their weak enemies, and ships are often taken there.

To the east was Melilla, a city controlled by the Christians today, may God return it to Islam. We docked among the islands of Malwiyya, three islands near each other, where the river Moulouya flows into the sea. There, we stayed two days, delayed by a strong easterly wind that turned up the waves of the sea. The inhabitants of Tetouan told us that the Christians, may God destroy them, followed us in eight ships from Ceuta. But God defeated them and sent them back empty-handed because of this eastern wind, which enabled us to escape them, God be praised. We were told this after we had returned.

We cast anchor near Hanin, a walled city that is desolate today. Nothing remained there except its wall, its mosque, and some fig trees. We left it and passed by the city of Oran, which is controlled by Christians, may God destroy them and return it to Islam...

We left Tunis and passed Ras Adar (Cap Bôn), the mountains stretching out into the sea. It is quite frightening because Christians lurk there and capture ships, sailing out from the nearby islands of Malta and Sicily. Sailors say in the dialect of Tunis that he who passes by Ras Adar, let him first prepare his ransom money at home...

We travelled to Monastir, very near Sousse, actually visible from it. In the past, it used to be a flourishing city, with scholars and seekers of knowledge. It has a *ribat*, designed for the learned, just like an educational institution. It is spacious and octagonal in shape and includes mosques for prayer, student housing, and large book depositories. In the distant past, it used to be a residence for scholars and students and was supported by many charitable foundations from every city in Africa and al-Andalus. Food and subsidies were sent to it to cover the expenses of the students. In recent times, however, the *ribat* has fallen into disrepair. It is still the most fortified spot in the city, however, and whenever Christians attack from the sea, the inhabitants seek shelter inside it, where they hide their children...

We first sighted the Turkish mainland on the evening of Wednesday. The captain had hoped to see land in the morning. When he did not, he became despondent and anxious. Afraid, he kept on standing and sitting, fearing that he might have miscalculated, and an easterly wind would rise from the land and push the ship backward, which was certain perdition, or cast it onto the land of the enemy. He was brought lunch but could not eat. He sent everyone he knew who had sharp eyesight up the mast to look for land, until a Turk saw it and called out from the top of the mast.

The passengers on the ship broke out in joy and hope and congratulated the one who had had the first sighting of land. The captain then said, 'Bring me my food. I will eat now.' By the end of the third part of the night, we reached land and cast our anchor in the port of Modon...

The two ships in which we sailed returned from Algiers to Istanbul carrying large sums of money, the tax revenue, and gifts to the Sultan, the vizier, the captain, and others. They also carried merchants, ammunition for soldiers, and other things. Many Muslims sailed in them, including the judge of the city, with all his possessions, wives, and children, along with merchants, pilgrims, and others. After they had sailed for a night, the *renegado* slaves and their captains along with the Christian rowers and other Christians attacked and killed the ship captains and all who resisted from among the Muslims. Some Muslims hurled themselves into the sea, some of whom swam to safety while others drowned. The Christians sailed in the two ships to their countries, seizing the money, women, and children, and all the Muslim men who surrendered and who had neither fought nor thrown themselves overboard.

A man who was knowledgeable about the affairs of the Pasha, the ruler of the city, told us that he had lost a thousand thousand *mithqals*. Another said that he lost 18 gold *quintal*s, not including jewellery, clothing, merchandise, carpets, and Christian slaves. There was great lamentation in every house in Algiers because of what had happened to Muslim property and persons.

Some time later, captain Arn'ut returned, having been away corsairing off Christian coasts. He had captured eight ships and eighteen Christians from the two ships that had been taken.

The Christians reported how they had sailed back to their country on the captured ships. They explained that when they reached Christian lands, they divided the booty, each taking a thousand *mithqals*, after leaving 20,000 *mithqals* as offering to their church. They reported that they had planned on their perfidy and assault while they were on the ship with us, before reaching Algiers. The reason that they delayed their attack was that they deliberated, and one said, 'The two ships are carrying people only. Wait until they return from Algiers, carrying money and ammunition.'

And so it was. The Istanbul captains are stupid and careless. Nothing like this has ever happened to the Algiers captains.[3]

Barbary corsairs did indeed do terrible things—as the stories in this book show—but it is salutary to keep in mind that Europeans did so as well.

Part of the problem perhaps was that human trafficking was *profitable*. It is worth remembering here the writer Upton Sinclair's famous line: 'It is difficult to get a man to understand something, when his salary depends upon his not understanding it.' In order to maintain their profits, the people of the time—North Africans and Europeans alike—engaged in brutal acts... all while viewing the 'enemy' on the other shore as entirely reprehensible and justifying their own actions as completely appropriate.

Something we should all remember, maybe.

---

3. These excerpts from al-Tamjruti's travel journal come from *Europe Through Arab Eyes, 1578-1727*, by Nabil Matar, pp. 149-157. *Europe Through Arab Eyes* is a fascinating book, well worth reading if you're at all interested in the view from the other shore (so to speak) of the Mediterranean.

# Bibliography

The following is a list of works cited in this book.

Archenholz, Johann Wilhelm von. *The British Mercury, or Annals of History, Politics, Manners, Literature, Arts etc. of the British Empire*, Volume 7. Hamburg: B. C. Hoffman, 1788.

Aranda, Emmanuel de. *Relation de la captivité et liberté du sieur Emanuel d'Aranda, mené esclave à Alger en l'an 1640 & mis en liberté l'an 1642*. Bruxelles: Jean Mommart, Imprimeur ordinaire des États de Brabant, 1656.

Barker, Andrew. *A true and certaine report of the beginning, proceedings, ouerthrowes, and now present estate of Captaine Ward and Danseker, the two late famous pirates: from their first setting forth to this present time*. London: Printed by William Hall, 1609.

Brooks, Francis. *Barbarian Cruelty: Being a True History of the Distressed Condition of the Christian Captives under the Tyranny of Mully Ishmael Emperor of Morocco, and King of Fez and Macqueness in Barbary*. London: Printed for J. Salusbury at the Rising-Sun in Cornhil, and H. Markman at the King's Arms in the Poultry, 1693.

Brown, Horatio F., ed. *Calendar of State Papers and Manuscripts Relating to English Affairs Existing in the Archives and Collections of Venice, and in Other Libraries of Northern Italy*, Vol. XI, 1607-1610. London: His Majesty's Stationery Office, 1904.

Calixte, le R. P., ed. *Les plus illustres captifs : recueil des actions héroïques d'un grand nombre de guerriers et autres chrétiens réduits en esclavage par les mahométans*, tome 2. Lyon : Delhomme et Briguet, 1892.

Castries, Henry de, ed. *Les sources inédites de l'histoire de Maroc, première séries, dynastie saadienne : archives et bibliothèques des Pays-Bas*, tome IV. Paris: Ernest Leroux, 1913.

Des Boys, René du Chastelet. *L'Odyssée ou diversité d'aventures, rencontres et voyages en Europe, Asie et Afrique, divisée en quatre parties*. In *Revue Africaine*. Alger: A. Jourdan, Libraire-Éditeur. Volume 10 (1866) 91-101, 257-266; Volume 11 (1867) 157-167; Volume 12 (1868) 14-32, 350-363, 436-454; Volume 13 (1869) 371-383; and Volume 14 (1870) 193-199.

Dan, Pierre. *Histoire de Barbarie, et de ses corsaires, des royaumes, et des villes d'Alger, de Tunis, de Salé, et de Tripoly*, Seconde Édition. Paris: Imprimeur & Libraire ordinaire du Roy, 1649.

Dan, Pierre. *Les plus illustres captifs: recueil des actions héroïques d'un grand nombre de guerriers et autres chrétiens réduits en esclavage par les mahométans*, tome 2, Le R. P. Calixte de la Providence, ed. Paris : Delhomme et Briguet, 1892.

Garcés, María Antonia, ed., & Diana de Armas Wilson, trans. *An Early Modern Dialogue with Islam: Antonio de Sosa's Topography of Algiers (1612)*. Notre Dame: University of Notre Dame Press, 2011.

Grammont, Henri Delmas de. *Relations entre la France & la régence d'Alger au XVIIe siècle, première partie*. Algiers: Adolphe Jourdan, 1879.

Heeringa, K., ed. *Bronnen tot de geschiedenis van den levantschen handel*. 's-Gravenhage: Martinus Nijhof, 1910.

Jowitt, Claire, ed. *Pirates? The Politics of Plunder, 1550-1650*. New York: Palgrave Macmillan, 2007.

Lithgow, William. *The Totall Discourse of the rare Adventures, and Painefull Peregrinations of long nineteene yeares Travailes from Scotland to the most famous Kingdomes in Europe, Asia, and Affrica*, 1632, reprint, Glasgow: Glasgow University press, 1906.

Manwaring, G. E., & W. G. Perrin, eds. *Publications of the Navy Records Society: The Life and Works of Sir Henry Mainwaring*, Volume 2. London: Printed for the Navy Records Society, 1922.

Marsh, Elizabeth. *The Female Captive: A Narrative of Facts Which Happened in Barbary in the Year 1756, Written by Herself*, Volumes 1 & 2. London: Printed for C. Bathurst, 1769.

Marsh, Elizabeth. *Narrative 1: Narrative of her Captivity in Barbary*. MS 170/604, Charles E. Young Research Library Special Collections. Los Angeles: University of Los Angeles.

Mascarenhas, João de Carvalho. *Memorável relaçam da perda da Nao Conceição que os Turcos queymárão à vista da barra de Lisboa vários sucessos das pessoas, que nella cativarão, E descripção nova da Cidade de Argel & de seu governo & cousas muy notáveis acontecidas nestes ultimos annos de 1621 atè 1626*. Lisbon: na officina de António Álvares, 1627.

Matar, Nabil. *Europe Through Arab Eyes, 1578-1727*. New York: Columbia University Press, 2009.

Monnereau, Dr. MM. & A. Berbrugger, trans. *Topographie et histoire générale d'Alger* (trans. of *Topografia e historia general de Argel* by Diego de Haedo/ Antonio de Sosa), 1870. Reprint, Algiers: Éditions Bouchène, 1998.

Morgan, Joseph, *A Complete History of Algiers, from the Earliest to the Present Times*, Volume 2. London: J. Bettenham, 1721.

Nixon, Anthony. *News from Sea of two notorious Pyrates, Ward the Englishman, and Danseker the Dutchman, with a True Relation of all or the Most Piracies by them Committed unto the sixth of April, 1609.* London: [by Edward Allde] for N. Butter, 1609.

Okeley, William. *Eben-Ezer, or, A small monument of great mercy appearing in the miraculous deliverance of William Okeley, William Adams, John Anthony, John Jephs, and John _____ carpenter, from the miserable slavery of Algiers.* London: Printed for Nat. Ponder, 1675.

Pananti, Filippo. *Narrative of a Residence in Algiers: Comprising a Geographical and Historical Account of the Regency; Biographical Sketches of the Dey and his Ministers; Anecdotes of the Late War; Observations on the Relations of the Barbary States with the Christian Powers; and the Necessity and Importance of their Complete Subjugation.* London: Henry Colburn, 1818.

Pellow, Thomas. *The History of the Long Captivity and Adventures of Thomas Pellow, in South-Barbary.* London: Printed for R. Goadby and sold by W. Owen, 1740.

Phelps, Thomas. *A True Account of the Captivity of Thomas Phelps, at Machaness in Barbary, and of his Strange Escape in Company of Edmund Baxter and others, as also of the Burning of Two of the greatest Pirate Ships belonging to that Kingdom, in the River of Mamora upon the Thirteenth day of June 1685.* London: Printed by H. Hills, Jun. for Joseph Hindmarsh, at the Golden Ball over against the Royal Exchange in Cornhill, 1685.

*Processo Criminal Contra Juan Rodelgo Natural de Villacañas, en La Mancha*, manuscript dated October 10, 1622 – July 6, 1633. Museo Canario, Código de referencia: ES 35001 AMC/INQ-148.001. Las Palmas, Gran Canaria, Canary Islands.

Purchas, Samuel. *Hakluytus Posthumus or Purchas His Pilgrimes: Contayning a History of the World in Sea Voyages and Lande Travells by Englishmen and others* (originally published 1625), Volume VI. Glasgow: James MacLehose and Sons, 1905.

Schoolmaster of Oostaan. *'t Begin, midden en eynde der zee-roovereyen van den alderfamieusten zee-roover Claes G. Compaen van Oostzanen in Kennemer-landt: vervattende sijn wonderlijcke, vreemde en landtschadelijcke drijf-tochten: waer in verthoont wordt, hoe hy met weynigh schepen de zee onveyligh ghemaeckt, een ongelooffelijcken buyt, en groot getal van schepen van alle landen gheroost, en afgeloopen heest.* Netherlands: Gedruckt by een liefhebber van alle nieuwigheden (Printed by a lover of all novelties), 1659.

Smith, John. *The True Travels, Adventures and Observations of Captain John Smith into Europe, Asia, Africa, and America, from Ann. Dom. 1593 to 1629.* London: Printed for Awnsham and John Churchill, 1704.

Ternaux-Compans, Henri. *Archives des voyages ; ou, Collection d'anciennes relations inédites ou très-rares, de lettres, mémoires, itinéraires et autres documents relatifs à la géographie et aux voyages.* Paris: A. Bertrand. 1840-41.

Teyssier, Paul, trans. *Esclave à Alger : récit de captivité de João Mascarenhas.* (trans. of *Memorável relação da perda da nau Conceição* by João Mascarenhas, originally published in 1627.) Paris: Éditions Chandeigne, 1993.

Thompson, James. *A New, Improved, and Authentic Life of James Allan, the Celebrated Northumberland Piper, Detailing his Surprising Adventures in Various Parts of Europe, Asia, and Africa, Including a Complete Description of the Manners and Customs of the Gipsy Tribes.* Newcastle upon Tyne: Mackenzie and Dent, 1828.